G. A. CHENEY

MODERN EUROPE: AN ANTHROPOLOGICAL PERSPECTIVE

LAPLAND

LAPLAND

LAPLAND

LAPLAND

● Kiruna

LAPLAND

FINLAND

URAL MOUNTAINS

● Leningrad (St. Petersburg)

ESTONIA

LATVIA

● Moscow

RUSSIA

LITHUANIA

Viriatino ●

WHITE RUSSIA

POLAND

UKRAINE

LOVAKIA

CARPATHIAN MOUNTAINS

● Átány

MOLDAVIA

CAUCASUS MOUNTAINS

HUNGARY

RUMANIA

Belgrade ●

BLACK SEA

Orašek ●

YUGOSLAVIA

BULGARIA

● Sofia

ALBANIA

MACEDONIA

DARDANELLES

PINDUS MTNS

GREECE

TURKEY

● Vasilika

● Athens

CYPRUS

CRETE

GOODYEAR REGIONAL ANTHROPOLOGY SERIES

Edward Norbeck, Editor

ANTHROPOLOGICAL PERSPECTIVES OF:

MODERN EUROPE
Robert T. Anderson

INDIA
Stephen A. Tyler

INDONESIA
James L. Peacock

CIRCUMPOLAR PEOPLES
Nelson H. Graburn and Barry S. Strong

ABORIGINAL NORTH AMERICA
William W. Newcomb, Jr.

Additional Volumes Forthcoming:

Southeast Asia

China

Africa

Philippines

Polynesia and Micronesia

Middle East

Latin America

MODERN EUROPE: AN ANTHROPOLOGICAL PERSPECTIVE

ROBERT T. ANDERSON

MILLS COLLEGE

GOODYEAR PUBLISHING COMPANY, INC.
Pacific Palisades, California

Library of Congress
Catalog Card Number:
72-76938
(Paper) Y-5821-7
(Cloth) Y-583X-3
ISBN: 0-87620-582-1
        (Paper)
        0-87620-583-X
        (cloth)

Current printing (last
digit):

10 9 8 7 6 5 4 3 2 1

Printed in the
United States of America

FOR SCOTT

CONTENTS

PREFACE

This book represents one man's effort to describe modern Europe in all its complexity and fascination. It strives to be easy to understand, yet sophisticated. It also seeks to emphasize people and problems in our time rather than in the past.

The writing draws upon more than two decades of experience and training, a background made possible by the special advantages given an American for a career in science. In my case these included years of study at the University of California in Berkeley, governmental funds for graduate work, including two years each at the universities of Copenhagen and Paris, and support on numerous occasions which freed me to follow research interests. Most recently, a grant from the National Science Foundation (GS-28677) for the academic year 1971–1972 allowed me to do field work in Denmark. For judicious administration of this grant I am grateful to Dr. John B. Cornell, program director for anthropology.

Operating in the belief that for students to grow in wisdom and knowledge their teachers must grow as well, Mills College has given me generous, unfailing support and encouragement for twelve years.

Several anthropologists helped bring this book to fruition. Professor Edward Norbeck of Rice University provided the opportunity for publication and contributed from his rich experience as a specialist on Asia and a prolific author. Professor Michael Kenny of Catholic University of America read an early draft and offered helpful comments and criticisms. In final form the manuscript benefited from a careful editing by Professor Barbara Gallatin Anderson of California State University, Hayward.

ONE

TRADITIONAL EUROPE

Anthropologists have been slow to bring Europe into their thinking about man and his ways. For decades the continent was there only tangentially for us. Fossil hunters searching for clues to the early evolution of *Homo sapiens* found the continent a rich treasure trove. Heidelberg man was found near the well-known university town. A valley in Germany gave its name to Neanderthal man. Archeologists also recovered early human tools in Europe. It was from such materials that the now-classic sequence of Stone Age, Bronze Age, and Iron Age first was worked out. Europe was central to the ideas we had about prehistory, but it was neglected in our thinking about contemporary men.

To the extent that anthropologists interested in the cultures of living peoples did look to Europe, they tended to look for survivals from ancient times. Those doing studies of primitive folklore drew heavily upon richly documented collections from Europe. Linguists attempting to reconstruct the evolution and diffusion of world languages found guidelines in conclusions drawn from Indo-European philology. Early anthropologists, including Edward Burnett Tylor, Louis Henry Morgan, and Sir James Frazier, found data for evolutionary hypotheses in survivals of antique practices discovered in Europe, as well as in the customs of non-Western peoples throughout the world. No one seemed greatly interested, however, in strictly contemporary life styles in Europe.

As anthropologists, we were slow to rectify this shortcoming. The first modern ethnography of a European community was not undertaken until the early 1930s, when Conrad Arensberg began field work in Ireland's County Clare with the collaboration first of W. Lloyd Warner and later of Solon Kimball. When Arensberg published his findings, first in 1937 and then in 1941 in a volume co-authored with Kimball, not only had he published the first ethnography of a contemporary European community, he had produced one of the earliest studies to be done anywhere in a complex society (Arensberg, 1968; Arensberg and Kimball, 1968).

A few others had been slightly earlier to do community studies in modern nations other than in Europe: Robert S. and Helen M. Lynd and W. Lloyd

Warner in the United States, Robert Redfield in Mexico, and Horace Miner in Canada. Complex nations had not been neglected by carelessness or design, however. Anthropologists were few in number and had a prior commitment to the study of simpler, less complex societies. We were engaged in a race to learn as much as possible about such peoples before they might become extinct. Our research methods and theoretical concerns were developed for this purpose. It took time to move from the study of vanishing tribesmen to the inhabitants of modern nations. When the move was made, it took us almost simultaneously to China, India, and other complex societies as well as to Europe. As a footnote to history, the earliest of all modern ethnographic work in Europe was carried out in 1928 in Sicily by Charlotte Gower Chapman, but the manuscript she produced in 1935 got lost, and was not rediscovered and published until 1971 (Chapman, 1971).

The late thirties and early forties were inauspicious for research in Europe. Irwin T. Sanders managed to finish field work in a village in Bulgaria before the war started, but his findings were not published until 1949 (Sanders, 1949). During and after the war, Ruth Benedict, Margaret Mead, Rhoda Métraux, Geoffrey Gorer, and others did studies of Great Russian, French, Rumanian, and British personality, using a technique characterized as the study of culture at a distance (Benedict, 1946; Gorer, 1955; Gorer and Rickman, 1949; Mead and Métraux, 1953; Métraux and Mead, 1954). Unable to get into the field, they collected information from interviews with refugees, travelers, and migrants; from available moving pictures; from novels, newspapers, and magazines; in short, from whatever they could get their hands on that might incorporate cultural clues.

During the war, Robert H. Lowie used library resources to prepare lectures on European culture for military students at the University of California. After the war, he visited Germany to update and amplify his observations. The result was one anthropologist's view of German culture (Lowie, 1954). David Rodnick produced another such view, also drawing on materials collected in Germany shortly after the war (Rodnick, 1948). Others quick to get into the field at about this time were J. A. Barnes in Norway, H. H. Turney-High in Belgium, and Dorothy Keur in the Netherlands; while in Portugal, Jorge Dias turned from work in Africa to undertake two community studies in his own country (Barnes, 1954; Dias, 1948, 1953; Keur and Keur, 1955; Turney-High, 1953).

As the 1950s gathered momentum, a new generation of anthropologists became active. Established universities got bigger and new ones were founded. Increased employment and research opportunities brought new people into the profession. Many were especially influenced by Robert Redfield, whose provocative books did much to get anthropologists started in the study of civilizations (e.g., Redfield, 1956). It took time, though, for the postwar generation to finish their training, do their field work, and get into print.

At that time young anthropologists wanting to specialize on contemporary Europe had to get their training as best they could. They read what Robert Redfield, George M. Foster, and others had to say about complex societies, with a heavy emphasis on peasant societies (e.g., Foster, 1953). They spent a couple of years acquiring background from European history, folklore, philology, and geography. They learned European languages. But the anthropological literature that dealt specifically with modern Europe still was so limited that it could be covered in a month or so. Much, perhaps most, of their training as specialists consisted of field work. It was a slow, inefficient, and frustrating way to master the field.

The 1960s brought immense improvement. Hard work in field research by a growing number of specialists during the 1950s began to pay off in publications that appeared in the late fifties and sixties. The size and complexity of modern Europe as an ethnographic field is great, so the documentation remains incomplete and spotty, a still serious problem. Yet, by the end of the decade, for all of its gaps, the literature had become rich in both factual content and ideas. The problem in becoming a specialist on the anthropology of Europe became one of mastering a large and growing literature. It is time, then, to look over what has been written, to pull it together, and to present it in a form that will give some idea of where we are, what we know, and where we are going.

TRADITIONAL EUROPE:
TIME AND SPACE

The concept of Traditional Europe is our beginning (Anderson, 1971). Europe today is in cultural upheaval. To understand a changing present, we must identify some baseline in the past from which change can be measured. Yet an ethnographic baseline is itself difficult to delineate, since in its time it too was a changing, ephemeral thing. To cope with this problem, we need some analytical tools, some concepts which can help in finding our way through the historical maze. The concept of Traditional Europe is such a tool. It constitutes an intellectual map, a model, of Western civilization as a system and as a process. It is a way of describing the preindustrial world so that once done, we can turn to the present and hope to identify cultural continuities as well as cultural changes. To identify both continuity and change, and to evaluate them somehow, ultimately must be our goal.

Traditional Europe is a statement about both time and space. It defines certain consistencies of cultural process as well as certain continuities of cultural tradition which set apart the tenth to the eighteenth centuries. Because we are concerned here with the present, the time of our baseline may be taken as the eighteenth century, the end of this period.

The territorial dimension did not remain unchanged during the many centuries of Traditional Europe. European civilization was confined in the Middle Ages to the western part of the continent. Only later did it push eastward to cover Russia and the other Slavic nations. By the end of the period, however, this expansion was complete. It remains substantially unchanged to this day. Our baseline, as a consequence, comprises that eighteenth-century civilization which extended from the Mediterranean to the Arctic and from the Atlantic to the Urals.

To be somewhat more precise, the geographical boundaries of Europe extend westward to the shorelines of the Atlantic and over adjacent islands as far into the ocean as Iceland. The latter is part of Europe because it lacks Eskimos and had been settled by Norsemen since the ninth century. Greenland, however, does not belong, since it has a resident Eskimo population and its Norse settlement became extinct. The present Danish colony on Greenland dates from the eighteenth century, but it is customary to exclude from ethnographic Europe all colonies established in the post-Columbian period. Because they have had unique histories of adaptation and acculturation, but also because the effort to include them would be very strenuous, they are not usually considered "peoples of Europe," even though they remain predominantly European in social inheritance.

The eastern border of Europe always has been comparatively fluid, since no major topographical barrier prohibits the interpenetration of peoples at this meeting place of Europe and Asia. In broad terms, however, Europe terminates along the low Ural Mountains, the Caspian Sea, across the north of the Caspian Sea, the Caucasus Mountains, and the Black Sea to the Mediterranean at the Dardanelles (Evans, 1968). For the most part, the eastern boundary separates settled European peasant communities in the west from nomadic herding people of different traditions in the east. These nomads include reindeer-herding peoples in arctic Siberia, some of whom have home territories on the European side of the Urals. The northern region of Europe, topographically delimited by the Barents Sea, is thus a zone of cultural heterogeneity where Europeanized circumpolar peoples—Lapps and Samoyeds—long have lived in contact with settled peoples more thoroughly European in origin.

In the south, Europe extends over the islands of the Mediterranean, including Malta, Cyprus, and Crete, but ends at the coastline of Africa and the Near East (Anderson, R. T., 1972b). The circum-Mediterranean societies which are excluded have much the same ancient peasant-village tradition as Europe, once were part of the Roman Empire, and as Muslims share generously in the Judeo-Christian past. Since the lands around the Mediterranean additionally constitute a unified ecological system—are similar environmentally—one may speak meaningfully of Mediterranean peoples as a culture area. By further extension, Conrad Arensberg identifies a culture area of Old World peoples, a large expanse of anciently contiguous, mostly Indo-European-speaking, peasant villagers, enveloping Europe and the Middle East as far as India and Ceylon (Arensberg, 1963). Europe never has been isolated from adjacent parts of Asia and Africa, so continuities with these areas as well as with distant areas of former colonization can be documented. Such contacts and similarities, however, do not obscure the integrity of Europe within its own boundaries. It is that Europe which will occupy us in this book.

CULTURAL UNIFORMITY

Europe in the eighteenth century was home to a variety of cultures. These included Lapps in the far north, Basques in the Pyrenees, Jews in urban ghettos, and Gypsies ever on the move. Overriding such variety, however, was the pervasive uniformity of three distinctive major cultures which coexisted, side by side, throughout the continent as a whole (Anderson, R. T., 1971, 9–18).

Nearly everywhere one found a society of aristocrats—whether titled or not was unimportant—whose life was molded by their control of power, wealth, and leisure. In towns and cities, living side by side with aristocrats and others, yet very different from them, burghers pursued a second distinctive mode of existence shaped by the demands of commerce or artisanry. A third culture had its roots in the fields and forests of the countryside, where peasants lived in a world oriented to the demands of producing food. These three pan-European cultures—aristocratic, burgher, and peasant—more than any and all others gave shape to that complex of cultures we call the traditional civilization of Europe.

Aristocratic Culture

Aristocratic culture in each nation tended to be uniform within that nation (Anderson, R. T., 1971, 83–120). The social structure that gave shape to upper-class life provided a basis for ongoing homogenization. From antiquity, noblemen held country estates as the foci of family solidarity. Residence on the family estate, particularly in the spring and fall when trees were in color and the air was fresh, was one of the perquisites of the rich. To manage an estate was hard work. But if management of a large estate had its onerous side, it was more than offset by the delights of a comfortable home, a staff of servants, a well-stocked larder, high social standing, and the company of one's own kind.

Manors in most places were scattered throughout the countryside, each nestled in its own forest, park, and fields. But the masters of such manors were generally not isolated. Their horses and carriages with liveried coachmen drove them where they liked. And they liked to visit one another. Afternoon coffee and cakes drew ladies and their children into a ritualized round of visiting. A nice afternoon was a time to visit up the road a few miles or to receive visitors. Dinner parties for adults in formal dress, though less frequent, threw the net wider. At least a few times a year, to travel several hours by coach to a dinner party was an accepted thing to do. In the hunting season, gatherings lasting several days took place. More informally, men consulted with other local noblemen on agricultural problems and matters of local government. In other ways, too, they met. Meetings had to be infrequent where large estates were widely separated, yet some visiting and collaboration was typical in every nation. In many places it was intense.

Each estate nestled in a network of nearby estates with which it had social ties. Through socializing within the network, traditional mores were upheld and new ideas were disseminated. The process could result in uniformities, either of tradition or of innovation. And since the visiting networks overlapped from area to area, wide expanses, whole nations, and even larger regions tended to be culturally homogeneous.

Some people lived on their estates year in and year out. Many, however, changed residence seasonally. Summer was a time for sunny beaches or mountain resorts where the waters reputedly were beneficial for bodies made sluggish by rich meals and good wine. Winter attracted an elite to provincial and national capitals. Away from their estates, families resided in elegant apartments, town houses, or hotels and took part in a busy cycle of banquets, balls, and theater parties. Walks in manicured parks, carriage promenades on fashionable boulevards, and conversations in coffee shops, elite clubs, and private salons also brought people together. The royal court often centralized these activities, setting a pace which others followed as best they could. But princes and lesser nobles also held court at times, and often the final arbiters of taste were those who frequented the salon of a distinguished lady. In all, the capital city was a busy place where members of the upper class gave allegiance to traditional virtues and rendered verdicts on proffered new ideas.

The face-to-face socializing of these residents of urban centers and vacation resorts was a mechanism, in effect, for deciding which aspects of culture would continue and which would change. Culture was modified in this way. With dispersal at the end of the "season," an elite within the elite, relatively uniform in what they did and valued, moved back again to the smaller networks of which their estates were a part. Back in the countryside, their return, welcomed with parties big and small, assured that what had spread among residents of the capital and spa eventually would diffuse even to small, remote, provincial estates. The nation, even when it was as large as Great Russia itself, had an upper-class social structure which worked efficiently to ensure cultural sharing throughout its territory.

The culture of the aristocracy had national dimensions. In Spain, the haughty demeanor, the pronounced Catholicity, the touchy pride of a Castilian nobleman set him apart from his more light-hearted and urbane counterpart in Italy, from a baron caught up in the intrigue and status dueling of a small princely court in Germany, from a nobleman of Sweden, Lithuania, Bulgaria, Hungary, Greece, or France. In each nation, aristocratic culture was distinctive to some extent. Yet, by means of a cultural network which reached across all the nations of Europe, that diversity was overshadowed by uniformity. The culture of the aristocracy was pan-European in basic contours.

Many social ties cut across national boundaries. Marriage alliances often did so importantly, particularly within royal lines, but also among the higher aristocracy. In addition, young gentlemen customarily traveled before settling down, taking a year or two to visit the major capitals of the western world, a practice which allowed them months to get acquainted with high society in Rome, Paris, London, and beyond. Older gentlemen traveled too, as princes of the Church, as diplomats, as invited men of letters, often as exiles, and sometimes just because they wanted to visit. Even when nations were fighting one another, ties within the upper class could remain strong. Horace Walpole and Gibbon circulated in the salons of Paris while France and England were at war.

Because aristocrats nurtured ties of kinship and friendship which cut across national borders, they kept in touch even when they did not travel in person. Postal service was improved. The eighteenth century was a time when the custom of corresponding became something of an international mania. Long and frequent letters united individuals across the widest expanses of the continent.

The upper class also learned through literature. The *belles lettres* were enthusiastically cultivated, and when a noble lady or a gentleman pulled up beside the fire to read something of Montesquieu, Marivaux, or Beaumarchais, the result was more than simply to be entertained. The reader gained instruction in what was appropriate for a noble person to think, to do, and to want. Plays acted out on the stage were even more effective, no doubt, for in watching them an audience was exposed to an audiovisual demonstration of appropriate class behavior. Illustrated magazines clearly taught the latest fashions as well as, unconsciously, appropriate posture and mien. Books of instruction, such as *An Honorable Mirror for Youth, Or a Guide to Deportment*, could be read by those eager to conform, just as in our time one may pick up Emily Post or Amy Vanderbilt. And since books, magazines, and plays circulated among aristocrats throughout the continent, they fostered everywhere a sameness that was pervasive.

Upper-class culture evolved more or less uniformly throughout Europe through a process which tended to be centralized. Some nations had greater wealth, power, and prestige than did others. In the eighteenth century, France, with its focus on Paris and Versailles, was the single most powerful nation in Europe. The French elite functioned as cultural arbiters for European aristocrats in other nations. The French king, his courtiers, and other prominent members of the aristocracy provided examples of a life style eagerly imitated throughout Europe. The princes of small domains in Germany re-created Versailles in miniature, sometimes bankrupting themselves in the process. By the time of Catherine the Great, the nobility in St. Petersburg not only emulated life in France, but circulated French gossip along with their own. So French had they become, they spoke French as their preferred tongue, leaving Russian to the peasants. London also was a center of innovation in this century—the Enlightenment was as much English as French—but even London was French in many ways. In all, the social structure of the upper class made it possible for prominent individuals in the salons of Paris or the halls of Versailles to approve the old or adopt the new as decision-makers for members of their class everywhere.

Burgher Culture

Burghers also had a culture in which a uniformity of continental dimensions overlay local and national diversity (Anderson, R. T., 1971, 121–134). They too had social institutions that fostered sharing, though less completely than was so for the upper class.

Burghers generally were townsmen, though some lived in villages. They were distinguished by a commitment to trade and craft industry which did not normally make them rich or even well-to-do but shaped their lives in distinctive ways. Many were merchants who worked out of warehouse-homes in urban centers selling imported cloth, spices, and exotic foods to urbanites who could afford them, acting as middlemen in the sale of agricultural surpluses and locally produced goods or as bankers in the lending of money. Others were artisans who spent long hours in their shops, which, with a back room or two, served also as storehouses and living quarters. Small entrepreneurs, they specialized in making and repairing shoes, blacksmithing, lockmaking, tinsmithing, clock-making, furniture-making, cutting glass, producing tableware, binding books, tailoring clothes, carpentry, building in stone or brick, and in other activities as well, providing all of the goods and services needed by their contemporaries.

Every town had a commoner population of tradesmen and artisans. Within the town, these burghers lived in intimate circumstances. Most preindustrial centers were small by modern standards. Though urban in the sense that they housed peoples of diverse origins, and in the sense that many residents engaged in commerce and trade, they were not urban in the modern sense of social anonymity. Town populations were comparatively small, so that often all burghers knew one another, at least by sight. Further, all members of the burgher class were brought together regularly at the marketplace in the give and take of trade. Often, leading burghers—wealthier, more powerful men— served in the municipal government, taking active part in town affairs. Guilds still existed in the eighteenth century, uniting men with others of the same or similar occupation. Feast days provided occasions for townwide celebrations which brought out the various guilds to parade in ceremonial spirit and attire. Most importantly, during quiet evenings, beer halls or wine cellars attracted men to drown the cares of a long hard day in the conviviality of the drinking mug.

Preindustrial cities and towns were relatively intimate places for their burgher inhabitants. In the inn, the marketplace, the church, and the street, townsmen met. To some extent, they remained heterogeneous. Each craft or trade to some extent tended to create its own unique personality. The special activities of the shoemaker, to take one example, shaped him differently from, say, the more rugged and active routine of the blacksmith, or the less energetic work of the merchant. Some were more prosperous than others. But counteracting this tendency to diversity was a force for uniformity within town walls. All burghers were subject to municipal laws and occupational restrictions, to sumptuary regulations and market restraints. Every burgher was caught up in an economy that removed him from fields where he might grow his own food, and captured him in a system of monetary exchange. Above all, burghers lived as neighbors to one another, able in face-to-face communion to work out a shared view of what was right and proper as a way to live and a life to hope for. In spite of differences, the burghers of a preindustrial town tended to be culturally homogeneous.

A powerful mechanism functioned very efficiently to extend the burgher uniformity of individual cities and towns to a uniformity that covered all of Europe. That mechanism was the custom of the journeyman's tour. To learn a trade, a boy spent some years as an apprentice. After he had put in his time and finished his journeyman's piece—perhaps a chest of drawers for a cabinetmaker, a silver bowl for a silversmith, some structure, the completion of which proved his command of basic skills—he provided food and drink for a party which graduated him as a journeyman. About twenty years old, still unmarried, employable, he was felt then to need the experience of working a few additional years in other shops and especially in areas highly regarded for the quality of their artisanry. He took to the road to see the world and to perfect his craftsmanship.

Without responsibility, he needed little money to travel. He could cover hundreds of miles by walking, since he had time and could expect a small handout, a place to sleep or a bite of food, from the masters of workshops in each town. Generally, these "wandering birds" traveled in pairs or small groups. On entering a town, they made the round of shops of their craft to get a coin or two in each place for food and drink. In good weather they could sleep in the open. In bad they were put up, perhaps in the guild hall or, for a small fee, in a guild-supported hostel or private inn. At their destination, they found employment for a couple of weeks, a few months, often for a year or two.

After working for a while, the young journeyman could collect his earnings and move on. Eventually he would return to his homeland to settle down. There he would work for master status, marry, and raise a family. Most likely, once returned, he never would travel again. Yet each year, new journeymen went out and others came back, so always, transients kept alive ties which bound all of Europe into a single network.

These travels cut across national boundaries. Passports and visas were not needed in those days. On his tour, a journeyman did not think of borders he must cross, but only of towns he must reach. The Germanic part of the continent was central in this. From Scandinavia, Balkan towns, the islands of Britain and elsewhere, young men made their way to workshops in central Europe. The most respected ateliers were found in what is now Germany, Switzerland, and Austria. As a consequence, the international language of tradesmen was not French, but German.

The journeyman's tour functioned with particular success in making burghers throughout Europe similar in culture because of the way journeymen were housed. For those months or years when the journeyman worked in a foreign shop, he generally resided with the family of his master. Throughout Europe, the burgher family was uniform in that regard. Apprentices and journeymen, both foreign and local, took their meals at the master's table and slept under his roof. Such an arrangement exposed the traveler to every intimate detail of local burgher life and led him to imitate what he observed. It behooved an impressionable young man to conform to the customs of that family. He was thought strange and was ridiculed if he did not. The arrangement did not favor rapid change or major innovation: burgher custom tended strongly to be conservative. But the conservatism it nurtured had pan-European dimensions.

Peasant Culture

In cultural terms, aristocrats and burghers were major constituents of the mix that was Old Europe. As residents in castles, manors, and palaces, or as townsmen crowding marketplaces and narrow streets, they were prominent to contemporary observers. As producers and consumers of art, music, literature, fine architecture, boulevards, monuments, high cuisine, theater, parks, *haute couture*, furniture, household utensils, jewelry, and the other creations that distinguish a civilization. aristocrats and the artisans who served them did much to enrich Europe. Yet, in terms of population size, they were not preponderant. Perhaps 75 to 80 percent of the population lived as peasants, and it is to them we must turn if we truly are to lay hold of the ethnographic reality that once was Europe.

In Traditional Europe, the uniformity of peasant culture was much less apparent than was the uniformity of aristocratic or burgher culture (Anderson, R. T., 1971, 135–151). Peasant activities did not unite group with group across nations and beyond. True, some individuals wandered among villages as beggars, peddlers, minstrels, or pilgrims. Others moved seasonally to seek harvest work as field hands or migrated to towns to join the ranks of burghers. In places, shepherds covered great distances going from pasture to pasture or from field to market, and fishermen at times dropped anchor in harbors not their own. But contacts of these kinds did not add up to the sort of international matrix which united burghers or aristocrats throughout Europe. Lines of travel did not cut across one another to establish a peasant network of pan-European dimensions.

In a way, international ties did exist in the eighteenth century as an unrealized potentiality. Except for remote mountain, forest, or wasteland settlements—places isolated by the absence of roads and rivers—communities normally had frequent and regular contact with neighboring communities. In general, marriage alliances brought at least some brides from other villages to live in the communities of their husbands. Every locality had peasant markets which attracted a peasant clientele. From time to time, a fair or town festival attracted visitors from farther afield. However parochial in habit and vision, every peasant normally knew about peasant custom in villages nearby.

Since peasants customarily were familiar with other peasants in the vicinity, only mountain ranges in Scandinavia, the Balkans, central Europe, and northern Spain, or water barriers such as the English Channel, the Irish Sea, and the Kattegat, seriously interfered with contacts between communities which *in toto* covered Europe end to end. Certainly, from the west coast of France, through Germany and Poland to the eastern border of Russia, the physical basis of a network was at hand. Yet culture traits did not generally spread over distances that great.

The contact of community with community did not normally encourage imitation for peasants as it did for burghers and aristocrats who were in touch. At most, imitation spread among the villages of a restricted locality: along a river valley, a coastal stretch, the expanse of a grassy plain. For the most part, diffusion was circumscribed in the territory of a single village by itself or a cluster of villages. The result was village or local differentiation. The peasants of Europe tended to be culturally diverse.

The fact of diversity is not in dispute. All observers agree in that. What is in dispute is why it should have been. It has been widely assumed that peasants differed because they were isolated and out of touch. But as we have seen, that was not actually the case in most instances. For an explanation we must look rather to the symbolic function of culture.

Peasant communities were not so clearly ranked in prestige hierarchies as was true for aristocratic centers and towns. Most frequently, each village or locality of villages held itself the equal—morally if not materially—of every other. One community did not normally feel impelled to imitate another in a quest for high status and prestige. On the contrary, since each felt superior or at least equal, but also because each felt a sense of local solidarity, each seemed to want to stay different, as though it were important that its customs should dramatize symbolically an independent status. Culture traits did not usually diffuse far through community-to-community connections, it appears, because culture traits tended to acquire a local identification, to come to symbolize the local integrity of the societies that possessed them.

The facts support this conclusion. As concerns clothing, for example, it is significant that in the busy marketplace, every peasant saw the costume of every other peasant. He could easily copy if he chose. That he did not suggests he chose not to. The clothes one wore were symbols. To copy the hat, the blouse, the shoes of another was to say, in a symbolic code, "You and I are the same." A peasant might alter his dress, but not in the direction of imitating neighbors. To do that was to confuse mutually understood symbols of communal loyalty. And what was true of clothing was generally true as well of details of architecture, household furnishings, dialects, beliefs, and other practices. A tendency to diverge was characteristic of peasant culture change. It tended to keep each village or locality different. Contacts which might have functioned as a peasant network to diffuse cultural uniformities over major parts of Europe were not much activated so long as these attitudes held sway.

In spite of the tendency to differentiate culturally, and in spite of only a small amount of ongoing diffusion, European peasant culture was not endlessly diverse. The tendency for each village or locality to grow different never completely obliterated many uniformities which survived from earlier centuries. A few traits, and those rather generic or nonspecialized in quality, remained sufficiently widespread to constitute pan-European characterizations. They included the village form of settlement, Indo-European speech patterns, folk animism, reliance on magic, Roman relics in the festival calendar and in concepts of medicine, fundamental Christian beliefs and practices, including the central place of the church and its congregation in village life, and the attitudes and expectations of people accustomed to an exploitive social system with concomitant rural poverty.

The oldest of these pan-European uniformities appear to have resulted from prehistoric population movements. They were carried by peasants themselves as they expanded over the continent. Later shared traits apparently resulted for the most part from a very different process, that of mediated acculturation. That is, such traits did not spread as peasants acculturated to neighboring peasants. Diffusion in that way tended to abort. Rather, certain customs became widespread because they diffused among members of the dominant class as traits foreign to their own way of life, yet imposed by them upon villagers. In particular, subordinate personal status (in times and places, serfdom) characterized European peasants because the upper class tended to be uniform in techniques for managing subordinates. Only rarely—though importantly as concerns religion—did peasants resemble one another because they came to share (acculturated to) a cultural characteristic of the upper class as such.

Other peasant uniformities were more limited in geographical spread, each unique in its distribution. The most apparent of these comprised the major linguistic groups (especially Romance, Germanic, Slavic, and Celtic), peasant urbanism in the Mediterranean area, single-farm settlement along the Atlantic fringe, church and sect adherence, systems of land management, and types of animal husbandry and fishing. These more limited regularities seem mainly the products of older folk movements and later mediated acculturation, though some represent shared adaptations to similar ecological circumstances.

CULTURAL SIMILARITIES
AND DISTINCTIONS

It is not enough to distinguish three major cultures—peasant, burgher, and aristocratic—a triad spread side by side over the larger expanse of Europe. Fully to grasp the nature of Europe as a civilization requires that we also look at how these cultures were united with one another, yet kept distinct (Anderson, R. T., 1971, 165–174). Generally it has been assumed that the quality or style of a civilization derived from shared culture traits which permeated the various parts and gave them all an underlying commonality. Further, it has been assumed that the very integrity of a civilization as a social system required that the parts be substantially the same, as though only subsocieties which were alike could stay together. When European culture history is looked at more closely, however, civilization as a process appears to have been something quite different.

In one important way, the major cultures of Traditional Europe were similar. All were Christian. Religion provided not only a shared response to the religious needs of Europeans, it gave them as well a shared view of the world. And one most important component of that world view was a system of ethics that justified for everyone the invidious class distinctions by which they lived. In the Christian view, it was right and proper that a minority lived as lords and kings while the majority remained subservient and impoverished. The place each had in life was God's will. As part of their religion, peasants and burghers were brought to believe they should be faithful in their tasks and in their poverty, for their reward would come in a glorious life after death. No doubt, the persistence of class inequities was facilitated by these shared myths.

In other ways, however, the classes tended to be different from one another. But in considering this fact, take care to keep the time dimension clearly in mind. Because many traditional customs persisted into the industrial period, it is easy to confuse preindustrial with later cultural processes. One tends to think about earlier classes as though their styles of life had some or many of the characteristics of later, much changed descendants. Often people talk or write about peasants as though they had the mentality of farmers and about burghers as though they were bourgeois or middle class somehow. Subsequently, we shall examine postindustrial changes in class cultures, and the process whereby classes tended to acculturate to one another. In premodern times, however, the classes tended on the whole to remain very different in culture. Cultural processes functioned effectively to make them that way, and to keep them so. We can identify those processes.

Cultural differentiation constituted a key process in the development and maintenance of Traditional Europe. Each class tended to become culturally different from the others. Acculturation, the growing similarity of societies in contact as they borrow from one another, functioned above all as a force for uniformity within a class. In particular, diffusion within the aristocratic and burgher classes was a part of civilization as a process, and without it Traditional Europe would have been very different from what we know it to have been.

Acculturation also took place between classes. Religious beliefs spread that way. Always, some additional traits moved downward. At times, the trickle of upper-class traits that moved into burgher and peasant strata grew into a heavy stream, as in the sixteenth and early seventeenth centuries when unaccustomed prosperity in the Renaissance carried major uniformities into burgher neighborhoods and peasant villages. But for the most part, and particularly in the eighteenth century, acculturation from high to low, what Charles Erasmus refers to as invidious emulation, was blocked. It was not able to take place.

For each class, its culture stood as symbol of its special place in society. The aristocracy, above all, took its whole way of life as symbolic of unique high status. The upper class regarded itself as different and superior from all others. Correspondingly, aristocrats seemed to take delight, at least unconsciously, in making their customs as distinctive as possible. In the eighteenth century, they were characterized by powdered wigs, abundant lace, tortured rules of etiquette, grammarians to tell them how to talk, elaborate cuisines, and daily and seasonal rituals of balls, the theater, the hunt, and conversations in salons, cafes, and courts. In everything they did, as well as in what they thought about and valued, aristocrats were culturally as different from the other classes as were Chinese mandarins or Mogul princes.

Naturally, burghers and peasants envied the good life with its many comforts. They simply could not borrow very much, however, because to live the life of the privileged required wealth, power, and leisure they did not have. An artisan in his shop or a peasant in his fields could not imitate very much. Insofar as he could, he was discouraged or even forbidden by custom. When some, the more well-to-do, did imitate clothing styles, jewelry, or etiquette, the customs borrowed tended to be abandoned by the upper class. Various elements of clothing, especially, sifted down from above. Yet, clothing always functioned clearly to distinguish classes.

The cultural relationship of burghers with peasants also discouraged acculturation. Traditional burghers were not wealthy. But they did have a higher status than most peasants. Though their lives were actually deprived and monotonous by modern comparison, confined for the most part to the four walls of a small shop, as town-dwellers they had the excitement from time to time of market activities, of travelers passing through, of floggings and hangings, and of church and civic processions. Since the Middle Ages they had been free men. They felt greatly superior to the "country bumpkins" whom they knew. And they gave expression to that feeling of superiority. They symbolized it for themselves and all others, in their whole way of life. Burghers took care, however ragged and tattered, to dress, talk, live, and relax in town ways.

The work they did and the things they aspired to were different to begin with. They embroidered on those differences as much as they could.

No one wanted to imitate peasant customs (see Lopreato, 1965; Redfield, 1956, 64–65). It did become an upper-class fad in the eighteenth century to play at being peasant. Marie Antoinette had a hamlet of straw-roofed peasant dwellings constructed at Versailles where she and her friends could relax in rustic surroundings. I would not call that acculturation. At about that time, an adapted form of a peasant straw hat was produced for milady by some milliners. That was a genuine imitation. It was not much.

Acculturation between the classes was limited. When it took place, the direction almost always was from top to bottom. To some extent, more successful burghers and peasants borrowed what they could from the upper class. Elements of clothing, tastes in food, and items of household furnishing and art could be found in some eighteenth-century burgher apartments or peasant houses. But on the whole, class cultures were very different, little changed by such exceptions.

The differentiation of cultures persisted in spite of peasants who moved to towns, and burghers, less commonly peasants, who became rich.

Every generation witnessed the movement of great numbers of peasants into burgher communities. An excess of children on the land and an inability of town families to reproduce themselves made this sort of village-to-town migration normal and necessary. But social mobility did not blur cultural differences. The process of social movement assured it would not. Peasants moving to town not only changed their work routine, they moved into a society where peasant speech, dress, and habits were burned out with the powerful acid of ridicule. This commonly took place as the migrant took up residence in the house of an employer, often under the formal terms of an apprenticeship contract. Old customs were abandoned and new ones adopted with great completeness under these circumstances, even in the realm of beliefs and values, for the family functions with special effectiveness to enculturate its new members.

The human personality, it appears, is very flexible. We have been wrong to assume that once an infant has enculturated—that is, has internalized the culture of its parents and community— it cannot change again. It is clear that individuals can enculturate a second time, and just as completely (see Mead, M., 1966a, 411). This is especially so in circumstances where a migrant moves into a family-like situation.

Wealthy burghers also tended to move socially and to experience secondary enculturation. A successful merchant normally tried to emulate the upper class completely. Customarily, he bought land, established a manorial household, and sought out the company of the upper class. Often, he gave up his business to achieve this end, which speaks more powerfully than words for the determination he had to abandon burgher ways and adopt those of the aristocracy. And when such a man entered aristocratic society, he did not somehow act as a bridge between cultures. Aristocrats did not emulate lesser men. Rather, the lesser man changed as completely as he could in an aristocratic direction. Freequently, his success was incomplete. Often he was not admitted to upper-class society. Normally, he was not allowed to enter as intimately into it as did a peasant who moved into burgher society. Often he lived on as one of the *nouveaux riches*, a social isolate to some extent. His children, however, might better hope for social acceptance, and with time the family typically merged indistinguishably into the class to which it aspired, changing completely itself but bringing no appreciable change in its wake for the society it joined.

Traditional Europe, then, can be looked at as a civilizational system made up of parts and processes. Three major cultures constituted its major parts or elements. Each was kept more or less uniform throughout Europe by the process of acculturation within networks (aristocrats and burghers) or by processes of conservatism and mediated acculturation (peasants). Acculturation between these classes or elements was very limited, countered by a strong tendency to differentiate. Social mobility did not generally counteract cultural differentiation, because it normally was accompanied by the secondary enculturation of mobile individuals. Only the myth which justified class relationships tended to remain a shared trait, a product of early acculturation. As Christians, nearly everyone regarded differences of class as ordained by God.

TWO

THE UPPER CLASS
IN OUR TIME

The upper-class style of life has persisted into the Age of Aquarius. It remained until World War I as a pan-European uniformity. Russia since 1917 and the rest of eastern Europe since 1945 have diverged in an important way from the west. Yet in both east and west, older aristocratic traditions still shape upper-class habits in many ways.

To survive, an upper-class way of life has had to persist through armed revolutions, legislative sieges, economic transformations, and ideological upheavals. Yet survive it has. To understand how this can be, we need to look at three key nations: France, where the Revolution of 1789 constituted an attempt to replace aristocratic privilege with liberty, equality, and fraternity; England, where the industrial revolution promised a new popular culture in the nineteenth century; and Russia, the land that gave birth to the communist dream in 1917. Change and continuity in the other nations of Europe reflect changes in which these nations led.

FRANCE: LIVING NOBLY
THROUGH REVOLUTION
AND RESTORATION

In France, revolution inaugurated a decade of discord. On the night of August 4, 1789, the Constituent Assembly revoked all noble privileges. The assembly envisioned a new aristocracy of talent and service that would give recognition to artists, scholars, and literati as well as to governmental and military leaders. Before the new upper class could be born, however, the revolution entered a phase in which the recognition of any elite other than that of power was out of the question. Between 1792 and 1794, the badge of the new power elite was humble origin and unsophisticated demeanor in which the *sans-culottes*, rough working-class men, established the character of government and set their stamp upon society. Those who refused to conform lost their heads to the guillotine. Old upper-class customs were wiped out with blood (Cobban, 1965, 120–131; Moore, 1966, 101–110).

In the early 1790s, aristocratic culture in France was dealt a blow from which it must have seemed it never could recover. Yet the corpse had life in it still. In 1794, Robespierre was executed. As the century ebbed out, military officers rose more and more to the top. One of these was Napoleon Bonaparte.

Under Napoleon, a new society of aristocrats was born (Geyl, 1949; Thompson, J. M., 1952; Wright, 1960, 86–106). In principle, it was an aristocracy of achievement. Yet aristocrats normally had been achievers of power and wealth, and in that the new were not truly different. Further, the elite soon resuscitated aristocratic habits which for a time had seemed dead. Once-hated symbols of high status were refurbished for new use. From 1808, noble titles came into favor again, rank in governmental and military hierarchies providing the criterion for appropriate honor. Generals became marshals, princes, and dukes; ministers and senators became counts; presidents of departmental electoral colleges, higher judges, and mayors of large cities became barons; members of the Legion of Honor became knights.

The old aristocracy also survived. Many former noblemen remained impoverished by the Revolution. But others had retained their property, a source of wealth even without feudal privileges, and even their titles reappeared, in spite of the law, since the usage "former count" (ci-devant comte), "former baron," and so on, became customary. Titles have never identified all who were bearers of aristocratic culture. Yet the reappearance of titles at that time was diagnostic. The prerevolutionary culture of the upper class had many years of life still to come.

Not since the Middle Ages had the Aristocracy of France been so dominated by a military ethic. More than half of the letters of nobility went to army officers, and about one-fifth to men in governmental posts. For the rest, 6 percent went to wealthy or influential men, 3 percent to prelates of the church, a mere 1.5 percent to scholars, writers, physicians, and members of the liberal professions, and practically none to businessmen.

High society learned to favor uniforms, the dress saber, and military honors. Some of the new leaders made no effort to disguise the unpolished manners of the barracks, showing disdain for civilian softness and sensitivity. But for the most part, genteel habits were revived. The court itself became a social center, gay and ornate, carrying neoclassic modes to a new epogee.

Napoleon wanted to create a nobility of achievement that would revive and perpetuate a noble way of life in a neoclassic mold. With this goal in mind, an individual was allowed to pass his title on to his heirs only if he also passed on a fortune large enough to support an appropriate standard of life. Consistent with the emperor's penchant for order, the amounts of such fortunes were explicitly defined. A prince of the empire had to leave his son an estate with an income of at least 200,000 francs per year; a count's estate must yield a minimum of 30,000; that of a baron, 15,000; and that of a knight, 3,000.

The emperor had been working toward a gradual amalgamation of his own titled courtiers with the older aristocracy. In this respect, evolution gave place to revolution when the empire collapsed in 1814. Restoration of the monarchy restored the old aristocracy as well.

The Restoration was culturally as well as politically reactionary, for the king returned to France with a coterie of diehard defenders of the old way of life (Sauvigny, 1955). Absent from changing France for years, their ultraconservatism was so strong that they had turned down earlier offers of amnesty accepted by many. When they arrived with Louis XVIII, who soon was succeeded by Charles X, the frivolity of an imperial generation died down, and in its place an ethic of piety and morality diffused.

Fields and villages became important again for most members of the upper class. Feudal tax and status privileges were not restored. Most lived well, however, from the land they had either retained or regained. Loss of old special privileges was balanced to a degree by the more complete control they now exercised over their estates. No legal and few customary restrictions on exploitation of the land had survived. *Noblesse oblige*—a sense of responsibility for tenants and villagers— lost its force. Many ignored its demands completely.

Rather than mere landlords, some became active farm managers who rationalized their estates economically. This was not an innovation. The Old Regime had known a few such gentlemen farmers. Now there were more. The general backwardness of industry did not favor experimentation with better equipment, however, so most efforts went into stock improvement, with the introduction of English cattle, Spanish sheep, and improved horse breeds.

The royal court became as status conscious as of old and grew extravagant in its pageantry. But it could not match prerevolutionary Versailles. The king no longer dispensed pensions and sinecures to attract courtiers, and factionalism within the nobility led many to seek alternative social circles. The courts of the Comte d'Artois and the Duc d'Orléans competed with that of the king, while numerous salons, including those of the successful bankers Lafitte and Rothschild, attracted still others. Yet, on the whole, social leaders were identifiable, and the upper class conformed to resurrected ideas about the good life.

A new political upheaval took place in France with the creation of the July Monarchy in 1830 (Brogan, 1963, 52–92). When Louis Philippe became king, the old nobility, loyal to the Bourbons and to a traditional style of life, retreated to country estates. Some devoted themselves to rational development of their farmlands; many simply idled their time away. As the historian D. W. Brogan notes, "The 'émigré of the interior' became a familiar figure, sulky, hostile, living in a world of dreams and resentments." (Brogan, 1963, 55.)

Louis Philippe gave titles to men who thought and felt as he. The new elite lacked both the elegance of courtiers under the Restoration and the military bearing of noblemen in the time of the empire. Rather, they were men in trousers, top hats, and umbrellas, in many ways imitative of the old aristocracy, but without the éclat of earlier times. Their rise to importance represented a break in the continuity of upper-class lineages. For the most part, these were not the scions of old aristocratic families. Neither were they businessmen in charge of commercial and manufacturing concerns. Rather, most of them came from the liberal professions, from administration, and from the world of finance. They were men of wealth and ability, capable of assuming positions in government.

This change in the personnel of upper-class society was not without precedent. A similar change had taken place in the time of Charlemagne. Another occurred in the seventeenth and eighteenth centuries when power shifted from the older sword nobility to a class of successful administrators, the newly created nobility of the robe. Once again, the composition of upper-class society changed under Napoleon. It is important to realize that a change in personnel did not necessarily imply a change in culture.

It is customary to speak of the new upper class of the July Monarchy as bourgeois, implying they abandoned the culture of the aristocracy for that of the so-called middle class. "Henceforth it was the bourgeoisie that set the tone," writes Professor Gordon Wright, "no longer in brazen imitation of the nobility but in conformity to its own developing set of semiaristocratic, semi-bourgeois standards and ideals." (Wright, 1960, 213; see also Landers, 1965, 131–133.) The same had been said of Louis XVI in the eighteenth century. He too was accused of propagating bourgeois tastes. The implication is distortive in both instances.

True, culture change took place in the 1830s. It was long overdue. Aristocratic customs during the Restoration had become anachronisms in their own time. They had grown increasingly out of step with other developments. The moment had come when it was appropriate to shift to trousers, top hats, and umbrellas. But the resultant standards and ideals were not partly aristocratic and partly something else. They were completely aristocratic. The new upper class updated and modernized a style of life shaped by the control they had of wealth, power, and leisure. Gentlemen in long pants and top hats can be as noble as those who wear breeches and lace, particularly when such dress is associated with manorial housing, formal entertaining, seasonal recreation, and the enjoyment of power.

The most prestigious of the upper class even continued to assume court titles. Louis Philippe granted titles. So did Napoleon III shortly after the Second Empire began in 1848. And under the Third Republic (1870–1914), the number of new titles grew in what the historian Albert Guérard has characterized as a "stupendous" manner (Guérard, 1965, 174; see Wright, 1960, 355). By then, titles had lost all economic and political advantage. They were merely symbols. But they were symbols of allegiance to noble standards and the genteel life.

From World War I to the present, an upper class has continued to persist in France. The sociologist Jess Pitts estimates that the upper 3 to 4 percent of the total population presently includes only about 15 percent aristocrats, the remaining 85 percent being "bourgeoisie." (Pitts, 1963, 236.) But whether noble or nonnoble in lineage and title, this small elite still lives in a way shaped by the control of wealth, power, and leisure. It is a culture which has changed enormously since the Middle Ages and before, yet its continuity is unbroken, and it remains an aristocratic culture insofar as it is a proud and prestigious tradition based upon the control of power and wealth. In Europe as a whole, the essential thing for the upper class always has been to live nobly. The elite in France still does this well.

ENGLAND:
ADAPTING TO CHANGE

In England, too, an aristocratic culture survives to our time. During the nineteenth century, industry created a new basis for the control of wealth and power. But newly rich businessmen did not compete with the ruling class, they joined it. Typically, the successful factory owner fell victim to that old deference, "a sneaking kindness for a Lord," as Gladstone put it, an habitual respect that many Englishmen still have for social superiors (Briggs, 1963, 11, 91–92). Typically, a *nouveau-riche* merchant purchased a landed estate, emulated upper-class mannerisms, adopted aristocratic living habits, sent his children to exclusive schools, and married them into the highest social stratum. By the time his offspring had finished school and married, the new generation, at least, had broken completely from older family custom.

The continuity of aristocratic culture remained intact, although it changed somewhat in content. Perhaps the absorption of businessmen in an atmosphere of capitalistic expansion was a source of change. Perhaps, too, concern for the consequences of envy played a role. "The aristocracy live in fear of the middle class—the grocer and the merchant," it was written in 1867. "They dare not form a society of enjoyment as the French aristocracy once formed it." (Cited in Lewis and Maude, 1950, 62.) In all events, the Victorian Age witnessed elaboration of a comparatively austere mode of life for the ruling class. The tone was one of regularity of habit, of sober conduct, of homes filled with heavy, ornate furniture. Queen Victoria herself became the embodiment of "ideals of family life, of earnestness, morality, and patriotism." (Lewis and Maude, 1950, 67.)

The stolid refinement of the Victorian upper class gave place to a rediscovered elegance when coronation of a new king inaugurated the Edwardian Era (1901–1914). For the first time since 1837, and for the last time in history, the royal British court showed how a carefree upper class could live. Open to a wealthy elite in Britain, it became a center for French urbanity and American extravagance. Customs, of course, were those of the period, and to many they seemed inferior to earlier standards. " 'Society' still keeps its end up," it was observed, "but in Edwardian days it was far more self-conscious than now. Sex was not openly discussed. The conventions bred oversensitiveness to absurdly subtle class distinctions." The writer also felt good taste had declined in art and in dress. Women's clothes in particular came in for censure. "It was noticed in Paris on the occasion of a royal visit," he states, descending now into mere gossip, "that the French ladies had politely brought out their dowdiest hats so as not to outshine their exalted British guests." (Bloomfield, 1955, 168.)

Yet, for the ruling class, the Edwardian Era "was incredibly free and comfortable." It was "an age of boisterous wealth and prosperity . . .," as one commentator put it (cited in Havighurst, 1962, 40). Other authors agreed. "Their assured, curt voices, their proud carriage, their clothes, the similarity of their manners, all show that they belong to a caste and that caste has been successful in the struggle for life," wrote Arnold Bennett in 1909. And with the novelist's ability to grasp what often escapes the social scientist, Bennett noted that "It is called the middle class, but it ought to be called the upper class, for nearly everything is below it . . . ." (Cited in Lewis and Maude, 1950, 17.)

The first decades of the twentieth century brought changes of great significance for the upper class. In 1920, Paul Cambon, the French ambassador to England, described them in these terms: "In the twenty years I have been here I have witnessed an English revolution more profound and searching than the French Revolution itself." He then went on to explain, "The governing class has been almost completely deprived of political power, and to a very large extent of their property and estates, and this has been accomplished almost imperceptibly and without the loss of a single life." (Cited in Lewis and Maude, 1950, 89.)

Precedent for this change was established in 1909 when Lloyd George proposed his People's Budget. That budget provided for disproportionate taxation of the wealthy to finance welfare projects. It introduced the practice of high inheritance taxes, special taxes on unearned income, and supertaxes on higher incomes even when earned. This shift in the tax structure escalated in subsequent years, and particularly after World War II. Income tax and surtax now reach 97.5 percent on the highest incomes, and death duties have reduced wealthy old families to penury.

Yet the upper class with aristocratic tastes still exists in England. As Roy Lewis and Angus Maude have observed,

> The Royal Enclosure at the Ascot race meeting, the Eton and Harrow annual cricket match, a fashionable wedding at St. George's, Hanover Square, a coming-out dance for debutantes in Mayfair—a glimpse of one of these ritual gatherings may satisfy a working man or a suburbanite that the upper class exists, that society continues, powerful, monied and exclusive. (Lewis and Maude, 1950, 11–12.)

The upper class now finds it difficult to support old luxuries, however. Great estates have broken up or turned to new purposes. Very few can afford the leisured life of the country gentleman. Rather, we find an upper class with business and professional responsibilities, people now forced to fit their social lives into the interstices of a busy routine different from that of the old days.

Under contemporary circumstances, it is perhaps remarkable that old customs survive as much as they do. Newspapers still display "pictures of titled men and women at meets of the Quorn or the Pytchley, at shooting parties, at Goodwood or Ascot, at the Eton and Harrow match, at Cannes or Biarritz." (Mowat, 1955, 204.) Gentlemen's clubs still exist in Piccadilly and Pall Mall, though they are the haunts of business and professional men as well as aristocrats as such. Clothes, which used to provide clear signs of class, no longer so clearly distinguish. Speech, on the other hand, provides a clue, since the upper class uniformly speaks "U," the dialect originally associated with Oxford and Cambridge Universities.

It is customary to brand contemporary upper-class culture as "middle class," and the characterization is derogatory. It reflects an implicit allegiance of the observer to the stylistic mandates of an earlier society and an unexamined assumption that upper-class culture must continue largely without change to be truly upper class. In fact, the dominant class has always had to adapt to changing circumstances, and their way of life has necessarily balanced continuities with significant discontinuities throughout history. Upper-class culture in contemporary Britain is the legitimate descendant of a noble lineage in that regard.

RUSSIA: A NEW
PRIVILEGED CLASS

With the October Revolution in 1917, Russia became the dominant component of the Union of Soviet Socialist Republics, bringing a communist regime not only to Russians, but also to White Russians (Byelorussians), Ukrainians, and other ethnic groups (Black, 1960; Mazour, 1962). After 1945 the other nations in eastern Europe also became communist, Yugoslavia doing so independently of the USSR, while East Germany, Latvia, Estonia, Poland, Hungary, Czechoslovakia, Albania, Rumania, and Bulgaria became satellites.

The intent of Lenin, Stalin, and other communist leaders was radically to change the class system. Ultimately they hoped to eliminate all but the working class, the proletariat, as augmented by a proletarian-adapted peasantry. In fact, they brought about enormous changes, but these changes did not constitute as sharp a break with the past as may at first appear.

The old aristocracy of Russia was eliminated by the revolution. Deprived of their land, wealth, and influence, the well-to-do disappeared as a recognizable class. Many escaped to surrounding countries, where they became a familiar sight in the twenties and thirties. The lucky ones—able to smuggle jewelry and gold out of the country, foresighted enough to establish bank accounts abroad, possessed of professional skills with which to earn a good living, helped by influential friends and relatives, or married to monied foreigners—they perpetuated something of the old way of life in new surroundings. Many, however, saved only their lives. In Paris, London, Rome, and other cities throughout Europe and America, Russian aristocrats, ruined, took what jobs they could get. Waiters, musicians, and even doormen at restaurants and night-clubs in major Western cities often were escapees from the Revolution. Some had been noblemen of rank and influence.

Fighting and bloodshed came to an end. The Bolshevik government turned from revolution to consolidation. As they invested themselves in the gargantuan task of modernizing a war-devastated, underdeveloped nation, they aimed to create a truly classless society. Yet the very act of governance, including management of the state-controlled economy, silently and unintentionally created a new class of privilege. Some saw what was happening, and objected. But the trend proved inexorable. To run the nation, skilled, experienced, educated leaders were needed. As high-ranking bureaucrats in charge of governmental operations or the management of industry, leaders claimed rewards, and they got them (Djilas, 1957, 35–47).

This so-called new class crystalized out of the masses of east European society and now perpetuates itself from one generation to the next. The American economist David Granick finds for Russia that the children of executives and professionals have a much better chance than the children of ordinary citizens to get into high-priority engineering schools, and ultimately to end up in top managerial positions. "The Russian October Revolution itself could not break the traditional pattern," he concludes. Apparently, the motivation to achieve, an attitude of self-confidence and experience in thinking abstractly—qualities essential for success—are more likely to be nurtured in executive and professional families than in the families of the working class. Even an avowed Soviet bias in favor of worker and peasant children has not overcome these advantages (Granick, 1961, 39–42).

A former vice president of Yugoslavia, Milovan Djilas, has described the new class as enjoying a way of life characterized by the right to use, if not to own, country homes, the best of housing, good furniture, automobiles, and resort facilities for vacations (Djilas, 1957, 57). The proletarian ethic discourages and punishes those who conspicuously consume wealth, so these advantages appear very modest by comparison with the West. Nothing approaching the opulent luxuries of former Russian noblemen or contemporary Western millionaires exists now in eastern Europe. Yet, modest though they are, the new upper class is set apart from workers and peasants by their control of wealth, power, and leisure.

Soviet sources offer no information on this new class. Milovan Djilas was expelled from the Yugoslav Communist Party and condemned to ten years in the notorious Srenska Mitrovica Prison because he spoke out on these and other issues. David Granick gives us some idea of how the new class lives in Russia. In the absence of other documentation, we can accept his findings as at least roughly suggestive of how the upper class lives in eastern Europe as a whole (Granick, 1961; see also Miller, 1961, 125–147).

The Russian managerial family enjoys an income that is much greater than that of ordinary people. There are limits on what the money can be used for, however. Good housing is unavailable, and a fine house, if it could be obtained, would evoke criticism as unacceptably luxurious. So the manager and his family must make do with an apartment of perhaps two medium-sized rooms, a small kitchen, a toilet, and a bathroom. Good-quality, ready-made clothing can be bought. Most managers are not able to own a private car, but they are very likely to have exclusive use of a factory car, perhaps even with a chauffeur. To some extent, such cars may be used for family driving and Sunday recreation. Just as often, however, managers and their families rely on public transportation, as workers do.

Perhaps the most luxurious acquisition a manager can hope for is a summer cottage (*dacha*) in the countryside for vacations. Small, with outdoor plumbing, these *dachas* provide welcome retreats from crowded cities. In some areas a member of the new class may also invest in a boat, perhaps even in a small yacht with galley and berths. But in general, consumer durables are limited in quality and availability. The comparatively affluent bureaucrat possesses a small refrigerator, a radio, a television set, and a tape recorder. His furniture will be relatively good. There is not much else he can buy to put in his home or on his back.

With these restrictions on the consumption of wealth, the culture of the new class tends to emphasize other aspects of European upper-class custom. Well-to-do families enjoy good dining. Restaurants are well patronized, though nightclubbing is limited, with very few hotels providing a band and the opportunity to dance.

Unable to develop a traditional kind of aristocratic material culture, members of the new upper class have focused on esthetic and intellectual interests. Even in smaller cities, the Soviet state provides excellent opportunities for theater, ballet, musicals, and concerts. "In this respect, the Russian is part of the general European culture," observes Granick. "But he goes even further. Imagine a four-hour dramatic performance in the United States! Only Eugene O'Neill could get away with it. But in Russia, the four-hour five-act play is standard fare." (Granick, 1961, 103.)

The Russian upper class also reads a great deal. Unlike most American businessmen and technocrats, but like those of western Europe, the Russian reads more than newspapers, trade publications, and technical reports. A Russian executive who looked only at such materials would be considered "uncultured." In devoting his leisure to fine literature, the Russian is in part merely illustrating how limited are his opportunities to utilize leisure. But in part he seems also to be living up to old upper-class ideals insofar as he is able. "Perhaps," Granick concludes, "he is responding . . . to old European traditions, well ingrained in Russia, where the term 'uncultured' is one of the strongest forms of damnation." (Granick, 1961, 103.)

The new class in eastern Europe appears to have adapted more-or-less traditional customs for affluent living to the restrictions of a relatively limited pocketbook and an austere ideology. Compared with surviving upper-class culture in western Europe, the new elite culture represents a very impoverished version of old traditions. What is remarkable is that old traditions survive at all to structure a life of relative luxury.

Today, the trend appears to favor a rapprochement to the prevailing western version of the good life. Tastes in eastern Europe increasingly reflect those of the west. Modern art, *avant-garde* music, and extreme styles of dress and comportment in the past have occasioned severe censure by the government. Yet this kind of xenophobia is in decline. Eastern Europe seems enchanted with modern western culture, and as contact with the West has grown easier and more intensive in recent years, the old drive to emulate western styles of affluence have reasserted themselves.

MODERN ARISTOCRACY:
JET-SET SURVIVORS

Throughout western Europe, a modern form of the traditional culture of the aristocracy survives (e.g., Brügge, 1966). The bearers of this culture wear elegant clothes and expensive jewelry. They live in mansions and townhouses, some in modernized castles and palaces. In Rolls-Royce or Mercedes sedans they still are driven by liveried chauffeurs. To reach their country estates for weekends and vacations, they may fly, often in their own privately owned airplanes. Cocktail and dinner parties need not always require formal attire, but uniformed maids are *de rigeur* and liveried man-servants desirable.

In their homes these people may display collections of paintings and *objets d'art* which are quite traditional in character. But they are just as likely to favor contemporary painters, sculptors, and interior decorators. Some modern estates incorporate television sets in bedroom ceilings, art galleries separate from the dwelling, flamingos in the estate park, and concrete bomb shelters outfitted for protection in the event of atomic warfare.

Even the traditional "season" survives in adapted form. Modern modes of communication have changed it in many ways. In a quieter century, when horse carriage and railroad moved noble families between town and country, most movement took place within a region or nation. Today, seasonal moves span all of Europe, and reach Asia and the Americas. The upper class has become the jet set. Its leaders find their way to private residences and resort hotels along the French Riviera in the summer, and to the Swiss Alps for skiing in the winter. At St. Moritz, some habitués maintain private mountain-top residences, while many reside in the old Hotel Palace, where society may include such world-famous names as Niarchos, Onassis, Ford, and Agnelli, and where the "ins" will recognize the distinguished names of Prince von Thurn und Taxis, Princess Bismarck, Prince Alfonso zu Hohenlohe, and others.

The jet set also rallies at estates all over the continent for weddings, silver anniversaries, and other events, and spends time in capital cities for seasons of drama and music. Even with family time in country homes, it all adds up to a very fast pace, one possible only because the old way of life has adapted to the potentialities of modern technology. Attaché cases and business suits are deceptive. They make powerful men look little different from many more ordinary people. Yet members of the upper class perpetuate traditions as old as the aristocracy itself.

Item: In Germany, Professor Dr. Ernst George Schneider is a leading industrialist. In his Düsseldorf Castle estate he keeps a large collection of old Meissner porcelain as well as paintings by Paul Klee. He is patron of the medical academy and the town theater. For his sixty-fifth birthday, he invited 850 friends and employees to the Düsseldorf Opera House to enjoy a special performance of a rarely played Haydn opera.

Item: Another West German, Duke von Württemberg, apparently thought nothing of turning the weddings of his children into folk holidays for the villagers of his enormous estate. As a "morning gift" to the bridal pair, traditionally presented at breakfast the day after the wedding, and not to be confused with the wedding gift itself, he gave a white Mercedes, a leopard coat, and two arabian mares.

Item: Prince von Thurn und Taxis, in spite of enormous losses of land in East Germany, still is a large landowner. A banker as well, he celebrated the opening of a new central office for his firm by inviting 500 guests to attend a private performance in a Munich Theater, after which a buffet dinner was served. Each guest was presented with a commemorative gold medal struck for the occasion. The grand old manner lives on, at least for some.

Thus an upper-class way of life still exists in Europe today. It has changed as modern technology, modern tastes, and contemporary political and economic realities have changed. But upper-class culture always has changed in that way. Insofar as the eighteenth century is our baseline, the twentieth century is no more different in terms of basic cultural content that is the sixteenth century. Both are part of an ancient tradition which always had been flexible and innovative.

It is not change in cultural content that makes twentieth-century members of the upper class different. It is change in the relationship of upper-class culture to the cultures of other classes within the system that is Europe that makes Modern Europe markedly different from Traditional Europe. (For one nation looked at in this way, see Anderson, R. T., 1972a.)

Effects of a Large Middle Class

One way in which upper-class culture differs in our time is in its relationship now to a large middle class. For many centuries, the culture of the aristocracy belonged to a tiny elite. Since it required wealth to perpetuate itself, it always included some individuals who shared goals with the wealthy, but could attain them only in attenuated form. Many such people were old gentry who had fallen to relative impoverishment, and were forced to adjust older family customs to contemporary financial realities. Others had risen from humble status, attaching themselves to the upper class as clerks, priests, teachers, artists, or functionaries of various sorts. Still others became successful as businessmen. As industrialism grew, especially during the eighteenth century in England, and throughout Europe in the nineteenth, the number of these families increased at a rapidly accelerating pace. They are identified now as the bourgeoisie or middle class, and they are far more numerous than the old elite of wealth, leisure, and power.

The style of life of the middle class has always been that of the upper class, but modified to fit more limited pocketbooks and a different work routine. Their housing is more modest, their dinner parties less elaborate, their wardrobe more restricted. Unable to sponsor hunting parties or to travel extensively for seasonal recreation, they place emphasis on those activities not so expensive to pursue.

Bourgeois individuals give over some of their evenings to musical gatherings, and spend leisure hours reading old classics and contemporary novels. They attend concerts, the theater, ballet performances, and the opera. The gentlemanly art of conversation is cultivated or, at least, those habits of dining and relaxing in which conversation may be appropriate. Pleasure gardens occupy them as well as touristic vacation trips. Above all, they live in terms of a shared world of discourse partly learned in school.

Middle-class individuals tend to be relatively well educated. In the classroom, young people carefully and systematically are taught speaking mannerisms, values, interests, norms, beliefs, and facts appropriate to their class, all under the strict discipline of a schoolmaster. The process provides a very effective supplement to family training as well as a powerful enculturative institution for individuals moving upward from the lower classes.

Upper-class society includes a large middle-class element now. It also plays a greatly diminished role in creativity.

The old elite was the class that created traditional European civilization. In literature, art, music, architecture, science, and manner of life, members of the ruling class either were creators themselves, or were the patrons of creators. Insofar as they were patrons, the artists, scholars, and builders who did their bidding shaped their creations to suit aristocratic tastes. So civilization evolved as the plaything of the aristocracy, in a manner of speaking. It reflected aristocratic ideals.

In Traditional Europe, innovation within upper-class culture was structured by a pan-European network of personal interaction. Further, the network was centralized, so that certain capital cities played leading roles; within such cities, a hierarchy of social circles and prestigeful individuals made it possible for a rather small coterie of people in intimate contact to play a dominant role in reaffirming norms or introducing novelty.

The aristocratic network survived to World War I for Europe as a whole. In those prewar years, royalty enjoyed its final moments of cultural supremacy. The czar in Russia, the emperor in Germany, and less powerful monarchs elsewhere gained new visibility as social leaders in a time when photographs and well-circulated newspapers and magazines were dominant in the field of mass communications. Above all, the court of Edward VII of England was cultural leader for the upper class throughout Europe.

The cultural network of the aristocracy did not fully survive the war. The Russian czar and the German emperor were dethroned. The king of England became unglamorous, and popular democracies or fascist movements elsewhere threatened other surviving relics of the old order. Of course, royal courts were never essential to the network. Private salons could serve the same purpose. And the upper class did continue to congregate in capital cities and in seasonal retreats. To that extent, the old network survives still in western Europe. But though it survives, it is superseded by other, more effective mechanisms for cultural continuity and change.

Since the Great War, especially, cultural creativity has broken free of the old elite structure. The role of the fashion leader is different now. He still is identified by his place in a social structure, and his effectiveness still is determined largely by how he is placed. But the social structure is a new one. It is peopled by store managers, salesmen, wholesalers, and the clerks who help you try on a suit or test a sofa. It includes ministers, priests, and teachers. A few individuals possess influence that can circle the globe: in clothing, top couturiers; in home and landscape design, top architects; in industrial products generally, designers in major industrial concerns. In a changing family code and personal morality, religious leaders, newspaper and magazine columnists, movie directors, playwrights, novelists, leading scientists, and physicians assert a pervasive influence.

Decisions which can influence conservatism or change within a whole civilization may now emanate from manufacturing and sales concerns, religious, educational, and scientific institutions, and the organizations of politics and government. Advertising and mass media transmit and inculcate innovations. Style leaders, however, still must have norms to live by. They must have values by which to judge. And where do they find them? In the search for guidelines leaders turn to working-class norms or peasant ideals, especially in the arts. Importantly, they look to a new youth culture. But for the most part, the leaders in change and continuity look where leaders always have looked, to the tastes and demands of the upper class. It is an upper class, now, with a large middle-class component. And much creative talent is turned to making this bourgeois mode of life available to people of lesser income. In this sense it is a modern, transformed version of aristocratic culture above all that one sees purveyed in our time to the masses of an industrialized Europe. An occasional reaction, a bohemian revolt, merely dramatizes the over-whelming loyalty Europeans still show to upper-class standards.

Acculturating the Working Class

Not only does the upper class now include a large middle class, and not only does it possess a different structure of creativity, but for the first time it is acculturating working-class and farming-class culture to its own norms, a change of revolutionary proportions.

At the end of the eighteenth century and into the nineteenth, the upper class continued as always to behave as though it was important to them to be different and "better" in culture. They are that way to this day. Yet a highly significant new trend was introduced. As a product of the Enlightenment, leading members of the upper class became distressed about the poverty and degradation of poor peasants and workers. As a matter of conscience and of rational commitment they felt living standards had to be raised. To make this possible, they worked for new factory legislation and educational reforms. These efforts, however, set in motion a process of civilizational change destined to end the centuries-old condition of three distinctive cultures kept separate through a process of cultural differentiation. Slowly, but with increasing momentum, the classes of Europe acculturated.

European civilization as a process in our time, then, is very different from what it was in Traditional Europe. The dominant process is that of the acculturation of working-class and farming populations to bourgeois standards. In the perspective of history, the process seems far advanced already. Yet it remains unfinished. In a survey of the continent a distinctive working-class culture can still be identified, though it is changing rapidly. A distinctive farming-class culture also persists. Yet it too is changing, slowly in some areas, explosively in others. Much of what anthropologists have written about Europe in recent decades deals, in fact, with these developments. We shall examine them in detail.

THREE

RISE OF THE
WORKING CLASS

In the towns of Traditional Europe, craftsmen and tradesmen set the tone for ordinary people. If days normally were filled with the drudgery of hard work, they offered some compensations as well. Artisans were free men, proud of their skills. Apprentices and journeymen worked long hours under the supervision of stern masters, yet in their servitude they nurtured the hope one day of being masters themselves. Further, although men kept to their work benches every day of the week, with time off for church on Sundays, the pace was set by people, not by machines, and at times men slacked off to down a pail of beer or a bottle of wine and to talk. Periodically, the church calendar gave days off, and in each merchant, master, and journeyman guild, elaborate celebrations customarily were organized annually to honor the anniversary day of the patron saint of the guild or of the town. The latter event in particular provided an occasion for the whole community to take on a circuslike atmosphere, featuring a formal parade of guild brothers in church processional as well as a carnival of entertainment in the square.

The townsmen of Traditional Europe did not lead the exciting, thoroughly self-fulfilling lives romanticists often attribute to them, but they did enjoy some excitement and some self-fulfillment. Although unskilled workers and hangers-on were denied the special advantages of guild membership and craft privilege, they bathed culturally in the backwash of others. So long as the dominant members of society worked in commerce and craft manufacturing, town life had cultural rewards for common men, whether skilled or not.

EFFECTS OF
INDUSTRIALIZATION

By the eighteenth century, some towns had large populations of factory or mine workers. Yet through the eighteenth century, artisans and small merchants survived, and their guilds continued to give color to town activities in most places. Trends in earlier centuries became dominant realities in the nineteenth, however. With time, in cities throughout Europe, craftsmen lost their trade to rising manufacturers. Guilds were suppressed, destroyed, or transformed. Surviving artisans, with just a few young apprentices, held on marginally in many parts of western Europe as repairmen and specialists serving a diminishing clientele, or as inefficient, microscopic factories. Towns that once had sheltered thriving colonies of solid burghers became slums for a depressed proletariat. The age of the working class had arrived (Mumford, 1961, 414; Nef, 1963, 273–301).

In the larger view of the economist, industrialization brought with it the diversion of national income from consumption to investment. It brought "a substitution of foundries for beefsteaks." (Hobsbawm, 1968, 72.) To this end, the working class was pauperized. Worse, it was deprived of traditional forms of relief. Where employers formerly felt some obligation to provide for the old and the sick, and where guilds provided explicitly for such needs, factory employment offered only a small cash income which could be cut off precipitously and completely. A man without money was a man abandoned. Unable to pay for food, he starved; unable to buy fuel and clothing, he froze. Not every working man lived in deep poverty but, because cash and cash alone assured survival, every working man lived always with the threat of deprivation. Slums were part of the lives of all working men, whether they lived in them or not (Booth, 1882–1897; Pfautz, 1967, 61–76, 196).

Home and neighborhood for the working class became sad, dreary places. "The town which at one time in English history had provided artists, players, minstrels, great pageants and guild festivals, represented now the meanest and barest standards of life." (Hammond and Hammond, 1920, 50.) Gardens and parks disappeared or were walled in for exclusive use by individuals of higher class, and the skies grew cloudy with smog. "There was no change of scene or colour, no delight of form or design to break its brooding atmosphere," write historians J. L. and Barbara Hammond. "Town, street, buildings, sky, all had become part of the same unrelieved picture." (Cited in Pfautz, 1967, 61–76, 196.)

Housing was deplorable. By the end of the nineteenth century, sociologist Charles Booth found in central London that many a family with several children lived in a single filthy room so infested with vermin that some reported they sat up all night in hot weather because fleas and bedbugs tormented them if they tried to sleep. Small yards intended to serve six or seven families were dominated by garbage heaps and containers of drinking water on which flotsam reposed, the refuse in at least one case including a dead cat. Children played in trash-filled hallways and stairways or were sent out to amuse themselves on unpaved streets. Whole lives were lived out in the filthy, crowded, miserable surroundings of such houses and streets (Pfautz, 1967, 61–76, 196).

For many, nothing gave meaningful relief from the urban slum. There were almost no rewards for the wife who cared for undernourished children in a waterless, one-room flat. There was little pleasure for the husband who returned bone-weary to a damp room filled with wet diapers and cranky people. Sundays in the afternoon and evening were the best times, yet even then escape was limited. Men smoked pipes and drank beer on their doorsteps with other men and women, while children played in the mud and youths gambled in the middle of the street. By evening, many were drunk, at the cost of food, fuel, and clothing needed by their families (Pfautz, 1967, 61–76, 196).

The factory itself, with power-driven machinery and clock-conscious bosses, had dehumanized the working environment. Unskilled laborers functioned as mere tenders of machines, each man trained only to carry out a small part of the total production process. Managers were powerful and remote. Skilled mechanics—master craftsmen in a new guise—though they worked as specialists, became wage workers themselves, alienated too by machinery from intimacy with the products they created.

Long monotonous hours to earn starvation wages bred men of extremely limited personal attainment. They swallowed tasteless helpings of starchy food, drank what they could to seek temporary warmth or oblivion, snatched a few hours of sleep in stinking, crowded hovels, suffered fevers and pain, and worked from dawn to dusk for six and a half days of the week.

NEW RIGHTS
OF CITIZENSHIP

In its early nineteenth-century nadir, working-class culture reduced many people to such an animal-like existence that even Karl Marx dismissed them as the *Lumpenproletariat*, too degenerate to save or reform. Those who got regular work were relatively better off, yet they too lived in poverty and insecurity. In the early stages of industrialization, the dominant class explicitly rejected older paternalistic responsibilities toward the poor. Ordinary town families were stripped of traditional rights and expectations, yet it was a long time before they got new ones to take their place. Workers had no civil rights. In most of Europe, trade unions were regarded as criminal organizations. Restrictions on voting rights deprived proletarians of any voice in government. Lack of education left them nearly helpless (Bendix, 1969, 69; Sturmthal, 1968, 523).

The plight of the working class became desperate, but elements of current ideology offered hope. Philosophers of the Enlightenment nurtured the idea of equal rights for all men (Bendix, 1969, 75). Under the influence of these ideas, working-class protest could be raised, and sympathetic responses in some quarters could be heard. "In the late eighteenth and through the nineteenth centuries," writes sociologist Reinhard Bendix, "the civic position of the common people became a subject of national debate in Europe." (Bendix, 1969, 77.)

As the nineteenth century unfolded, men of the working class gradually were granted the rights of citizenship. Above all, as Bendix has stressed, during the century the lower classes became a political force as they gained two civil rights hitherto denied them. One was the legal right to form associations. Only when they could unite to bargain with employers could they hope to improve their circumstances. The other was the right to an elementary education. "To provide the rudiments of education to the illiterate appears as an act of liberation." (Bendix, 1969, 105.) It is not possible to give exact dates for the granting of these rights. They were won gradually and at different times in different countries. On the whole, however, they were present but incomplete by the beginning of the twentieth century.

RISING POLITICAL POWER
AND LIVING STANDARDS

Time moved on. The working man of the year 1900 lived quite differently from his ancestors of 1800. Many could read, which gave access to political pamphlets and newspapers. (By that time, too, workers generally could hear public speakers agitating for reform.) Political and labor organizations still were weak, though in England, the pacesetter for industrialization everywhere, unions became legal in 1825 and got the right to strike in 1875. Further to consolidate these advances, workers were beginning to gain power as voters. After the revolutions of 1848, movements for representative democracy spread throughout Europe. Residential and property restrictions for decades denied full voting rights to workers, but with time more and more workers were enfranchised (Bendix, 1969, 74–89, 112–122; Eckersley and Seaman, 1949, 137–141; Hobsbawm, 1968, 137–139).

It also took time for governments to regulate the conditions of work in industry. The Act of 1833 in England attacked some factory abuses, for example. But it applied only to textile workers, and while it limited child labor, it set such low standards that children as young as nine could be employed if they were given a few hours off for school. It took a decade for even these minimal regulations to be applied to other industries in England. Yet, by World War I, the eight-hour day had begun to spread, a series of workmen's compensation acts made employers liable for injuries suffered by men on the job, and a Trade Boards Act set a minimum wage in certain "sweatshop" industries. Laws were enacted to encourage wage workers to purchase land on which small homes could be raised, and an old-age pension law granted a small government income to workers over seventy who were needy. The law also provided workmen's insurance against sickness and unemployment and set up labor exchanges to help the jobless find work (Hobsbawm, 1968, 137–139; Rickard, 1951, 176–177).

By 1914, in short, much of the legislative foundation for raising living standards had been laid in England and elsewhere. It took time, however, for laws to become cultural realities. "The stagnant mass of poverty at the bottom of the social pyramid remained nearly as stagnant and as nauseous as before." (Hobsbawm, 1968, 135.) Even so, in England, where progress was most pronounced, "between 1870 and 1900 the pattern of British working-class life which the writers, dramatists and TV producers of the 1950s thought of as 'traditional,' came into being," writes historian E. J. Hobsbawm. "It was not 'traditional' then, but new." (Hobsbawm, 1968, 137.)

Turn-of-the-century workers were better nourished than they had been. Increasingly after 1870 they purchased more meat. Canned sardines became available. For the first time they could afford to buy jam, and to apples they added bananas, newly available at reasonable prices. Margarine, still peculiar in flavor, was welcomed as a cheap substitute for butter. Changing food habits were perhaps epitomized by the appearance and spread after 1870 of what remains to this day the preeminent culinary institution of the British working class, the fish-and-chip shop (Hobsbawm, 1968, 135; Reader, 1964, 92–100).

Workers dressed better too. Factories and cooperative or chain stores developed a working-class market for ready-made clothing and footwear. Shoe stores set the pace. As early as 1875, England had 300 chain shops specializing in footwear. By 1900 there were 2,600 of them. A few cheaply priced consumer's durables also made their appearance. Although only the most successful of workers could afford them, sewing machines fit into the budgets of some during the 1890s (Hobsbawm, 1968, 136; Reader, 1964, 92–100).

By the end of the century, life had begun to brighten again. The music hall had its first major success in the 1880s and became a proletarian mainstay from the 1890s. The Factory Act of 1867 gave factory workers Saturday afternoons free. To fill these leisure hours, professional spectator sports were organized. Association football became a national passion. The County Cricket Championship was founded, rugby was organized, and the Queensberry rules were introduced into boxing. By 1890, amateur sports were well organized, and in 1896 the Olympic Games were reestablished for the first time since antiquity (Hobsbawm, 1968, 136; Reader, 1964, 92–100).

Workers became mobile. For traveling long distances, the railroad added third-class passenger carriages to serve people of small means. A few workers found they could afford recently improved bicycles; later the working class was to be liberated from urban captivity by this invention. Horse-drawn streetcars were perfected. By the 1800s, even men on low wages could afford this convenience. Bicycles and trams permitted Sunday afternoon picnics in the countryside. They also made it feasible to live away from central-city ghettos (Hobsbawm, 1968, 136; Reader, 1964, 92–100).

The end of the century is remembered as the Gay Nineties, and it is right to take note of a new and growing capacity for fun. But the nineties are also remembered as the years of the Great Depression. Falling prices made living costs cheaper for those with money. But many were out of work. The working class and the upper class remained different,

> and the immensity of the gap between the top and bottom of society was merely underlined by the orgy of conspicuous waste into which a section of the rich, headed by that symbol of the luxury class, King Edward VII, launched itself in the decades before 1914. (Hobsbawm, 1968, 139.)

WORLD WAR I:
EAST-WEST WATERSHED

World War I marks a watershed in the development of working-class culture, as east and west each went their separate way.

Eastern Europe

In eastern Europe, the Soviet Union began its rapid ascent in industrial development. For long a backward, agrarian nation, by 1957 it had sent Sputnik on its historic voyage into space. But though Soviet technology developed fast in some areas, it developed slowly in providing consumer goods for the new masses of workers. In our time, proletarians eat well and have warm clothing, but they eat plain food and dress austerely. The housing shortage remains a major problem, with the lucky ones settled in the tiny apartments of new high-standing apartment buildings, while many still must share old apartments with other individuals or families. Sometimes strangers share a single room. Privacy remains rare for the urban working class (Novak, 1964, 15–35).

Consumer durables also remain largely out of the reach of ordinary workers. Automobiles are beyond their reach, and motorized bikes or scooters are uncommon. Only a few own small refrigerators, though anyone may possess a radio, and television sets are spreading in metropolitan areas. In all, as concerns levels of consumption, Russian workers in the twentieth century resemble west European workers in the nineteenth. The profits of industry benefit the managerial class, but otherwise go into capital development. For the Russian worker in our time, as for English workers of yore, low wages and high prices channel money into building industry rather than into improving the quality of life (Miller, 1961, 97–124).

The lot of the Russian worker has not been as hard as that of earlier west European workers, however. Basic needs are taken care of. They have food and clothing, elementary education, basic medical care, and state support in sickness or old age. On the other hand, they pay in a special way. They have security, but they lack privacy. The pervasive police security system of an enormous totalitarian state reaches into every factory, school, apartment house, and home. No deviation from the party line goes unnoticed. No marked deviation from acceptable working-class behavior goes uncensured. Conformity to a strict, austere code is the price Soviet workers pay for security and the promise of a better future (Novak, 1964, 68–99).

Western Europe

In western Europe, the working class has realized some of the potential of pre-World War I reforms. Major change, however, did not take place until the 1950s. Earlier, at a time when success seemed imminent, an aspiring proletariat found their needs and demands postponed by the Great War, tensions and uncertainties in the 1920s, the harsh depression of the 1930s, shortages and destruction during World War II, and several years of postwar reorganization in the late 1940s. Finally, however, in the fifties, sixties, and seventies, high employment and peace brought about changes only dreamed of before (Cantor and Werthman, 1968, 133–134, 273–276; Graves and Hodge, 1963; Hobsbawm, 1968, 233–250; Marsh, 1958).

Consumption goods have become available. In the middle and late 1950s, motorcycles, motorscooters, and motorbikes challenged bicycles, buses, and streetcars. By the late 1960s, small automobiles appeared in working-class neighborhoods: the European worker entered the automobile age, as unprepared for it as Americans were in the twenties and thirties.

Neighborhoods improved as worker housing has gone up in green belts around cities. Although many old working-class neighborhoods survive in town centers, they are overshadowed now by tall apartment buildings. Refrigerators as well as bathrooms with flush toilets, absent or rare in working-class apartments in 1945, now are common. Home furnishings in other ways demonstrate a new if incomplete affluence. Mass housing at times has been imperfectly planned. But in historical perspective, workers have never lived so well (Cantor and Werthman, 1968, 133–134, 273–276; see also Chombart de Lauwe et al., 1959, 47–67; 1960, 65–90).

The higher standard of living created by the new consumption society includes more leisure than ever before. The capacity to move around combines with free time to allow workers to do now what only the wealthy once could do. They can attend distant sports events, visit friends and relatives in the suburbs, go to a movie across town, or simply drive for the pleasure of it. In recent years, they even have been able to take vacations in such old bastions of upper-class privilege as the French Riviera or La Costa Brava in Spain. Workers get paid summer vacations, and tourist agencies offer very low-priced group trips which can place a north European worker and his wife on a beach by the Mediterranean for a price within their means. So many Danish workers have visited the Portuguese Madeira Islands in recent years that some restaurants there now offer *frikadeller* as a popular substitute for Portuguese dishes alien to the Scandinavian tongue.

The world has widened for workers. They travel. Elementary education is virtually universal. Nearly all workers now are literate. Newspapers and magazines are sold everywhere. Since the 1920s, radios have become the common possession of all. At the same time, movies became popular, serving as microscopes which allowed workers to examine other classes and people in detail. In the 1960s, television began its conquest of leisure hours, and today television sets are so widely owned that the cinema has become a threatened industry. Workers often still seem very circumscribed in their interests and activities. A bottle of beer and the "tellie" seem to represent the highest aspirations of many. Yet that very tellie is a formidable means of exposure to other life styles, although the full implications of that exposure have not yet been realized.

URBAN LIVING AND
THE WORKING CLASS

Slums in our time no longer provide an inevitable background to proletarian lives. They still exist. In and around cities such as Lisbon, Madrid, Rome, or Palermo, streets lined with decrepit old houses give shape to neighborhoods as shabby as any in the eighteenth and nineteenth centuries. On the edges of these cities, urban immigrants unable to find proper housing have built small tin, tar-paper, and scrap-wood shacks to form communities so unsuitable for human habitation that in some places the authorities tear them down from time to time because they are eyesores and health hazards. But their inhabitants have nowhere else to go (Anfossi, Talamo, and Indovina, 1959, 28–35; Chombart de Lauwe et al., 1952, 182–192; Kenny, 1966, 182).

In general, as one moves northward in western Europe, slums tend to become less conspicuous or to disappear. In modern times, shanty towns have not grown to substantial size around central and northern towns, although there have been exceptions, as around Paris (e.g., Hervo and Charras, 1971). Central-city slums were once characteristic nearly everywhere, but since the 1950s they have begun to disappear as part of urban-renewal schemes. Their inhabitants are scattering. Often they move into nearby housing, in that way converting older middle-class areas into proletarian neighborhoods. In and around every city, recently constructed, low-priced dwellings, usually in the form of large, often graceless, apartment buildings, have created new alternatives for many of these people (Chombart de Lauwe et al., 1959, 11–25, 47–63, 103–122).

Although housing can be very bad in eastern Europe, the socialist approach to housing tends to eliminate both compact ghettos in the inner city and squatters' colonies on the outskirts. Rather, good and bad housing tend to be interspersed throughout the city. This is the pattern described for Belgrade, Yugoslavia, by the American anthropologist Andrei Simić. A shanty town has grown up in one place, but otherwise, modern apartment houses have been raised in areas where one also finds family dwellings created out of dilapidated wooden barracks, damp cellars, adobe hovels, and shacks quickly and illegally constructed from salvaged materials (Simić, 1970, 178–181).

Building practices of this sort make it difficult to designate any one area as substandard, a circumstance which in part led Simić to speak of "dispersed" slums (Simić, 1970, 178–181). Dispersion in this sense is not unknown in the west, however. In some sections of Paris, for example, new and old housing are located side by side (Chombart de Lauwe et al., 1952, 182–192). The critical difference between capitalist and communist nations appears not to be the neighboring of new and decrepit housing, but rather the fact that in the east families from higher levels of society may live under conditions as deplorable as those of the humblest unskilled worker, while in the west higher-class people enjoy comparatively good housing.

A Culture of Poverty?

From research carried out in Latin America, Oscar Lewis contributed an anthropological perspective to our view of slum living. He defined the life style of certain slum dwellers as a culture of poverty. It is a life style characterized by social marginality. On the national level, the extremely poor do not participate effectively in national institutions except for jails, public-welfare systems, and military conscription. On the local level, too, social participation is ineffective, in spite of crowding and the gregariousness of neighbors. The result is that people depend primarily upon the family. Yet family solidarity is weakened by informal or common-law unions, frequent abandonment of wives and children, sibling rivalry, and competition within the family for money, food, and maternal attention. The result for the individual is apathy and fatalism, "a strong feeling of marginality, of helplessness, of dependence and of inferiority." (Lewis, 1968, xlii–lii.)

It seems likely that some west Europeans are characterized by a culture of poverty. Oscar Lewis felt slum conditions tended to create such a culture in urban centers here and there throughout the world. No anthropologist has yet demonstrated the existence of a true culture of poverty in contemporary Europe, however, so we can only observe that in some nations, particularly around the Mediterranean, but perhaps also in other places, conditions suggestive of a culture of poverty exist (e.g., Coing, 1966, 84). These conditions include a capitalist economy in which workers are paid low wages, a rate of unemployment and underemployment that is high for unskilled workers, an absence of effective organizations of the poor, including kinship groups bigger than the nuclear family, and a belief among the higher classes that poverty results from personal inadequacy or inferiority (Lewis, 1968, xlii–xliv).

The culture of poverty probably constituted a prominent feature of industrial western Europe during the eighteenth and nineteenth centuries. Professor Lewis felt it likely that the culture of poverty flourished in "the early free-enterprise stage of capitalism." (Lewis, 1968, l.) But if it once was characteristic, it now is nearly gone. Modern developments have worked against it all over Europe. In the west, if it exists, it is certainly not widespread. As Lewis has pointed out, "in highly developed capitalist societies with a welfare state, the culture of poverty tends to decline." (Lewis, 1968, l.) Almost certainly, it does not occur in the east. Unskilled workers in a socialist economy may be very poor, but characteristically they are highly organized and, as citizens in a state dedicated to a proletarian ideology, they have a sense of commitment, a feeling of power and importance (Lewis, 1968, xlix–l). A culture of poverty cannot exist under such conditions. Many people in Europe still are poor but, at most, very few live in a culture of poverty (Lewis, 1968, xlviii).

Neighborhood Solidarity

Relatively impoverished proletarian neighborhoods make up part of every west European city. Such neighborhoods do not usually engender that deeper sense of community which may appear in country villages. "The 'we-feeling' of the rural community is insignificant at the urban parish level," concludes Michael Kenny from his study of San Martín, a downtown neighborhood in Madrid (Kenny, 1966, 139; see also Bott, 1971, 96). Yet old urban communities are not faceless, anomic masses either. Social intercourse tends to be less diffuse and less personal than in villages, yet it may exist as a valued ingredient all the same.

San Martín is not without significant communal solidarity. The daily comings and goings of residents create an atmosphere of mutual awareness and common identity. This atmosphere is enhanced by hours of leisure spent in neighborhood surroundings. Nightly before dinner, parishioners join other Madrileños in the traditional *paseo*, a stroll up and down the boulevard to get a bit of air, to look at one another, to court, to chat. Cafés, taverns, and even new fluorescent-lighted, plastic- and chrome-decorated cafeterias draw people together. "The café is . . . a social necessity in the main streets and squares where . . . friends can be met, business discussed, and the world passed in review." (Kenny, 1966, 216.)

The church adds to this sense of community, particularly as it sponsors popular neighborhood fiestas such as the feast of Our Lady of Mercy at the monastery on Silva Street. "It is on these occasions that the parish as a cohesive unit can most easily be defined," writes Kenny, "since they become a focus for parish or district loyalties." (Kenny, 1966, 215–219.)

Old working-class neighborhoods in other cities appear to have at least as much social solidarity as does San Martın. In Rome, sociologist Arnold Rose studied a community that appears to be similar in the extent to which residents know local shopkeepers and peddlers, converse with other residents as they sit in cafés, taverns, or parks, and pause during walks to chat with acquaintances (Rose, 1959, 76–77, 101–102). Sociologist Paul Chombart de Lauwe found in France that working-class neighborhoods tended to become small, closed worlds for their inhabitants. Most of their social life took place within its confines, and community ties were important. "The difficulties of daily life," he writes, "made frequent help from nearby neighbors an indispensable necessity." (Chombart de Lauwe, 1956, 91.) Similarly in the working-class borough of Bethnal Green in London: "Most people meet their acquaintances in the street, at the market, at the pub or at work." (Young and Willmott, 1957, 84.) There too, long residence, familiar surroundings, and facilities such as pubs, markets, and sidewalks contribute to a sense of solidarity (Young and Willmott, 1957, 81–93).

Modern housing developments, on the contrary, become very impersonal worlds for their residents (Chombart de Lauwe et al., 1959, 59–61). Arnold Rose found that working-class families in a new quarter of Rome felt relatively isolated as well as dissatisfied with their lives (Rose, 1959, 77, 102). Chombart de Lauwe's research team of social ethnologists in France reports that working-class families moved to housing settlements frequently feel quite "lost" as they first settle in, that the move breaks down contacts with old friends, and that when neighborhood interaction eventually is reestablished in the new locality, it tends to be limited almost exclusively to the women of the households (Chombart de Lauwe et al., 1960, 240–256).

Bethnal Green Londoners who moved to the Greenleigh housing estate report similar isolation and disenchantment. Frequently they complain of unfriendliness in their new surroundings. Cut off from old friends and acquaintances, they fail to find new ones. Mutual suspicion and distrust isolate people who find themselves no longer living among people they have grown up with. Further, the estate does not provide convenient places to meet (Young and Willmott, 1957, 106–140).

> The pubs and shops of Bethnal Green serve so well as "neighborhood centres" because there are so many of them: they provide . . . small face-to-face groups with continual opportunities to meet. Where they are few and large, as at Greenleigh, they do not serve this purpose so well. (Young and Willmott, 1957, 127.)

Finally, television is available to provide a substitute for missing activities. "Instead of going out to the cinema or the pub," write sociologists Michael

Young and Peter Willmott, "the family sits night by night around the magic screen in its place of honour in the parlour." (Young and Willmott, 1957, 117.) As one Greenleigh father happily reports, "The tellie keeps the family together. None of us ever have to go out now." (Young and Willmott, 1957, 117.) The proletarian families that moved to Greenleigh exchanged the relative intimacy of Bethnal Green for a settlement which seems unconsciously contrived to make them anonymous.

Kinship Ties

The presence or absence of neighborliness in working-class society is correlated in part with differences in the ecology of urban surroundings. Neighbors who have grown up together in old settlements which preserve traditional cafés, shops, and meeting places tend to interact more intensely with one another than do neighbors in most new apartment-house complexes. The intensity and importance of family ties also show correlations with ecological differences. In old, long-established neighborhoods, kinship ties beyond the domestic family appear more likely to shape the social life of workers than in new settlements.

In working-class society, ties beyond the domestic family can be constricted and weak. This is so in France according to sociologist Henri Lefebvre (Lefebvre, n.d., 327, 333). But such ties are not inevitably weak. On the contrary, they may provide an important component of the proletarian social network. Raymond Firth and Judith Djamour report for a working-class borough in London, for example, that kinship ties beyond the elementary family are significant in part as the means to organize mutual aid, but more because such ties provide companionship and a sense of security derived from long familiarity (Firth and Djamour, 1956, 62). But though the British working class nurtures such ties, their kinship system does not develop great genealogical depth. Normally, people more distant than one's grandparents and their descendants are neglected and forgotten, so that people generally cannot trace ties beyond first cousins (Young and Willmott, 1957, 65–66).

The strength of kinship appears to weaken with resettlement. The study of Londoners who moved from Bethnal Green to Greenleigh reveals that people see their relatives less frequently after making the move. Furthermore, distance or the cost of travel make it impractical to resort to kinsmen when in difficulty. If a man becomes ill, his wife can care for him, but if the wife becomes ill, she no longer can turn easily to her mother or to other relatives. These transplanted Londoners do keep up family ties, but residence on the housing estate is an impediment (Young and Willmott, 1957, 106–113).

In general, when individuals and families move from country villages to the city, kinship bonds may remain important to those who moved as well as to those who stayed behind. To the urbanite, such relationships constitute an ultimate source of security. They permit old ties to be maintained while new, nonkin ties are evolved (Denitch, 1969; Friedl, E., 1959; Simič, 1970, 262). So long as the migrant has brothers and cousins in the countryside, he has an ultimate refuge when unemployed and hungry. Keeping in contact with his country cousins gives him a sense of belonging as he enters the strange new world of the city as well as a place to recharge spiritually as he spends his vacations in his home village. It means occasional parcels of fresh fruits and vegetables, sausages, and wine. But above all, it perpetuates a sense of community into an alien environment. In modern Belgrade, according to Simić, "ties with kin are still governed by strong moral imperatives, and their maintenance is an important aspect of contemporary Serbian social life." (Simić, 1970, 219.)

Frequently, migrants seek solidarity in the city in other ways as well. They may establish or join formal voluntary associations which unite them with others like themselves. Most major cities have meeting places which attract immigrants from one province or another. Newcomers congregate with others from the same region in a particular café, church, park, or social club. This is true of migrants within a nation, and it is true of those who cross national boundaries. Ukrainian peasants who migrated to Paris initially met nearly all of their social needs in the context of Ukrainian voluntary associations. Later, Ukrainian churches became the foci for urban congregations (Anderson and Anderson, 1962c). Italians in London also established voluntary associations (Firth, 1956, 67–69).

The ultimate refuge of the working-class individual, however, is the domestic family, comprising a married couple and their unmarried children. Working-class families differ somewhat from the families of other classes. In some cases, at least, they appear to be strikingly matrifocal. When men must be away at work all day, when their wages are low, and particularly when their jobs are insecure, wives may assume a comparatively authoritarian role. This can happen even though the father always remains the legal and moral head of the family.

The findings of Michael Kenny concerning working-class fathers in Madrid confirm this conclusion. He found that poor working conditions often make it difficult or impossible for a father to fulfill his role. The more a man falls short of the ideal pattern in this regard, the more his status and authority within the family is reduced. In formal, ideal terms he remains unchallenged as the head, but mother-centeredness is apparent in that the wife mediates between the children and their father, in that it is her relatives rather than his who normally stay with them, and in that it is her family which may have provided the apartment in which they live (Kenny, 1966, 170–173).

In Bethnal Green, mother-centeredness is even more pronounced. The key to family solidarity there is the tie between a mother and her children, and particularly between a mother and her daughters. Married women tend to live near the homes of their mothers, whom they see often (Young and Willmott, 1957, 29). In some cases, young married women spend part of every day in the mother's flat. "When my husband's home in the evenings we eat separate," remarked one informant. "But in the day we usually have our meals with Mum, or she comes up with us." (Young and Willmott, 1957, 31.) Young and Willmott refer to such merged households as extended families. More than two families may be included.

"All my family," said Mrs. Shipway, "gather at Mum's every Saturday afternoon. We sit jawing, and get amused with the children . . . , play cards and listen to the wireless. No one leaves until tenish at night. It always happens on a Saturday." (Young and Willmott, 1957, 33.)

And in each case it is the mother who is central. Not only is she the focus of warm attachments, she performs important services for her daughters, helping them to find places to live when they marry, aiding them when children are born, looking after babies later on, assisting in shopping, and giving advice and help in any emergency. So long as the wife's mother is alive, the fundamental social unit in Bethnal Green often is an extended family of this sort rather than the nuclear family as such (Young and Willmott, 1957, 28–43).

The closeness of a mother and her children in British working-class families stands in contrast to the relative segregation of the husband and wife from each other. Of a working-class couple in east London, social anthropologist Elizabeth Bott reports that they engaged in almost no joint recreation, and rarely spent their leisure time together except to visit relatives or occasionally to take the children on a Sunday outing (Bott, 1971, 84; see also Bott, 1957). They appear to be typical, not of the British working class as such, but of the working-class residents in old neighborhoods.

Once again, differences in urban ecology appear correlated with differences in social structure. In this case, it helps to understand the nature of the social structure if one thinks in terms of a network of social ties which each individual may possess. The concept has been applied to European problems by John Barnes:

Each person is, as it were, in touch with a number of people, some of whom are directly in touch with each other and some of whom are not. . . . I find it convenient to talk of a social field of this kind as a *network*. The image I have is of a set of points some of which are joined by lines. The points of the image are people, or sometimes groups, and the lines indicate which people interact with each other. (Barnes, 1954, 43.)

Elizabeth Bott finds that in old working-class neighborhoods, the husband and wife each participate in a network made up of friends, neighbors, and relatives, most of whom are born in the area and interact with one another as well as with the husband or wife. After marriage, each spouse can and does continue to satisfy social needs within these old networks. This allows the two to remain relatively independent of each other in many interests and activities. On housing estates, however, the networks are different. Each spouse has ties, but they are dispersed. They have no grouplike quality. Recreational and service needs cannot easily be met by activating such network ties, and consequently husband and wife find themselves significantly more inclined to share activities between themselves rather than with others. Their relationship becomes more joint or intense in that sense (Bott, 1971, 97–98, 101).

WORKING-CLASS
ACCULTURATION

As a process of acculturation, raising the standard of living for the working class has fallen short of final success. E. J. Hobsbawm can speak of the rapid and successful assimilation of the new middle class—what he refers to as the British business classes—to the "social pattern of the gentry and aristocracy," a process essentially accomplished in the last half of the nineteenth century (Hobsbawm, 1968, 141). But a comparable acculturation of the working class was later to begin and still remains incomplete.

In the mid-1880s, when conditions for some were improving, workers could be found whose incomes allowed them to emulate parts of the upper-class style of life in its middle-class version (Pollard, cited in Hobsbawm, 1968, 134). By the turn of the century, the acculturation of the lower class accelerated, becoming truly rapid after 1950. During the late nineteenth and early twentieth centuries, however, acculturation ceased to take place almost entirely as an accommodation of the proletariat to higher classes. In our time, the direction of diffusion remains predominantly from high to low, but the direction is not exclusive. Some culture traits first appear in the lower parts of society, from where they move upward.

That the direction of acculturative change can be from low to high is most apparent in women's fashions. In the 1920s, smoking cigarettes, using facial make-up, or wearing white stockings were among a number of traits which apparently began as affectations of prostitutes and entertainers, spread almost simultaneously to young socialites, bohemians, and working-class girls, and only reluctantly were adopted later by the more conservative women of the upper, middle, and lower classes. As Michael Kenny observed in Madrid of the 1950s, "Maids may try to imitate their mistresses in matters of dress, but a *marquesa* will dress up like her maid if she wants to look smart." (Kenny, 1966, 213.)

In part, we glimpse in the twenties the beginning of striking divergences in the culture of youth, anticipating the generation gap of present times. Today, many fads originate in a society of youth which to some extent defies class ascriptions. The upper classes have discovered new ways of having fun or of acquiring sex appeal by taking over youthful and working-class innovations (Cantor and Werthman, 1968, xxii–xxiii; Graves and Hodge, 1963, 39). But mostly, the diffusion of new traits still moves from top to bottom. Fundamentally, as anthropologist Eugene Hammel has demonstrated, even in communist Yugoslavia today, individuals tend to emulate the life styles of those above them (Hammel, 1969b; see also Goffman, 1959, 36; Simić, 1970, 64).

Emulation of the bourgeois style of life is retarded by relative poverty and the circumstances of traditional proletarian neighborhoods. In the San Martín section of Madrid, for example, Michael Kenny found mixed reactions to the stimulation of moving pictures depicting the modern way of life. To some extent, minor fashions were adopted. But much of what was seen could not be copied. It fascinated women to glimpse American kitchens, but to duplicate them in Madrid was financially impossible for workers. Beyond material possessions, much of what is seen has no place in the old parish. Adults tend to be bewildered or amused by foreign habits and the pace of modern life as they see them portrayed on the screen, though often the young are influenced as in Spain, too, the generation gap widens (Kenny, 1966, 227).

In England, Michael Young and Peter Willmott find a comparable inability to modernize in the old working-class neighborhood of Bethnal Green. Working-class families in the new housing estate, in contrast, acculturate very rapidly to middle-class custom. When they move into an unfurnished apartment, ". . . they make a first cup of tea after the removal van has driven away and look around their mansion," for in their eyes it is nearly a mansion or an estate, and "they are conscious . . . of all the things they need. . . ." In place of old furniture and simple goods brought from Bethnal Green, they feel a need for new belongings and changed habits, ". . . somehow to live the kind of life, be the kind of people, that will fit into Forest Close or Cambridge Avenue." (Young and Willmott, 1957, 129–133.)

London workers resettled in a suburb make a profound adjustment as they attempt to adapt their whole style of life to new surroundings. It is an irony of urban change that, as they search for guidelines in reshaping their lives, they find themselves caught up in the treadmill of "keeping up with the Joneses." Yet frequently this appears to happen. Above all, however, they seem to be groping toward bourgeois standards. "Middle-class morality claims its victim," whined Eliza Doolittle's father sadly when he struck it rich and appeared in a wedding suit to make his daughter's mother an honest woman. No doubt many a transplanted Cockney today might voice the same complaint, except that most do not share Mr. Doolittle's insight as a sidewalk philosopher.

From studies in several parts of Europe, it appears that patterns of family and neighborhood solidarity become less intense when workers move from old proletarian neighborhoods in the inner city to new housing developments. The move appears also to accelerate and intensify a long-range trend to acculturate to bourgeois standards. To the extent that this may be so, the construction of new housing constitutes a development with profound implications for the immediate future of European civilization, because now and in the next decade or two, we may expect an enormous part of the working class to be relocated in urban-renewal projects. The cumulative effect may well be revolutionary.

FOUR

FROM PEASANT TO FARMER

At one time, the great majority of Europeans were peasants. Have any survived to the present? The answer is yes, if by peasants you mean countrymen whose lives in some ways are similar to what they were in the past. In this sense, people living in simple hovels with dirt floors and geese under the table are peasants, insofar as their material culture remains old-fashioned. Agriculturalists who still thresh their wheat by beating it with flails are peasants, because they remain technologically primitive. Those for whom the cultivation of fields is more a way of life than an occupation are peasants, for they retain age-old attitudes and values.

In a different sense of the term, however, it is meaningful to state categorically that peasants are not found in Europe today. More, they have not existed in much of Europe for a century. This meaning of the term draws attention to civilization as a process rather than as an inventory of culture traits. It draws attention to a change in the structure of European civilization, as the relationship between different class cultures has taken on wholly new qualities. It draws attention to the profound consequences of a process of indirect industrialization which reached deep into the countryside in the second half of the nineteenth century and early in the twentieth.

INDIRECT INDUSTRIALIZATION

On the surface, indirect industrialization appears to modify traditional rural custom in rather minor ways (Anderson, R. T., 1972c; Anderson and Anderson, 1965, 103–112). It is a process which in its most visible aspect constitutes an expansion of commerce to bring some new mass-produced consumer goods into the countryside. Its most apparent consequence was that countrymen changed from homespun to factory-made clothing, substituted kerosene lanterns for oil lamps and candles, abandoned the fireplace or masonry oven in favor of cast-iron stoves, and in other ways adopted certain products of industry. To exchange traditional items of material culture for modern industrial products does not in itself constitute a change of large dimensions. In itself, a galvanized-iron bucket doing a job formerly accomplished with a ceramic pot has not transformed a culture.

Surface appearances are misleading, however. Indirect industrialization did far more than merely add a few objects to the peasant inventory. It transformed peasant culture into something different from what it had been. The purchase of industrial products was symptomatic of a withering away of cultural differentiation in the relationship of classes and its replacement by acculturation. In acquiring mass-produced goods, peasants, like workers, began to emulate their social superiors.

Indirect industrialization, then, constituted a change in the relationship of the parts. The structure of civilization became different. Further, the change was significant in magnitude, because new industrial products set off chain reactions. Rapidly, in the perspective of history, the quality of life was transformed. In this, surface indications are misleading. The purchase of new items of culture, seemingly trivial in itself, was associated with sequences of adjustment which had the impact of a revolution, a silent revolution.

Expanded Market Orientation

Indirect industrialization marked the beginning of a significant change in agrarian economics. An important part of the difference between a peasant and a farmer is that the former is a subsistence agriculturalist while the latter is commercial. The difference between the two is not simply that the one produces foodstuffs to eat while the other produces for sale, however. Both produce in part to sell, for peasants since the Middle Ages have had to have cash to pay their rents, dues, tithes, and taxes as well as to buy some things they could not produce themselves, such as salt or iron. Both also may produce in part to consume, for even modern farmers typically enjoy fresh meat, vegetables, and fruit from their own enterprise. Yet, the proportions of subsistence to commercial activities are quite different. The farmer is much more heavily oriented to the market.

Expansion of his market orientation did not take the countryman out of his fields, but it was associated with major changes in crops and equipment. The modernization of field technology tended to transform peasants into increasingly flexible food-producing specialists.

Bookkeeping began to become an accepted part of farm practice as early as the nineteenth century as cultivators in advanced areas learned to be aware of cost accounting. Farming became mechanized as well. Whether through cooperative societies, collective farms, or individual initiative, even in the nineteenth century many farmers came to possess or have access to steel plows, tractors, harvesters, threshers, and other labor-saving equipment. In addition, farmers early learned better techniques for soil management, including a more liberal use of fertilizers.

Crops also changed. In the 1870s, England, France, and Germany found themselves unable to compete with Russia and the United States in wheat production. Nor could they undersell Austrialian sheep merchants in the wool and mutton market. Modern transportation ended the monopoly they formerly enjoyed. For a time, they suffered deep economic depression. Ultimately, they shifted to other forms of husbandry. In turn-of-the-century Germany and France, pig and potato production increased while sheep and wheat production declined. The shift in these countries also included a move to beet cultivation, the raw material of a growing sugar industry.

In Holland, Switzerland, and Scandinavia, farmers shifted from wheat to dairy farming. Pig production also increased in these areas to provide breakfast foods for foreign tables, and poultry production developed to supply a large egg market. In Holland and in farming areas around all of the larger cities of Europe, cultivators learned to emphasize truck farming in order to provide fresh vegetables for local urban markets. More recently in Spain, Greece, and Italy, new commercial crops also have been introduced.

One consequence of this growing market orientation was that fundamental life values began to change. Traditionally, as Robert Redfield has pointed out, the peasant did not regard work as something he had to do in order to support the style of life to which he was accustomed (Redfield, 1956, 27). He simply did not divide his activities into work versus leisure. Rather, he plowed a field, celebrated a holiday, or did repairs on his house as a traditional calendar gave him guidance. Agriculture was part of a way of life rather than merely an occupation.

This changed with a growing orientation to cash crops and to the purchase of necessities and luxuries in stores. A new sense of what life is all about, of what one wants out of life, emerged. Slowly and in places still incompletely, agriculture changed from being a way of life in itself to becoming the job one did in order to support a family. This change took place gradually, almost imperceptibly, in Europe. It grew, however, as part of the process of indirect industrialization.

Availability of
Ready-made Goods

Another kind of change took place more rapidly, and in an equally thorough way changed the quality of daily life. Peasants traditionally not only produced most of the foodstuffs and raw materials they needed, they also processed both food and goods for their own use or for local sale. With modern technology, much of the food processing that formerly was done by hand with simple tools came to be done more easily with new machinery, often no longer on the farm itself. Further, many of the things formerly manufactured by peasants or peasant craftsmen came to be available in stores and markets. The whole realm of nonfield farm work changed, as a consequence, losing much of its complexity and difficulty.

Ethnologist Axel Steensberg has surveyed changes of this kind as they have occurred in Denmark in the last century (Steensberg, 1954b, 100). He finds that milking and threshing machines alone have greatly reduced barn work. Household work is also less time-consuming and less complicated as it no longer is necessary to brew beer, churn butter, make cheese, manufacture candles, card wool, prepare flax, spin thread, weave cloth, and bake bread. It might be added that farmers also have largely given up making sausages, butchering and smoking meat, repairing harnesses, and carving household utensils of wood. Further, village communities no longer include peasants who cultivate fields to supply their basic food needs, but otherwise specialize in quiet seasons as carpenters, masons, furniture-makers, harness-makers, tinsmiths, cobblers, potters, interior decorators, tailors, or what have you. In all, a vast range of local and family activities died out rapidly as industrial products and new machinery made them superfluous. The economic consequences of indirect industrialization were pervasive, even before factories came to be built in the countryside and villagers began to commute to town employment.

Culture Change through
Chain Reaction

To purchase mass-produced goods, then, the countryman shifted increasingly from subsistence to commercial cropping, and with that, shifted his sense of values, abandoning a wide range of traditional activities. The goods he purchased brought still other changes in tow, moreover. It is a fundamental premise of cultural ecology that even minor technological innovations can start reaction chains which terminate in a greatly altered relationship between man and his environment (e.g., Firth, 1951, 86). These alterations can include changes in social structure, in related cultural norms and values, and in personality. Chain reactions of this sort were set in motion in Europe in the late nineteenth century and continue in motion to this day.

A number of culture historians have written about the unintended consequences of technological innovations as the process has occurred in particular instances. Axel Steensberg and Holger Rasmussen, for example, have described developments of this sort that took place during the Renaissance as well as in recent times in Denmark (Rasmussen, 1963, 19–23; Steensberg, 1945a, 88; 1945b, 92–108). Recently, Suzanne Tardieu reconstructed such developments in the area around Mâcon, a town in south-central France (Tardieu, 1964). Her findings illustrate a process which in general terms characterized all of Europe.

Indirect industrialization in the Mâcon region began during the second half of the nineteenth century. Household inventories drawn up for inheritance purposes give detailed lists of what people possessed at time of death (Tardieu, 1964, 46–72). Before 1850, little changed in these lists from one generation to the next. As Tardieu points out, an inventory of 1750 and one of 1850 would be nearly identical. After 1850, innovations became increasingly common. These included a new kind of stove and new lamps, seemingly minor acquisitions. Along with other changes in material culture, however, they were associated with major alterations in style of life.

Changes in the methods of cooking, heating, and lighting were associated with major changes in the quality of country life. From antiquity, as historian Numa Fustel de Coulanges once pointed out, the hearth was the center of home life throughout Europe (Fustel de Coulanges, 1956, 25–33). It stood as a symbol of household integrity and functioned as the central point around which family activities were organized. In the area of Mâcon, the hearth was a chimneyed fireplace where food was cooked in large pots hung on pothooks or placed over tripods (Tardieu, 1964, 218–219, 221–223). The fireplace provided heat for the room and a secondary source of light as well as the place to cook.

As an early product of industry in that part of France, cast-iron stoves were purchased as early as 1845 in towns, and from about twenty years later in the countryside. With the adoption of stoves, the fireplace declined in use and importance. It remains still as a subsidiary source of heat and at times to keep a pot of soup, potatoes, or pudding simmering, or to heat food for the animals or water for washing clothes. But the primary source of heat became the stove in the nineteenth century, a wood-burning stove that could be lit with newly available sulfur matches.

Peasants adopted the new stove because they found it easier to light, easier to maintain, more economical of fuel, better at heating the room, and, for this region an advantage, portable enough to be moved to the porch in the summer for outdoor cooking.

When the open fireplace lost its central position in the household, much of the equipment associated with it went out of use. Pothooks, andirons, tripods, and firescreens were no longer needed. Cooking pots changed. With places on its flat surface for several pots, the stove permitted a more varied cuisine at a time when urban tastes were increasingly appreciated. In place of quite large cauldrons, each capable of holding the soup or stew that fed a family for days in a row, housewives began to use a collection of smaller pots of different sizes, each to cook parts of meals which included various dishes. Since the new pots sat rather than hung, their form was different. They also became lighter in weight, and were made of new, different materials. With this new kitchen equipment, seasonal variations in food consumption declined, but variety within individual meals increased.

Traditionally, the peasant wife stood to serve meals to her husband and sons, taking her own food separately. Greater ease of food preparation as well as new ideas about appropriate behavior allowed her a more equalitarian position. She came to sit at the table with the rest of the family to take her meals.

Household space became differently used. Formerly, activities centered on the fireplace. Tables and chairs were placed around the hearth in order to get the most out of its heat and light. With stoves, heat was more evenly diffused. The individual became less constrained in his indoor activities. The bed warmer, the brazier, and even the use of warm clothes indoors fell into disuse, although they were temporarily revived during World War II when fuel was in short supply.

Before 1870, homes were illuminated primarily with oil lamps in a variety of forms (Tardieu, 1964, 220, 223). New lamps came into use during the century. As early as 1822, oil-burning pressure lamps began to spread, appreciated for their better light and resistance to drafts, even though they had to be pumped every fifteen minutes. Around 1880, the petroleum lamp appeared. Much cleaner, easier to light, with a brighter and steadier light, it rapidly replaced older forms, and was itself improved around 1890 with kerosene fuel. Finally, electricity began to displace other lighting techniques. The first electric plant in the town of Mâcon went into operation in 1910. Soon thereafter, electric lines began their slow spread into the countryside. Between 1925 and 1930, most of the Mâcon area got electric lighting.

The introduction of better lighting further encouraged the growth of wider-ranging individual and family activities. In the days of poor heating and oil lamps, partly as a way of saving fuel costs, evening lighting was used primarily for *veillées*, occasional meetings in which members of neighboring families gathered in one house to pass the time together. In that way, a lighted and heated room got maximum use. The custom died out around the turn of the century, although until World War I the men often met in the evening to chat in somebody's stall.

In the old days, getting water was one of many chores that required daily work and attention (Tardieu, 1964, 220–221). Water had to be fetched from wells, springs, or fountains and stored in barrels and buckets. Because it involved so much work, peasants were inclined to restrict the amount they used. The piping of fresh water did not take place until after 1900. At first available mainly at communal taps, water eventually was led directly into houses, where faucets open into sinks with drainage outlets. The drudgery of household work was lightened by this easier access. The attainment of new standards of personal and household hygiene was also facilitated (Tardieu, 1964, 222–223). Perhaps because lighting got better, housewives became more conscious of dirt. No doubt, too, they were influenced by a growing awareness of higher urban standards. Further, cleaner houses became feasible. The chore became much less discouraging as stoves and lamps eliminated much of the smoke and grease of open fires. And it became less discouraging with plentiful water and new cleaning aids.

Piped water brought an end to the well or fountain as a social center where village women met daily to chat. Thus terminated a source of village or neighborhood sociability fully as significant in its impact and ramifications as the ending of the *veillée*. Both endings contributed to the decline of a sense of community and the increase of a sense of individual and family isolation.

In the old days, furniture was manufactured by the men of the family, or by local and regional craftsmen in their shops (Tardieu, 1964, 224). The result was distinctive styles of furniture in the various parts of France. At the end of the nineteenth century, new tools appeared in such shops and local styles began to erode. Craftsmen not only used new tools, they copied the techniques, and eventually the styles, of larger industrial producers. Ultimately, larger industrial concerns took over the market. The furniture countrymen put in their homes became the same as that of city people, more plentiful and more comfortable than before.

Warmer, better furnished rooms with brighter light created new possibilities for the use of evening hours. In the old days, peasants went to bed early if they did not participate in a *veillée*. Later farmers enjoyed other alternatives.

For example, the farmer might read, having become better educated with access to reading matter (mainly newspapers in the late nineteenth century). Early in the twentieth century he also got the radio.

Until the middle of the nineteenth century, the main route of communication in the region was the Sâone River (Tardieu, 1964, 224–225). A nineteenth-century railroad line introduced more rapid communication with the city of Lyon. More recently, electrification of the railroad placed Mâcon somewhat less than four hours from Paris. With railroads and automobiles, farmers no longer visited cities and towns only rarely and as country "hicks." Rather, they became familiar with urban modes and brought urban concepts to their villages.

In all, factory products in the countryside around Mâcon set off chain reactions of culture change which thoroughly revamped rural life. Even in the nineteenth century, modifications of the social structure appeared as communal solidarity declined, family-centeredness increased, and individualism was encouraged. Values and norms evolved as urban standards of comfort and cleanliness were adopted. Personality was involved, as individuals internalized these values and norms and gained a new image of themselves. People began to think of the good life in terms of money income from their work. In general, changes such as these in a part of France took place all over Europe, but our understanding of precisely how and when must await further research.

LAND REFORM

As specialists in a complex economy, farmers in Europe want secure, adequate incomes that will allow them to meet their needs and satisfy their aspirations in an industrial age. The income and security of an agriculturalist is very much determined, however, by the rules of land ownership and use under which he lives, so farmers and their supporters have agitated for land-reform legislation as part of the process of indirect industrialization.

Landholding laws and customs were far from uniform in Europe in the nineteenth century. Even within a single community, one might find large or small farms owned by their operators, plots worked by sharecroppers and rent-paying tenants, fields tilled by landless laborers, and estates managed by wealthy aristocrats.

It is possible to distinguish larger areas as dominated by one form or another of land tenure (Organization for European Economic Cooperation, 1959). In south Italy and Sicily, central Spain, Ireland, Hungary, eastern Germany, and England, much or most of the land was in large estates. The hard work of tillage in such places was done by hired workers, sharecroppers, or tenant farmers.

In other areas, sharecropping on smaller farms was common. The *mezzadria* of central Italy or the *métayage* of southern France would be prominent examples. In large parts of western Europe, in Scandinavia, the Netherlands, Belgium, France, Germany west of the Elbe, northern Italy, and northern Spain, small, family-owned farms were predominant.

Small family farms also characterized Russia, but the holdings of individual families were subordinate to a late-surviving form of traditional communalism, the *mir*, a village corporation which at times redistributed land ownership in an effort to assure that each family always would have enough to support itself.

In parts of the Balkans, large patrilineal joint families supported a different kind of communal land ownership, the patriarchal *zadruga*. Under this arrangement, a number of families related as the descendants of a single pair of grandparents or great-grandparents tilled their fields as a family enterprise.

Landless laborers, as distinct from landholders, were poor in every part of Europe. Whether employed by small landowners or by large, the field hand scarcely made enough to survive. Normally, he had to put his children to work at an early age. Such youngsters grew to adulthood with little if any schooling, and were conditioned to expect no more out of life than their elders had gotten. In Spain, for example, a field worker around the year 1900 get less than one peseta a day (15¢ or 20¢), plus enough coarse food to keep him alive. Without board, he might make twice that. Yet even such wages would have seemed high if he could have had them throughout the year. Part of the wage picture included unemployment much of the time. One estimate for Spanish field workers reckons them to have been without work for 115 to 165 days of the year. Their families had to manage in the off-season on what could be saved from busy periods. Sometimes they also found off-season work in the mines. Often they were forced to beg.

Day labor was widespread in Spain, Italy, and Hungary, and was common in France and Germany. In many other areas, however, field workers typically were hired for longer periods of time, often by the year, and sometimes as essentially permanent employees. Although term employment lessened insecurity, it did not assure more than minimal standards of living. The money salary was miniscule, and people worked essentially for payment in foodstuffs and lodging.

Field labor was brutal. The Spanish worker, for example, often put in 15 or 16 hours a day, beginning at 3:30 in the morning and continuing until 8:30 in the evening, only to begin again the next morning *if* he was fortunate enough to be needed again. Conditions were comparably bad in most places.

Landholders, if higher in status, were also impoverished, and sometimes they were scarcely better off than landless laborers. In areas of sharecropping or tenancy farming, they frequently had barely enough to keep their families alive after they had paid the landowners their share. Those who owned their own land typically possessed too little to support their families well. This varied, of course, and some cultivators lived better than others.

Throughout Europe, the average peasant lived in one or two rooms, frequently with only a dirt floor, the room inadequately heated in winter. He possessed little furniture beyond a bench, a table, a bed or two, and a few pots and pans. He suffered the threat of drought, flood, plant and animal disease, and the vagaries of a changeable market. Fighting the land with primitive equipment, he maintained life at minimal levels, working dispersed plots from sunup to sundown in the busy seasons, and huddling in cold, gloomy houses in the winter.

Any village might include a few thriving farmers. After the depression of the 1870s, many of the cultivators of the Lowlands and Scandinavia, having shifted from grain to dairy and poultry production, broke away from extreme poverty. Here and there in Europe, life was tolerable and even agreeable. But these were islands in a sea of discontent.

The peasant's view of his own life provided an essential ingredient in his aspirations for the future. As I have described him for the end of the nineteenth and the beginning of the twentieth centuries, he was discontented in the face of persistent low income and insecurity.

It is perhaps inevitable that when he thought of how life might be better, such thoughts were molded to the life he knew. To the extent that he might hope for improvement, he hoped for more of what he already had, or for escape. Typically, he felt that the essential way to end deprivation and insecurity was to own his own farm, one large enough to support his family in comfort (Franklin, 1969, 3).

In the last hundred years, the governments of Europe have almost universally agreed with farmers that future economic, political, and social well-being requires such farms (Organization for European Economic Cooperation, 1959). This changed in Russia after the revolution of 1917 and in other east European nations after 1945, as collective and state industrial farms received official sanction. In the west, however, the goal has persisted to the present.

In Western Europe

Even in west European areas where the family farm is old, reform has been necessary in order to make such enterprises viable. Often they have been too small. Those of Spain, for example, have been categorized as *minifundia*. Frequently fields have been too fragmented. Farms with ten or twenty tiny plots scattered in all directions have hampered the cultivator in many areas.

Creating or improving farms has required reform in land-allocation policies. It has also necessitated efforts to raise productivity by supporting improvements in soil, crops, livestock, machinery, and other modern methods and equipment. Legislation in support of such programs has appeared in various countries from the time of the French Revolution, and particularly from the latter part of the nineteenth century and the early decades of the twentieth. Much of it has been revised in the post-World War II period, however, and much of the legislation now in force is the product of the last twenty years (Coppock, 1963; Raup, 1969, 126–170). The result has been the creation in nearly every part of western Europe of the family farm as the basic agricultural unit.

In Eastern Europe

Developments in Russia took a different turn (Krader, 1960; Volin, 1960, 1970). Serfdom, late to develop, also was late to disappear. It was not officially abolished until the Emancipation Edict of 1861. That edict gave the peasant title to the land he worked if he paid an indemnity to the landlord, but the first real change did not take place until the early twentieth century when the government of Stolypin passed new laws, aimed not only at putting land in the hands of the peasants, but also at helping them to withdraw from the *mir* collectivity and to consolidate their scattered strips. By 1913, about 24 percent of the peasants owned their own independent farms. Rich peasants, *kulaks*, began to appear, men who had succeeded in increasing their acreage.

At the time of the October Revolution in 1917, peasants spontaneously seized the land of large landowners. The Bolsheviks, eager to gain peasant support, agreed to these seizures. The result was a proliferation of small family farms averaging 5 to 6 acres with only one horse, too small for successful farming. Peasant farms increased from 16 million in 1916 to 25 million in 1927, but so many were undersized that the condition of most peasants was not greatly improved.

Throughout this period, surviving drawbacks of the defunct *mir* system continued to plague agriculture. The usual peasant farm still consisted of about 16 separate plots, while some had as many as 100. It is estimated that millions of acres were wasted in boundary strips and unnecessary pathways, while much more than that lay unproductively fallow each year. In some areas fields were located an average of over three miles distance from the village, and one official rather dramatically calculated that a peasant had to walk 1,200 miles every year just going to and from his scattered holdings, four times what would have been necessary were the strips reallocated and consolidated.

Along with increasing inequities in land ownership and the persistence of outmoded land usage, agriculture suffered from the inability to mechanize and modernize. The government estimated in 1928 that about 74 percent of the spring grain still was plowed with wooden plows, that 44 percent of the grain area was harvested with scythes or sickles, and that 40 percent of the grain harvest was threshed with primitive equipment including the ancient and inefficient system of flailing.

Government policy abandoned, in effect, plans for peasant reform during the first decade of the socialist epoch, the period characterized as that of the New Economic Policy (NEP). The peasant urge for viable family farms continued along prerevolutionary lines, but with increasing inequities and persistent primitivity. Finally, in 1928, Stalin ordered massive socialization under the first Five-Year Plan. The program began with a war against the minority of prosperous farmers, the kulaks. Numbering about five million, they were killed, tortured, exiled to Siberian work camps, and dispossessed. Many survived but the prosperous family farm died with this program.

As late as 1927, scarcely any peasants had been organized into collectives, yet by 1930, one-fourth were collectivized, and only one year after that, the figure was about one-half. The program proceeded relentlessly for a decade, and by 1940, nearly all peasants in the USSR either worked on collective farms (*kolkhozes*), or on state farms (*sovkhozes*), the latter employing labor on a wage basis.

The transition from a peasantry with the family farm as its ideal to modern farmers organized in collective farms did not take place easily. Most peasants, however little they owned, resisted the new order. Rather than turn over livestock to the new kolkhozes, many slaughtered them, selling or eating the meat. Between 1929 and 1933 about half of the cattle population and two-thirds of other livestock were destroyed in this way. It took the cattle population until 1955 to regain its 1928 level. The loss of half of the horses of Russia in the 1928–1932 period left the new collective farmers extremely short of draft animals for field work. In the Ukraine, uncounted thousands starved to death as Soviet authorities used a planned famine to convert the reluctant.

Farmer resistance forced the government to allow a truncated form of family farming to survive. Although ideologically undesirable, each family is allowed to keep its own house, some implements, a few animals, and the key element, a small plot of land. Only 3 percent of the arable land of the USSR is allocated to private use, but remnants of family farming persist as a major interest and concern of the kolkhoznik, who labors on them whenever he can get time free from duties on the collective farm.

Collective farming, however, has not been unsuccessful. It has survived the reluctance of the peasantry and the persistence of family plots. The destruction in World War II made it feasible to consolidate kolkhozes into larger, more efficient units. By 1960 the number of collective farms had been reduced to 53,400 from a high of 250,000 in 1950. On these larger units, more efficient use can be made of the machinery which the developing industry of the USSR has made available. Systematic use of artificial fertilizers and a shift to new types of cropping techniques have also increased in recent years.

Agricultural underproduction still constitutes one of the most serious economic problems in the USSR, but it is a deficiency which must be looked at in Russian perspective. Before the revolution, the peasantry starved. It is estimated that in the old days, most peasants had enough to eat only from the harvest in August and September until Christmas. The relatively well-to-do might eat well until Easter. For the rest of the year, they scarcely had enough to stay alive, and occasionally they had nothing. Famines were common in the last decades of the nineteenth century.

Such harsh conditions no longer are typical. Most Russian peasants today have clothes on their backs, food in their stomachs and roofs over their heads. Their complaints are not that the old deprivation persists, but that they do not live as well as they would like, or as well as their counterparts in urban employment. This is a serious problem, but it is a problem of a different order from that of the prerevolutionary period. Nor does the kolkhoznik appear to hope any longer for the family farm. He now appears to see his future in the collective farm, or in escaping the farm, or in profiting from his family plot.

The domination of the rest of eastern Europe by the USSR after World War II led to efforts to impose the kolkhoz system and to terminate the trend to the family farm. As in the USSR, this program was resisted by the peasantry. Efforts continued, however, and by 1962, Bulgaria, Albania, Rumania, Czechoslovakia, Hungary, and East Germany had almost all of their arable land in either collective or state (industrial) farms.

Poland and Yugoslavia stand out as dramatic exceptions to this conversion (Franklin, 1969, 180–217; Portal, 1969, 419–429, 443–450). Polish peasants held to the ideal of the family farm, and as late as 1956, less than one-quarter of arable land had been socialized. Resistance came to a head in the disturbances of October of that year. In capitulation, the government permitted most collective farms to be dissolved, while the acreage under state farms was reduced. Today, only 13 percent of arable land is in the socialized sector. Communist Poland remains a land of family farms.

In Yugoslavia, the program of forced socialization was abandoned in 1951. By the end of 1953, most of the collective farms which had been established were disbanded, so that now only 15 percent of arable land remains socialized. The size of privately owned farms is limited to a maximum of 25 acres, and in fact, most farms have less than 12 acres. Since this leaves many holdings too small to support a family, part-time farmers (workers-peasants) have become common. The government still advocates collectivization, but so long as it attempts to encourage the change by voluntary means it appears destined to rule over a land of family farms.

In large perspective, the peasant of Traditional Europe has become a farmer.

In every part of Europe, some acculturation to modern bourgeois standards has taken place. Even in backward areas, one finds plastic buckets replacing older ceramic and metal containers and factory-produced clothing replacing local dress; growing literacy, access to radios, an occasional movie. One finds items such as eyeglasses, pocket knives, steel blades for plows, coffee or tea, and picture calendars. Elsewhere, acculturation is more complete. On the whole, countrymen differ greatly from one place to another in technological development and cultural condition. Because this variability is great, we need to look at the different parts of Europe in detail. The difference between communist and non-communist approaches to change makes it advisable to look separately at east and west. Eastern Europe can be dealt with as an undivided category, mainly because so little anthropological research has been possible there. Western Europe, in contrast, is well studied, and it must be dealt with in terms of culture areas.

The diversity of peasant cultures confounds any effort to delineate clearcut culture areas. Different scholars have come up with often quite different culture areas, simply because they have taken different culture traits as diagnostic (Bernatzik, 1954; Derruau, 1958; Erixon, 1938; Evans, 1968; Russell and Kniffen, 1951; Valkenburg and Huntington, 1935). Any culture area will suffer the dual shortcomings of not being completely homogeneous within itself and of not being thoroughly distinctive from every other area. Culture areas are useful, then, only as rough guides, as shorthand statements convenient for a preliminary orientation. I shall use them in that way only, as an organizational device, and little more. Occasionally, I shall disregard such boundaries as more distortive than helpful.

Europe as a whole has been divided into four culture areas by Conrad Arensberg (Arensberg, 1963; see also Anderson, R. T., 1972b). He distinguishes a Mediterranean Area, where countrymen tend to live in agro-towns as well as in villages; an Alpine Area, in which village life is seasonally disrupted by the movement of part of the population to high mountain summer camps; an Atlantic Area, which has a relatively high frequency of scattered farms in addition to small villages; and a Plains Area, characterized historically by large villages centered in open (unfenced) fields. It will help, in looking more closely at west European countrymen today, to organize our survey in the following chapters in terms of these categories.

FIVE

MEDITERRANEAN COUNTRYMEN: TRADITIONAL CULTURE AND CHANGE

Dramatic scenery and sunny weather have long made Mediterranean Europe a favored place for world travelers. To those who delight in capturing glimpses of the past in old villages and ancient customs, the area has a special appeal. Yet, in most cases, this very appeal indicates backwardness. Enchanting old villages and now-quaint customs survive in many parts of the Mediterranean area because these regions have remained conservative while other parts of Europe have modernized.

ITALY

If you drive slowly through the countryside in northern or central Italy, you will find yourself captivated by villages and farms which can be extremely attractive, with handsome tile-roofed buildings, shady trees, cool fountains, and green fields and hills covered with vineyards ripening in the sun (see Schnapper, 1971). If you drive into a village or town in southern Italy, including Sardinia and Sicily, your reaction is likely to be very different, particularly if you are alert to the details of your surroundings. South Italy is hot in the summer, with a parched dry landscape. It also is an area of pervasive rural poverty.

Poverty is not uniform within a south Italian community (see Moss and Cappanari, 1962; Silverman, 1966). A village studied by sociologist Joseph Lopreato may be taken as indicative of how social strata may vary (Lopreato, 1967). Professor Lopreato found that a few people live in spacious, well-kept houses with bathtubs, electric heaters, television sets, gas stoves, and refrigerators. They may even own automobiles. Others live more simply, but still are able to build new, spacious, and comfortable masonry houses, wear city clothes, and send their children away for a higher education which may even take them to the university. In all, about half of the families in the village live by the latter standards.

The other half of the families are impoverished. Many, almost one-third of the total village population, are poor without being destitute. The men work from sunrise to sunset to support their families on a few acres of land scattered so widely that they often spend two or three hours a day in walking just to get to and from work. A family of five or more typically lives in a house of only one or two rooms, and that shared with a donkey, goat, or pig. In the spring, just before the new harvest, the poor may find themselves short of food, although normally they have enough beans, vegetables, and bread to meet their basic needs. Inadequate housing, minimal food, and hard work often result in bad health, so that rheumatism, hernia, and other medical problems are a frequent source of complaint. Rarely are their children educated beyond five grades in the village school (Lopreato, 1967, 190–191).

Other families, about one-seventh of the total population, are destitute. Employment for the men in these families is erratic. They support their families on occasional low wages eked out with a few lire in unemployment compensation. Many live in subsidized apartment houses (*case popolari*), which often provide no more than a single room, perhaps two, with a kitchen they must share with a next-door family and a toilet that lacks running water (Lopreato, 1967, 194). Others live in old hovels. In her field notes, Ann Cornelisen, a social worker, describes one such home in the census she did of the poor in another southern Italian community.

> TEDESCHI, Paolo fu Angelo—6 children, between 6 months and 11 years. . . . One room, no window, back wall oozing brown, tarlike substance. Roof leaks, ceiling stain over bed. One bed, one hanging cradle visible. Jesus, St. Anthony, Grandfather with [votive] light, and framed dollar bill over bed. Four chickens and a rabbit in shoe box. Fireplace, no gas ring, twigs piled in corner, sink surrounded by water pots, two strips lard hanging on hooks. Unglazed brick floor weaves when walked on (stall underneath belongs to someone else). House very neat, but stench incredible. Curtain by door covers slop-feces chute. Only two chairs. . . .
> NOTE: see to X-ray Maria—pigeon-chested, black circles, fever and cough. TB? (Cornelisen, 1969, 196.)

How do you raise the living standards of poor countrymen in south Italy? Industry would help, but new plants usually are established in the north where they can profit from the presence of other factories, good transportation, and an experienced labor force.

Emigration to north Italy, other countries in Europe, and places as far away as the United States and Australia has helped the south. It reduces the population and brings remittances to those who stay. American dollars have come into the area this way for many decades. Unfortunately, emigration often leaves women, children, and the aged to struggle on without the help of adult males.

The modernization of agriculture is essential if the south is to progress. But it is difficult to modernize agriculture in an area which is devoted to grain, yet is better suited environmentally to cattle ranching.

In all, the hope of the future seems to lie in the development of as much industry as possible, in reducing the population through emigration and birth control, and in rationalizing agriculture as much as can be done. Planning and action on the national level are clearly necessary to achieve these goals, and the nation has not yet had great success. But even to the extent that help has come from the outside, programs have usually faltered and failed because they do not elicit local support (Barzini, 164, 244–261).

South Italians have shown themselves incapable of organizing on the local level in order to work for improvements in their lives. They have failed to make local government an effective institution for solving development problems.

The elected leaders typically are the local well-to-do. Often they are corrupt, caught up in a system in which, to be successful, political expediency rather than high ideals are allowed to shape policy. To get power and keep it, politicians administer patronage, doing favors for their supporters at the expense of others. Further, south Italy is an area in which criminal syndicates such as the Sicilian Mafia have been powerful for generations (Anderson, R. T., 1965; Boissevain, 1966b). Where criminals control politicians, they direct public investments into private gain.

Even where graft is minimal, very little gets done for the poor. Village leaders often feel no deep commitment to help them and nearly always have no real understanding of how they might be helped. The poor are thought "half-witted" or "lazy-do-nothings" who are themselves the cause of their own misfortunes. Worse, the poor fail consistently to promote their own cause.

As an alternative to working through local government, countrymen in south Italy have at times been mobilized through the establishment of formally organized voluntary associations. Voluntary associations have proven no more successful than local government in bringing improvements to the rural poor. In places, burial societies, festival committees, and political clubs have been organized. One of the most important voluntary associations was the *Unione Nazionale per la Lotta contro l'Analfabetismo*, established by teachers and social workers in 1947 to fight illiteracy. Hoping to encourage a new enthusiasm for cooperation and self-determination, the society achieved very little in its literacy program and probably even less in its efforts to create a new atmosphere of solidarity (Friedmann, 1960). South Italians do not usually commit themselves to voluntary associations and do not achieve much through them. Sad experience has taught them, it appears, that if they place their trust in leaders and organizers, they may expect to be cheated and deceived (Banfield, 1958, 19).

Other possibilities for wider forms of cooperation are equally undeveloped. The extended family ties of aunts, uncles, and cousins, designated loosely as relatives (*parenti*), provide a wider identification for the individual. Relatives get invited to baptisms, weddings, and funerals. Relatives feel obligations to one another. Mostly, however, they seem to concern themselves with the honor of their kin, insisting that related families live up to a strict code of feminine purity which makes a woman suspect if she merely is found alone with a man other than her husband, brother, or son. For minor matters, such kin may give advice or help, consulting one another about baby care, when to sow a new crop, or where to find a doctor in the city. But in more substantial matters, when economic assistance is needed, the extended family is nearly useless (Cronin, 1970, 50–66; see also Boissevain, 1966b, 204; Moss and Thompson, 1959, 38). As one Sicilian put it, "Sure you can go to the relatives for help, but if I have one hundred lire and I give them to my brother, then there will be nothing for my family if they need it, and what if my brother doesn't return them?" (Cronin, 1970, 62.)

Godparenthood is still another institution which defines wider ties of mutual interaction. Catholic dogma requires sponsors for the sacrament of baptism, and this tie of godparents to godchild or godparents to real parents, the *comparaggio*, provides yet another way in which wider social ties may be formed. By extension, godparenthood relations in Italy may be established in connection with events other than baptism, including ear-piercing ceremonies, confirmations, marriages, or the midsummer feast of St. John (Anderson, B. G., 1956; Moss and Cappannari, 1960, 30–31). Godparenthood is a common practice (Anderson, B. G., 1956, 19; Cronin, 1970, 49). But resultant ties seem to endure only so long as no party to them attempts to convert them into a means for the solution of major economic problems.

In a south Italian village, "A unifying web, not only of family ties (a first cousin was often as close as a brother), but of the acquired and symbolic kinship called 'comparaggio,' ran through the village," wrote Carlo Levi in his novel *Christ Stopped at Eboli* (Levi, 1947, 88–89). And such ties do give body to a wider world for the individual. They do not offer a mechanism for solving the serious problems of survival.

In the matter of survival, of satisfying basic needs for food and shelter, a south Italian finds his only strength in the smallest of traditional social groups (Cronin, 1970, 85–119; Moss and Thompson, 1959). "The Italian family is a stronghold in a hostile land," says writer Luigi Barzini (1964, 198). The disastrous shortcoming of the family in south Italy, however, is its weakness. A man with his wife and children can accomplish little against tough-minded landowners, unsympathetic bureaucrats, unscrupulous politicians, and the difficulties of underemployment, low wages, and agricultural primitivity. Under circumstances of this kind, a man's only loyalty is to his family, and he must assume all others will be the same. People relate to one another as though obedient to this rule: "Maximize the material, short-run advantage of the nuclear family; assume that all others will do likewise." (Banfield, 1958, 83; see also Brøgger, 1971; Cancian, 1961; Silverman, 1966.)

Where people obey such a rule, they may be said to suffer the difficulties of what political scientist Edward Banfield has termed "amoral familism." The condition is diagnostic of a vicious cycle of poverty and helplessness. So badly does every poor or destitute family need help that none dares risk giving it, for none has any surplus to spare. In their view of the world, they appear to have what George M. Foster has termed "the image of the limited good." They act as though wealth is nonexpandable and too limited to meet even the minimal needs of all villagers. As a consequence, each man and his family tends to see the success of a neighbor as constituting a loss to himself. It is not an attitude that encourages cooperation (Foster, 1965; see also Kearney, 1969).

This traditional social pattern and the ethos associated with it must change, but fundamental improvement in the agricultural system will be necessary first, and so far, in spite of the redistribution of estate land to small holders, such change is yet to take place. So argues Sydel F. Silverman, but she really describes a dilemma (Silverman, 1966, 17–18). Amoral familism and the related image of limited good hinder modernization; yet modernization is fundamental to the termination of amoral familism and the image of the limited good. It is small wonder that development is slow to take place.

South Italian villages are among the least developed in Europe. Yet they are changing. An incident that took place in Sicily in 1966 is illustrative. A girl was kidnapped and raped by a boy who wanted to marry her. The youth was attempting to get a wife in one of the traditional ways, since even if a girl and her parents are disgusted by the match, they are trapped by custom. To restore the honor of the girl and her family, she must be married to her abductor. Many have gotten wives this way before. In this instance, however, the girl refused to marry her kidnapper, and her father brought the youth and the twelve cousins who helped him to court, where they were sentenced to long prison terms. Many Sicilians applauded this challenge to what they consider a barbaric tradition, and when the girl married a soldier in 1969, the incident became at least a token of the new mentality emerging in southern Italy (Cronin, 1970, 53).

From the community study of Lopreato we also see clear signs of the new mentality. Well over one-fourth of the families in the village he studied belong to a social stratum, a part of the upper half of the village, which did not exist earlier. Now, "they are conspicuously adopting the ways of the city in diet, dress, and general behavior." (Lopreato, 1967, 184.) Their success represents a deep breach with tradition.

SPAIN

It is convenient to think in terms of nations, since political sovereignty results in certain distinctive nationwide uniformities. But though each nation in some ways is uniform, each in many ways is diverse within its own boundaries. Spain is no exception. Village culture varies broadly from one area to another (Baroja, 1946; Foster, 1951; Freeman, 1968, 44–48).

Spanish villages are changing. The anthropologically trained historian Carmelo Lison-Tolosana reports that by 1960, farmers in the village he studied in the region of Aragon in northeastern Spain already were trying out new seeds, fertilizers, machinery, irrigation channels, and land-use techniques. The well-to-do among them were investing in modern farming equipment and were emulating urban ways, while upwardly mobile families had gotten caught up in the "keeping up with the Pérezes" syndrome (Lison-Tolosana, 1966; see also Kenny, 1968b, 125; Pérez, 1966).

The magnitude of such changes in progressive areas becomes especially impressive when one considers how thoroughly undeveloped Spanish villages were until well into the 1950s. When Julian Pitt-Rivers studied a mountain community in the southern region of Andalusia around 1951, he found a community that was stagnating both economically and culturally. Modernization was scarcely thought of, as villagers adroitly "worked the system" to evade governmental demands for compulsory produce deliveries in order to sell on the more lucrative black market. Often caught between the demands of the local community and those of the central government, individuals utilized traditional social ties, and particularly those of patronage, to manipulate state authorities and others (Pitt-Rivers, 1954, 40, 154–159, 213).

Patronage defines the possibility open to a man (a client) to form an attachment to someone (a patron) who is sufficiently well placed to be helpful in getting things done, particularly when it concerns something a poor man needs from more powerful people. Professor Pitt-Rivers first drew our attention to the importance of this institution in Europe when he demonstrated how patrons intercede with governmental authorities to protect villagers from harmful application of the law. "Put in another way, the tension between the state and the community is balanced in the system of patronage." (Pitt-Rivers, 1954, 155.)

> There are many situations in which the *patrono* or *patrino* is of value. He is not only able to favour his protégé within the pueblo [village]. It is, above all, his relationship to the powers outside the pueblo which gives him value. For example, a *patrono* is required to sign the application for an old-age pension, testifying that the applicant was once employed by him. Many such applications are signed by persons who never in fact employed the applicant. He who can find no one to sign gets no pension. The *patrino* can give letters of recommendation to people who will do favours for him, who will protect his protégés. (Pitt-Rivers, 1954, 141.)

The institution that Pitt-Rivers described for a village in Andalusia is prominent in many other communities in Spain, though not in all (Kenny, 1960, 1968a; see also Aceves, 1971, 130–131). It also occurs in Italy and throughout the Mediterranean area (Boissevain, 1962, 1965; Campbell, 1964; Silverman, 1965; Wolf, 1966). As Jeremy Boissevain has pointed out, it seems to be associated with Catholicism and the religious custom of appealing to the saints as intermediaries between God and man (Boissevain, 1966a, 30). The ideology of using saints as intercessors is also that of the patron-client relationship.

Patronage seems also often to occur in association with amoral familism, functioning to hold society intact where other mechanisms of communal integration fail, as John Campbell has pointed out for villages in Greece (Campbell, 1968). Amoral familism does not occur in every village in Spain, but it is widespread (Aceves, 1971, 129). As a consequence, the social structure of a village in Spain seems no better suited to foster community development than is that of a village in southern Italy. Yet some development has taken place in recent years.

The village of El Pinar in the central province of Old Castile was a cluster of primitive shacks located along narrow, unpaved streets in 1949. Its byways stank from the excrement of people who lacked proper toilets, and strewn refuse swarmed with flies and mosquitoes to torment man and beast alike in the hot hell of a Castilian summer. Undernourished housewives kept their waterless houses neat and clean against nearly insuperable obstacles, while their husbands struggled to earn a living as small-hold farmers or forest workers in the resin industry (Aceves, 1971, 10–11).

Joseph Aceves first lived in El Pinar as a child in 1949. He has returned regularly in recent years as an anthropologist, and reports that when the village of 1949 is compared with the village as he knows it today, the differences are striking.

Today urban influences reach the community through trucks, automobiles, motorcycles, bicycles, and buses which travel the now-paved road connecting southward with Segovia and northward to the town of Los Encierros. Mail arrives daily, and brings with it copies of newspapers from Madrid and Segovia. Magazines are sold in a kiosk on the plaza. A new school was built in 1966. Nearly every home has a radio set, and television can be seen in each of the thirteen bars as well as in the homes of more prosperous inhabitants. In all, through education, travel, and the printed and electronic media, this community has gained a keen awareness of that modern urban world which in an earlier time seemed so remote (Aceves, 1971, 16–17).

This opening up of the village to new life styles is associated with a new mentality prepared for development. The villager has new aspirations. An atmosphere of amoral familism makes it difficult for progress to take place through local initiative, however. "Changes most readily resisted or rejected are those which force him into long-term contractual relationships with his fellows," writes Aceves, adding laconically, "long-term being anything over ten days or two weeks according to local reckoning." (Aceves, 1971, 126.) Several attempts to create farm producers' cooperatives have failed. Yet people have changed where this can be done as individuals or families. They have adopted a number of new seeds and crops, new techniques of irrigation and conservation, new methods of harvesting resin, and modern farm machinery (Aceves, 1971, 126).

The communities studied by Aceves and Lison-Tolosana are more progressive than most (see, for example, Mira, 1971). The key to success appears to lie in the creation of successful governmental programs. As Lison-Tolosana has pointed out, the great need of farmers in his area was for credit. In recent decades, agricultural production has improved in part because bank loans have been made available to those who need money in order to mechanize their operations (Lison-Tolosana, 1968, 330–333).

To make governmental programs work, however, agricultural-extension programs to inform and train villagers are of great importance (Aceves, 1971, 99–101). This seems especially so insofar as governmental policy has been formulated without consultation with the cultivators themselves. Planning is done by bureaucrats and technocrats (Aceves, 1971, 112). In his community, Professor Aceves finds that extension agents perform with great diplomatic skill as intermediaries between planners and farmers. "I never met an agent who did not realize that successful human relations was his most important tool and weapon and that people came before plants in importance," he observes (Aceves, 1971, 100). It is not clear, however, the extent to which extension agents are equally successful in other areas.

Writing of Greece in 1961, cultural geographer Irwin T. Sanders observed that one can find thoroughly modern as well as highly conservative countrymen in Greece, but most fall between these extremes (Sanders, 1962, 308). Ten years later, the description still would be accurate, for while the pace of modernization has continued, it remains incomplete. And always, even in the most modern of communities, one finds old traditions still very much alive. Among the most significant of such continuities in Greek history are the concepts of honor and shame.

We might have discussed these basic values when we looked at Spain. To comprehend the national character of that nation, you have to realize that behind the dignity and personal integrity of even the poorest Spaniard lies a value system oriented to honor (*hombría*), and its implied negative, shame (*vergüenza*) (Pitt-Rivers, 1966, 43, 45). As ethnographers Julio Caro Baroja and John Peristiany have pointed out, however, these concepts are important throughout southern Europe (Baroja, 1966, 81; Peristiany, 1966, 11). It seems most appropriate to discuss them with regard to Greece.

Dorothy Demetracopoulou Lee was one of the first anthropologists to describe how necessary it is to understand the importance of honor or self-esteem, the sense of personal inviolability and freedom known as *philotimo*, if one is to meet and get along with Greeks. *Philotimo* lies behind the ancient Greek dedication to equality and democracy. "Any Greek bootblack is equal to the king, to whom he may refer familiarly as *coumbaros*, wedding sponsor," she writes, "until some political agitator points out to him that the king is not Greek by descent, and therefore does not merit loyalty or respect as an equal." (Lee, 1955, 60.)

Planners must take concepts of honor and shame into account. It offends or violates a man's *philotimo* as an individual, as a representative of his family, and as a Greek to suggest that he needs to raise his standard of living. Honor is easily bruised or molested, and to speak objectively, or in purely scientific terms, of the shortcomings of his village is greatly to offend him. Harsh facts must be disguised in order to be acceptable. As Lee puts it, ". . . a Greek presents each fact wrapped in some subjective, protective covering. The fact is true and dependable, but it should not be naked." (Lee, 1955, 61.)

Greece is modernizing, and governmental programs have played a vital role. Loans from the Agricultural Bank of Greece have allowed villagers to buy irrigation pumps, tractors, and other machinery as well as fertilizers and pesticides (Friedl, E., 1968, 103; see also Bernard, 1970). A successful agricultural-extension program has also played an important role in preparing farmers to take advantage of new capital available to them. "Certainly the greatest change you will find," said development experts, of changes that took place between the beginning and the end of the 1950s, "is the development of the agricultural-extension program and the service it is rendering." (Sanders, 1962, 303.)

With basic economic improvement, the tendency to resist nonfamily commitments has been reduced if not eliminated. Agricultural cooperatives, some quite successful, have earned a place in village life where they function under the supervision of the Agricultural Bank (Sanders, 1962, 191–204).

Of the many factors that enter into the raising of living standards in the countryside, none is more significant than the creation of new channels of communication with urban centers. Where modernization has taken place in Greek villages, it has coincided with new forms of transportation, better education, and exposure to mass media, just as we have found elsewhere in the Mediterranean area. Two traditional institutions, however, have proved particularly effective as social mechanisms supportive of change, and in comparison with other parts of Europe, they give culture change in this part of the world a uniquely Greek quality. One is the coffeehouse; the other is the wedding dowry.

The coffee shop is a central feature of village life. "Like the English pub, it is a place of assembly, a communication center, a place to transact business, satisfy one's thirst, or find out about the health of one's friend." (Sanders, 1962, 205.) These are the traditional functions of an old, originally Turkish institution. But the coffee shop has always practiced an egalitarian ethic. Rich and poor alike are welcome to enter, and most of the men in a community come in nearly every day. Some are members of the local elite, which in larger villages would include teachers, doctors, and others who had been educated in the city. It also includes visitors from town centers, government officials, the bishop, and others. In this atmosphere, ordinary villagers are exposed to urban-derived habits in a particularly intimate way. As Ernestine Friedl points out, in drawing attention to this acculturation effect: "Visits to the coffeehouse enabled the farmers, from those least advantaged to those most prosperous, to observe the behavior and hear the conversation of the educated." (Friedl, E., 1968, 102.)

The practice of providing a dowry for daughters when they marry is also an old custom which now operates as a mechanism for communication with urban centers. By offering a large dowry, a village father can get a town son-in-law, a very prestigeful thing to do. During the 1950s, in the village studied by Ernestine Friedl, every bride whose father was in the more well-to-do half of local society married a man of respectable occupation who lived either in a provincial town or in Athens (Friedl, E., 1962, 65; for a similar custom, see Arensberg, 1968, 145–148; see also Schein, 1971a, 57).

Visiting customs subsequently turn such relationships into significant channels of culture change. The married couple returns to the home community of the wife at least twice a year for Easter and the annual celebration of the patron saint of the village. They also return for baptisms, weddings, funerals, and other family events, as well as in the summer for longer vacation stays. Conversely, villagers see their kin in the city, adults for brief visits, and young people often to stay for months or years as a place of residence while they learn a trade or attend school (Friedl, E., 1959, 34; 1963).

In order for the contact of town and village people to result in acculturation, it is essential that villagers view urban culture as something they might adopt. Without an inclination to borrow, very little diffusion from the city will take place. The situation must include what Friedl has referred to as "the attitude on the part of both peasant and elite that they are in the same social universe." (Friedl, E., 1968, 103; note Hoffman, 1971.) This has been true to some extent since the nineteenth century, but it has become overwhelmingly true since the end of the Greek Civil War in 1949. As a consequence, in addition to the adoption of new mechanical and chemical aids to cultivation, with attendant increases in production, Greek villagers have borrowed urban customs in a wholesale manner.

Such borrowing has not left them identical with urbanites. The process is not yet complete. Rather, what one sees today is the process in full operation, as villagers consciously emulate the manners, dress, and speech of city people. They worry about how properly to behave, "whether to serve coffee first, or a sweet and liqueur; where to seat the visitor; what the appropriate formal greetings are for specific occasions; whose hand to kiss as part of a greeting." (Friedl, E., 1968, 96.) They dress urbanely, even at work; and, perhaps the hardest to do, they are changing the dialect they speak, still using the local form in daily speech but increasingly speaking a more sophisticated form when talking with urban outsiders. In all, the modern Greek village is not nearly so distinctive in culture as it used to be (Friedl, E., 1968, 96–97).

MALTA

Strategically located in the Mediterranean, and a British colony for 150 years, the small islands of Malta industrialized earlier than any of the other Mediterranean areas we have considered. As an economic consequence of being a fortress, even in the nineteenth century only one out of five adult men worked in agriculture. The rest found employment in the garrison, administration, a large naval dockyard, and shipping.

Urban-industrial change became even more pronounced during and after World War II, a time when many shifted from farming to skilled or semiskilled industrial work. Somewhat more than half of the population today lives in the urban agglomeration centered on Valletta, while those who live in villages, even those most remote, are located now within easy bus and ferry distance from the city. Only one out of every ten adult men works in agriculture today.

The ongoing, rapid urbanization of this pair of islands can be seen in the village of Hal-Farrug. Before the war, one bus a day made the trip to and from Valletta. By 1967 this had increased to twenty-seven round trips a day, and villagers could do their shopping in the city when they wished. By 1960, three out of every four households were linked to the capital though redif-fusion loudspeakers, a wire service. By 1967, nearly one-third of the households had television sets.

In all, though Hal-Farrug was relatively isolated before the war, it now is so much a part of a wider urban world that three-fourths of the economically adult men are employed beyond its boundaries. A century ago, 77 percent of the adult men in this community were full-time farmers. Now only 15 percent farm full-time, although almost twice that number continue to work part-time in agriculture as worker-peasants, using their free time to produce potatoes and onions on small plots of land (Boissevain, 1969a, 9–11).

One still can distinguish village from city culture, but the distinction seems to be eroding before our very eyes. Jeremy Boissevain, whose repeated visits to the islands permit him to keep apace of changes, describes a situation in which urbanization is favored not only by easy communication, but by favorable attitudes as well. City culture has high prestige; village culture has low prestige. As a consequence, urban styles, often British in origin, find their way to Hal-Farrug as to other villages. Countrymen attempt to adopt habits and objects that symbolize urban culture. They dress like city people. Younger people especially are attempting to abandon the strong accent of the village in favor of urban Maltese. Automobiles, television sets, electric refrigerators, gas burners for cooking, and new furniture are acquired, often more because they symbolize urbanity than because they are useful (Boissevain, 1969a, 48).

The process remains incomplete, however. In spite of the disdain of urbanites, distinctive village customs, such as religious feasts, processions, and firework displays remain alive. Villagers continue to be perceptibly different. Reports Boissevain,

> When the people of Farrug go into the city, they put on their best (city-style) clothes and accents, but all too often the rough cut and slightly outdated style of their clothes, their sunburned faces, and their rough hands set them apart physically from the more sophisticated townsmen. The same is true of their speech. (Boissevain, 1969a, 48.)

In his work on the social structure of Hal-Farrug, Boissevain has built on the analysis of social networks in working-class culture carried out by Elizabeth Bott. From field work undertaken at times between 1967 and 1969, he has compared the network of an urban school teacher, Tony, with that of a village teacher, Cikku. The differences are striking.

Cikku's network is larger than that of Tony. It includes more kinsmen and the relationships are more intimate or personalized. The differences in these networks appear to reflect differences in personality. Cikku enjoys and encourages warm, diffuse relationships while Tony seems to prefer the more impersonal and limited ties of city people. Yet personality itself appears to be greatly infulenced by the differences between village and town environments, and is better seen as the product of different social structures than as a cause of them (Boissevain, 1969b).

Any conclusions must be tentative, based as they are upon the study of only two individuals. It appears, however, that with continuing urbanization, we may expect significant changes in the size, composition, and intimacy of social networks, as Maltese become increasingly like Tony and less like Cikku. We may expect corresponding changes in Maltese personality.

Further, in more specific ways, the kinship part of the network appears to be evolving in a predictable fashion. In his analysis of family relationships, Boissevain found a matrilateral bias very similar to that described by Young and Willmott for the working class in east London.

Maltese villagers reckon equally on both sides of the family. They emphasize the father's side formally insofar as he has legal authority over his wife, and the family is identified by his name. Nevertheless, informally, the wife's side is emphasized. When a couple shares a house, it more commonly is with relatives of the wife. Relatives of the wife are more frequently visited, and certain maternal relatives (uncle and grandmother) enjoy a warmer relationship with children than do their paternal equivalents.

As in London, this greater intimacy on the female side seems to build upon the strong tie that unites a mother with her daughter. Further, a matrilateral bias appears to be growing as urbanization increases, for it proves to be correlated with occupational and residential practices. When a man works outside the community, he is more likely to take up residence in the village of his wife when he marries. In this way, marriage may perpetuate mother-daughter ties rather than weaken them, as when the bride follows the older pattern of taking up residence in the village of the groom. In short, occupational and residential patterns are changing, and as they do, the kinship part of the social network appears to be developing an increasing matrilateral bias (Boissevain, 1969a, 23–25, 38–40).

In giving special attention to Malta, our coverage of the Mediterranean region is skewed. Malta is very small in territory to warrant so many pages in this chapter. It is very small in population as well. The total count of inhabitants numbers just a bit over 300,000, less than the population of a single large city in the region. Yet anthropologically, Malta contributes importantly to our understanding of Mediterranean culture because it is a place of extensive urban-industrial change.

Our coverage of the Mediterranean region is also skewed by the failure to discuss parts of two major nations. This too reflects the happenstances of research decisions. Southern Portugal, though west of Gilbraltar, belongs ecologically to the Mediterranean world. In spite of an informative book by cultural geographer Dan Stanislawski, however, not enough is written on this area to permit an extended discussion at this time (Stanislawski, 1963). Similarly, the southern coast of France, including Corsica, is anthropologically little known (but see Pomponi, 1962; Roubin, 1970).

SIX

ALPINE COUNTRYMEN:
ECOLOGY AND CHANGE

High in remote Alpine valleys, change comes more slowly than in villages on the plain. Peasant traditions hang on more persistently. You sense this as you drive along, ever upward, gradually realizing that settlements are becoming smaller and less frequent, that signs of business and industry are falling away, and as a turn in the road brings you to a panoramic view of unexcelled grandeur.

Where forest-coated, snow-capped mountains reach up to the sky, men seem still to live intimately as a part of nature. Crazy-quilt patchworks of fields in the valley, small houses clustered about steeple-topped churches, a great belt of evergreen trees, and high up patches of green where small huts give shelter to shepherds and herdsmen too distant to see, these signs of man suggest an older way of life.

FRANCE

In the late 1950s, when Robert K. Burns, Jr., drove his heavy-loaded Renault into the village of Saint Vérain, he drove some distance into the past of Alpine Europe. In spite of young men returned from military service, summer vacationers with urban ways, salesmen, and an open-all-year paved road to the outside, in spite of schools, radios, newspapers, and other contacts with the wider world of France, Saint Vérain in many ways had remained loyal to its past (Burns, 1959, 588).

The village itself was old. Some houses had been renovated, the work made possible by government loans intended for that purpose. But others remained antique, perpetuating a living arrangement that reached many hundreds of years into the past. The heavy-beamed houses with roofs of wood or slate clung top-heavy to the mountainside, each timbered, two-story top a hayloft where enough fodder had to be stored to feed livestock through at least six months of a snowbound winter. The smaller, partially recessed ground floor of masonry was the living area. That some people still occupied the ground floor in a traditional manner spoke eloquently of the conservatism of the village as a whole.

Entering the house by way of a narrow corridor, you might find a treasured grandfather clock standing darkly in the corner. It was inconvenient, but the hallway was drier than the living room, and less likely to rust the clock mechanism. In renovated houses, this entrance corridor might be changed into a small kitchen/living room with stove, table, chairs, and radio. In some houses, however, it still served its original purpose.

Where the traditional arrangement prevailed, one end of the living area centered on a small wood-burning, cast-iron stove with a long black pipe that angled awkwardly toward the wall. Sooty pots, pans, and cauldrons lay scattered in seeming confusion. Nearby, an unpainted wooden table provided the work area a housewife needed to prepare food and serve her family. Around about, wooden shelves recessed into the walls or standing against them along with smoke-stained, but once elegant stained-wood cabinets provided storage space for food, porcelain, or warm winter clothing.

Some interiors were freshly white-washed, though nearly every angle was crooked, as though folk still believed that the devil loitered in 90-degree corners. In certain houses, the walls revealed rough-finished timbers, peeling plaster, and bare stones. A faded touch of color could be seen here and there in the small checkered-cotton curtains that hung limply in front of shelves or recessed beds. An unframed printed picture or photo, yellow with age, might hang tacked to a convenient timber, and the most obvious sign of modernity sometimes was no more than a yellow-glowing light globe that dangled by its wires from the ceiling.

The tradition that reached far into antiquity was the custom of sharing this large room with animals. In basic ground plan, one end of the room was for animals, the other for human beings. In fact, chickens might roost on poles near the ceiling of the living room; and in the spring, each farmer bought a piglet which he fattened for eight or ten months in a pen usually kept at the foot of his bed. But larger animals were kept somewhat apart, though no wall or partition intervened.

Monsieur Brunet, for example, was one of a few who still lived this way. He kept six cows, a work mule, and four or five lambs in the stable end of his house, where the floor consisted only of dirt packed hard by the tramping of hoofed feet. Coming from pasture, the cows and mule sauntered cautiously through the front door, then were urged with dispatch across the wooden floor of the family area so that they could reach their stalls before they might leave droppings on the clean floor. In winter, when they did not leave the room, animal body heat assured warmth even in the coldest of nights. This moist warmth corroded the workings of grandfather clocks, but it also gave comfort, so that one learned to feel uneasy without animal noises, "the rattle of a halter chain, a hoof slamming down on packed earth, a moo or a bleat—and all of these accompanied by the soothing undertone of molars grinding hay." (Burns, 1959, 578.)

In the late 1950s, change was in the air, but it had not yet truly arrived. The old wooden scratch plow, for example, had been replaced by an implement with an iron point and a moldboard. Some farmers, with government aid, had acquired small gasoline-motored handmowers, though most reaping still was done with scythe and sickle. Claude Jouve, the village blacksmith, had argued that these handmowers, as well as tractors and other mechanized equipment, would be feasible for village use if each man's scattered plots could be consolidated into larger fields. But the plan was voted down, and mechanization was put off. Monsieur Jouve did experiment with building the first silo in the community, and though it was scarcely more than a hole in the ground, it kept the green grass more nutritious. Others copied him, and a few built cement silos with the help of governmental subsidies. On the whole, however, when one considers the degree of exposure to the outside world, change was minimal (Burns, 1959, 574, 576; 1961, 21,22).

Life in Saint Vérain remained in the fifties still tied to the basic demands of an Alpine economy. During the quiet coldness of winter, villagers experienced a confined leisure that required only a few hours each day to tend the stock. Spring arrived in May as the snow melted and fields could be plowed. On muleback, with implements across their shoulders, or guiding a cart of manure, farmers moved among their scattered fragments of land, preparing the soil for later planting. With the warmth of June, cows could be released from their stalls to regain their strength in nearby meadows, and by the end of the month, they were habituated once again to a summer routine in which the village herdsmen collected them each morning to be led to pasture for the day. June also was the month when Celestin, the village shepherd, took the sheep to Alpine pastures, where he would spend the summer alone except for his dogs and his flock.

The warmth of summer brought meadow grasses to maturity. For two hard months, enough hay was mowed to feed the stock through the winter. The whole family took part, children helping as they could, women raking, and the men swinging scythes in wide sweeps until their hands got as tough as leather and their muscles screamed to rest. From dawn to dusk, they cut and raked. Finally, the dried hay was gathered into large 200-pound bundles held together by rope nets, and during the last days of the season, mules carried these cumbersome loads to the village for winter use.

In September the harvest was brought in. When the first frost or snow was early, all the grain had to be brought in while still green. Normally, however, the rye was golden brown when cut down with flashing scythes, though sheaves of oats and barley were interrupted in their ripening and had to be spread along the large wooden-banistered balconies of the haylofts to finish maturing in the fickle autumn sun. The mules that carried loads of grain to the village were then turned to plowing the fields so they could be seeded with rye before the arrival of winter snows.

By late in the 1950s, the Alpine traditions of Saint Vérain already were dying out. Today they are nearly gone (Brunhes-Delamarre, 1970). In the community of Barcellonnette, south of Saint Vérain, such traditions also are moribund now. Barcellonnette is located in one of the most remote valleys of the French Alps. Its downriver exit is blocked by a gorge, and all of its French passes are located at over 6,000 feet of altitude. As in Saint Vérain, however, modern modes of communication brought an end to isolation. By World War I, trucks could drive in, and in subsequent decades the old economy weakened. By 1964, when Richard V. Wagner first did field work there, all of the higher settlements were abandoned, or nearly so, and Barcellonnette itself had become transformed. It once had been a community of subsistence farmers. By the mid-sixties it was a population of highly urbanized families, about half of whom had come in from outside the valley (Wagner, 1969, 90, 93).

Adjacent valleys in the Alps can be very different from each other in the way they are developing. No two valleys are identical. Yet, to the extent that it exchanged its Alpine economy for fuller participation in the wider economy of the nation, and to the extent that the old style of life was replaced with one much influenced by the city, Barcellonnette not only is typical of the French Alps in our time, it is typical of Alpine settlements throughout Europe.

SWITZERLAND

The distinctiveness of Alpine culture must be attributed to ecological processes in which both technology and environment are important (Burns, 1961; Netting, 1971). As Swiss ethnologist Richard Weiss once pointed out, not only does the whole of culture reflect the economic adjustment a community has made, but when that economic adjustment changes, the culture changes with it (Weiss, 1946, 80, 102–104). It is important to realize this, because often such differences are attributed simply to isolation.

Peasants are isolated but, even in hidden Alpine communities, such isolation is only a relative matter. From time immemorial, Alpine villagers have taken winter employment in villages, towns, and cities on the plain, returning each spring to their fields. For many generations, a surplus population that left to live elsewhere provided links between the valley and the outside world through correspondence and visits. In many cases, emigrants return to their home village after working outside for some years, bringing with them a knowledge of other styles of life.

In his work on Swiss folk culture, Richard Weiss drew attention in this regard to Engadin Valley, which has had a heavy, regular emigration since the seventeenth century (Weiss, 1946). The valley is of special interest, because emigrants from Engadin kept more closely in touch with their homeland than did those from other areas, and thus provide a better opportunity to estimate the amount of culture change which may result from communication of this sort.

Engadin emigrants typically retained ownership of their village homes, to which they returned with their families for a few months every year or two. The result of such recurrent visits was enough culture change so that Weiss could speak of this valley as less conservative than others. "But in spite of all, to this day," he concluded in 1946, "the valley retains a healthy and unique folk life." (Weiss, 1946, 122.)

To trace the breakdown of peasant culture in an Alpine village, John Friedl recently undertook a study of Kippel, a community in one of the most remote valleys of contemporary Switzerland. He found a community which in the early nineteenth century had been fully agrarian in the old Alpine manner. The first indirect impact of industrialization was felt in 1850, with the intrusion of a railroad line into part of the valley. By the turn of the century, modernization seemed underway, but the economy stagnated after World War I, and hit a deep low during the 1930s. Substantive change, therefore, was retarded, and did not occur until after the end of World War II (Friedl, J., 1971, 14–18).

A great change has taken place in recent decades, although not through efforts to modernize old practices. On the contrary, techniques of field agriculture and animal husbandry remain backward. Rather, the village has gotten caught up in a growing industrialization of the nation (Friedl, J., 1971, 250).

In the immediate postwar years, villagers worked at unskilled and semi-skilled jobs in newly built factories. Wages, and freedom from the endless chores of Alpine work, made it possible for workers to give their sons more schooling. Nearly all of these boys became skilled workmen, qualified as electricians, mechanics, locksmiths, and such. A few got into white-collar employment as draftsmen, salesmen, or bank tellers. As a result, by 1970 the village had three distinct occupational age groups: one made up of skilled workers under 35 years of age, a second of semi- and unskilled workers between 35 and 55 years, and a third made up of men over 55 who still were qualified only as agriculturalists. Even agriculturalists now find employment to some extent in the industrial sector, however. In 1960, 44 full-time cultivators still could be found in the community, but by 1970, only one was left (Friedl, J., 1971, 259–263, 285).

The contemporary inhabitants of Kippel are modern in dress, occupation, education, and in the enjoyment of industrial conveniences. They know how to be modern, for they not only work side by side with urbanized people, but the exposure of their village includes vacationers and, since 1969, television (Friedl, J., 1971, 240, 351). "The introverted pre-war Kippel has given way to the extroverted post-war Kippel." (Friedl, J., 1971, 311.) Village culture remains different from that of urban Switzerland, however, because villagers retain some aspects of a distinctive ecological adaptation. They continue to be part-time farmers.

Unlike Barcellonnette in France, where many of today's residents are immigrants, nearly all those of Kippel were born there (Friedl, J., 1971, 314). The inhabitants gave up their larger agricultural holdings to work in factories, but kept smaller holdings for part-time cultivation, and thus turned themselves into members of a class known popularly as worker-peasants (German, *Arbeiterbauern*; French, *ouvrier-paysans*) (Friedl, J., 1971, 250–251).

Worker-peasants remain part-time cultivators, but they retain very little of the traditional Alpine routine. Their basic rhythm is that of the factory with its daily hours and work week, though many arrange to work a swing-shift schedule in order to have daylight hours to cultivate their fields.

In cultivating their fields, worker-peasants now use some machinery. In particular, they rely upon a small tractor, the motor of which can be used to power various machines. The amount of land cultivated is much less than it used to be and is worked differently. Cooperative undertakings with other members of the community have fallen into disuse. Dairy cattle are fewer and only the most accessible fields are put to the plow. "Years ago the entire hillside was colored with ripened grain fields," recalls one old resident. "Today there are just a few rye patches—most of the hay fields aren't even cut any more. Everything looks different than it used to." (Friedl, J., 1971, 285.) Even the buildings are used differently, as some have fallen into disrepair and others serve new purposes. Further, they stand side by side today with tourist facilities, including a ski lift (Friedl, J., 1971, 251, 290-310).

The role of women has changed correspondingly. Wives do more of the heavy field work than formerly. Old cottage industry, for women as for men, has disappeared. In its place, women now work in their homes for local factories, producing sweaters on knitting machines provided for their use. Nearly every household has at least one woman thus employed (Friedl, J., 1971, 264, 291).

In all, the culture of Kippel residents is very different from what it was only a few years ago. It is strongly acculturated to urban custom, yet it remains different from the urban culture of people at lower altitudes. For the time, at least, it seems stabilized in a new ecological adjustment which has left Alpine residents more like other Swiss than they used to be, yet leaves them different all the same.

AUSTRIA

As elsewhere in the Alps, traditions hoary with age are disappearing in our time in Austria. In 1962, Leopold Pospisil took up residence in a Tyrolean village that had remained culturally conservative to that time. To reach it in that year, he still had to climb a narrow, winding path that mounted a steep, precipitous gorge. Inaccessibility kept the outer world at bay. The village still had an Alpine economy.

Those farmers had already begun to plan for change, however. The Olympic Winter Games were expected to bring an economic boom to that part of the nation in 1963. And by that date, several hostels were opened for business even in this remote village. Some of the farmers installed running water, showers, and flush toilets in their homes in order to be able to rent guest rooms (*Fremdenzimmer*). Meetings were held to discuss ways in which a permanent tourist business could be encouraged. By 1963, construction had begun on a paved road which, when finished, would open the area to tourist traffic. It seemed quite clear that there as elsewhere in the Alps, the old way of life was not to survive. It appeared to be just a matter of time (Leopold Pospisil, personal communication).

Such a community eventually will give up old habits, without doubt. How much time it will take will surely depend primarily upon the extent of economic change (note Brudner, 1972). Such a conclusion is consistent with the observations of Richard Weiss concerning Alpine ecology. It seems to follow from the findings of Raoul and Frada Naroll. The Narolls studied social change in a Tyrolean village as it was in the year 1956. The community they selected was one of the more remote, less modernized villages of Austria. Yet its conservatism could scarcely be attributed to isolation. A paved road connected the settlement with a modern highway, and nearly every family had at least one member who worked and lived outside the valley, yet considered himself still a member of the community, to which he returned frequently in off-season periods (Naroll and Naroll, 1962, 104, 106).

In spite of direct, recurrent contact with the wider world of Austria, this village had remained relatively unchanged. The lives of its people still were shaped by an Alpine economy, and the Narolls could say of them, "Alpine farming is not a way to earn a living but a way of life. . . . " (Naroll and Naroll, 1962, 105.)

Conservatism seemed to reflect the failure to develop industry in the valley. Alpine dairy farming was not sufficiently productive to provide surplus products for sale. The marketing of cattle and lumber brought in some cash, but not a lot. Money incomes were bolstered by catering to vacationers in July and August. But very few visitors came during the other ten months of the year. The community failed in its efforts to encourage a year-round tourist trade. Since they had no other industrial prospects, the population remained bound to a subsistence economy and the style of life it supported (Naroll and Naroll, 1962, 104–105).

By now, most of the communities of Austria have abandoned the old economy. This is true, for example, of Altirdning, a village studied by John J. Honigmann at various times between 1960 and 1966 (Honigmann, 1963a). Many members of the village now are employed as workers outside the community. Those who remain farmers have shifted from subsistence to commercial agriculture. They now have tractors, harvesters, electric fences, milking machines, silos, and modern barns. They no longer take their cows out of production during the summer to send them to Alpine meadows, but continue to milk them throughout the year. In their homes they have bathtubs, electric appliances, and other modern comforts (Honigmann, 1963a; 1964, 283).

In his analysis of culture change in this Styrian village, Honigmann draws attention to the adaptive role of surviving traditions. The old Alpine way of life is dead, yet it retains a sentimental hold on modern villagers. In romantic terms, they preserve selected aspects in song and fantasy (Honigmann, 1964; see also Honigmann, 1970).

In their taverns over beer or wine, men harmonize ballads and folk songs that speak of the joys of Alpine (*Alm*) life, interspersing hit tunes which they also like. In conversations, they talk of the goodness of *Alm* cheese and butter as compared with commercial varieties. The air of the high meadows is said to be purer, and summers there are remembered as carefree and fun, though in more realistic moments, older people undoubtedly can recall hardships as well (see Friedl, J., 1971, 351). On holidays, people walk to nearby *Alm* meadows, where they picnic. At village fairs an "*Alm* hut" is erected where a bar, tables, and benches are set up and drinks sold, much as in the old days when girls in the mountains provided wine or schnapps for visitors. In these and other ways, selected aspects of mountain transhumance are retained as a prominent part of modern life. "In imagination he fantasies the

Alm as a place of romance, gaiety, and release. He expresses this fantasy in song and, aided by alcohol, acts it out in the village summer festival." (Honigmann, 1964, 288; see also Honigmann, 1963*b*.)

Professor Honigmann concludes that these sentimental vestiges of the traditional life of the Alps make it easier for individuals to accept new habits and values in a time of rapid culture change. They provide "the bridge by which people span past and present. . . ." (Honigmann, 1964, 289.) Certainly, such retentions in no way interfere with objectivity in deciding what to retain and what to abandon or modify. Honigmann concludes,

> Their sentimental attachment to certain features of the past, which "costs" them nothing and provides emotional release without commitment or without obstructing new behavior, makes change even more palatable than it otherwise would be to a practical people hopeful of progress. (Honigmann, 1964, 289,)

Not all conservatism facilitates culture change, of course. In many Alpine villages one finds a reactionary mentality which works against completely rational modernization. Villagers tend to retain old traits when it is economically inadvisable. Swiss ethnologist Arnold Niederer has described villagers who continue to think in terms of a subsistence economy, when to do so is no longer either necessary or sensible (cited in Friedl, J., 1971, 278). Another Swiss ethnologist, Gérald Berthoud, notes that men in the village he studied continue to think of themselves as peasants, even though they work 45 hours a week in a factory or a hydroelectric plant, and John Friedl finds the same, pointing out that what he terms "the self-sufficiency complex" tends particularly to discourage innovation in the realm of agricultural practice (Berthoud, 1967, 165; Friedl, J., 1971, 279). In the community he studied, worker-peasants grow their own potatoes mainly because they cannot conceive of buying what they have always produced for themselves, and not because they have calculated that it is cheaper to grow them than to buy what they need (Friedl, J., 1971, 279–280).

ITALY

Regularities in the ecology of culture change occur in the Italian Alps as elsewhere. For change to take place, the mountain community must increase its contact with the outer world as roads and other modern forms of communication are constructed. People must aspire to a changed way of life. The economy must shift from traditional subsistence farming to some form of participation in modern industry (for example, see McConochie, 1971). And finally, people must come to terms with their past, for we have seen that the traditional way of life can maintain its grasp on changing peoples, helping them, as in an Austrian example, or hindering them, as in certain Swiss examples.

Now, from work in Italy carried out by Eric R. Wolf and John W. Cole, we find that how people come to terms with their past is itself a product of the past, at least in part. In the upper part of the valley of Nonsberg in the largely German-speaking province of Bolzano, the villages of Tret and St. Felix lie only fifteen minutes' walk from each other. Both communities share a common ecological patterning of their lives. Yet they differ in cultural heritage. Felixers speak German and remain loyal to the traditions of the German Tyrol, while Tretese speak Nones, a Romance dialect, and are oriented to Italian culture.

These villagers differ also in social structure and in the patterning of interpersonal relations, particularly as this concerns rules of inheritance. In St. Felix, the whole farm is inherited by a single son (impartible inheritance), with rights going by priority to the eldest son (primogeniture). In Tret, by contrast, the inheritance is divided equally among all children (partible inheritance) (Cole, 1970; Wolf, 1962, 1970).

The valley of Nonsberg, with its traditional Alpine way of life, felt the first stirrings of change in 1936, when a paved road brought it into closer touch with the surrounding region. Pervasive economic and culture change, however, awaited the period after World War II, when northern Italy industrialized with such success that even mountaineers felt its impact. In the villages of St. Felix and Tret, new job opportunities and new possibilities for working the land presented themselves. A whole range of alternatives is available now to villagers, and nobody need spend his life on a small mountain holding if he prefers not. The two villages, so similar in many ways, are adapting very differently to these new possibilities (Cole, 1969, 186–187, 197–201).

Tret as a community is adapting poorly. All of its young people leave now to find work outside the village, and most of them do not return. Nearly 40 percent of the holdings are in the hands of old couples over the age of 60, whose adjustment is characterized by diminishing production and limited aspirations. In spite of the availability of more consumer goods in greater variety than in earlier decades, they are consuming less than they did as young people.

Tretese men aged 30 to 50 who own medium to large-sized holdings are keeping production up better than the old couples. They are also shifting more successfully to commercial dairy farming. But they are not investing much in technological improvement, preferring, it seems, to put their cash into new clothing, home improvements, and furniture. Only three can be said to "have gone all out in the conversion to commercial farming, adding new types of equipment, such as tractors and mowing machines, automatic watering systems and other improvements in the stalls. . . ." Further, notes Cole, only these three "have sought out information on modern conditions of health and sanitation in handling animals." (Cole, 1969, 205.) Since 1945, six of the owners of medium and large holdings have sold their land, two others were attempting to sell in 1967, and a third had rented out his holding and moved to the city. Only in extreme financial emergencies have villagers ever sold holdings of this size in the past (Cole, 1969, 201–207).

But while Tret seems moribund as a community, St. Felix is thriving. Although many young people have left to find work elsewhere, the integrity and success of village farms is not in jeopardy. Some of the young people

return to live out their lives in the village. Impartible inheritance and primogeniture keep holdings intact and designate who eventually will succeed to
them. Consistent with this, at least one youth in every family plans to take
over the family holding, even when the latter is extremely small. With the
future of each farm secure, Felixers take full advantage of every opportunity
to make their operations more viable. Fields taken out of production in Tret
are added to holdings in St. Felix, either through purchase or through rental.
With more land to work, and less manpower, as wages tempt villagers into
industry, the German-speakers are willing to invest in new equipment, including washing machines for women and mowing machines for men. To finance
these efforts to modernize, they are willing to borrow, taking advantage of
governmental help in getting loans and putting their holdings up as collateral
when necessary, something traditional farmers avoided strenuously (Cole,
1969, 207–211).

In all, the traditional social structure and, in particular, traditional rules
of inheritance have channeled the adaptive tendencies of the villagers of St.
Felix in ways which allow them to modernize without abandoning their community and the continuity of family enterprise. Rules of inheritance in Tret,
on the contrary, are associated with abandonment of the village and of many
of its family farms. Renovated houses, fashionable clothing, automobiles, and
other industrial products give Tret the appearance of keeping up with the
times. But most of these goods are gifts from young people working elsewhere.
In fact, the population as a whole is unable and unwilling to modernize
through its own efforts. The community has become economically parasitic
(Cole, 1969, 212–213). Differences in traditional social structures rather than
ecological differences appear to have shaped differently the forms which modernization has taken in these two communities.

NORWAY AND SWEDEN

Scandinavia is not part of the circum-Alpine culture area. It lies too far distant.
Yet in its mountains, peasants were part of an ecosystem very much like that
of the Alps. There too, on high mountain pastures (Norwegian, *saeter*; Swedish,
fäbod), cattle were grazed in the summer, their rich milk turned into butter
and cheese. There too, summer was a time when the family was separated
in their diverse activities, though the young managed to meet in the time-
honored custom of night-courting (bundling) (Wikman, 1937). And there, too,
cattle were stabled during the cold, icy winter, and wood carving or embroidery
as well as other folk arts occupied long hours left largely free from farm duties.

The Alps and Scandinavia are so similar in environment and basic cultural
adaptation that since 1928 the Norwegian Institute for Comparative Cultural
Research (*Instituttet for Sammenlignende Kulturforskning*) has focused upon
the study of these two regions as its primary purpose (Bull, 1929). The emphasis, however, has been upon the traditional way of life. Further, traditional
mountain customs in Norway were largely abandoned in the nineteenth and
early twentieth centuries, earlier than was the case in the Alps (Blom, 1969;
Reinton, 1955; Solheim, 1952). The same is true of Sweden (Levander,

The old *saeter* economy is dead now, and with it, an Alpine-like way of life.

GREECE

Because the Pindus Mountains continue south from the Carnic Alps, the mountain peoples of Greece have been taken as belonging to the circum-Alpine area, even though they differ more from Alpine peasants then do Scandinavian mountaineers (Burns, 1963, 133). In cultural-ecological terms, they are similar in many ways to former pastoralists on the Iberian Peninsula, along the Mediterranean, and in the Balkans (Cvijic, 1918; Klein, 1920; Wace and Thompson, 1914). Of those still pursuing a traditional way of life, the best known are the Sarakatsani, whose scattered communities are mostly located in Greece, though some can be found in parts of Albania, Yugoslavia, and Bulgaria (Campbell, 1964; Kavadias, 1965).

Three distinct shepherding peoples can be identified in the rugged northwestern province of Greece. Koutsovlachs speak a Romance language related to Rumanian, though the men generally know Greek as well; Karagouni speak Albanian, although they understand the Romance language of the Koutsovlachs from whom they are descended; and the Sarakatsani, who are not considered Vlachs at all, speak Greek (Sanders, 1962, 106; for Koutsovlachs, see Schein, 1971a, b). Like Alpine peasants, these shepherds lead a life shaped by their environment and technology. They move sheep between high mountain pastures and valley meadows. In their way of life, however, they resemble the traditional Reindeer Lapps of arctic Scandinavia more than more southerly mountaineers, because they are nomads.

Alpine pastoralists and nomads each orient their lives to animal husbandry. Alpine pastoralists, however, maintain a permanent village, which is never deserted by everyone, and to which the herders return in season. The whole family does not normally move to the summer camp, for while some take charge of animals in the meadows, other remain in the village to harvest crops and mow hay.

Nomads, in contrast, move as families and communities with their animals. They do not wander randomly. The annual round of seasons normally brings them in a familiar cycle of high and low pastures that they visit every year. They may even have an encampment which they live in so regularly that they build more or less permanent buildings there. But if they possess such an encampment, it normally is abandoned by the whole group for parts of the year when they move with their animals to more distant places (Carrier, 1932; Frödin, 1940).

Living in impermanent, hive-shaped huts of reeds, and dressed in homespun black suits and goat-hair capes, the Sarakatsani are nomads who graze their flocks high in the mountains during the summer and along the coastal plains in the winter. To a large extent, they preserve to the present an old way of life. It is not without change. Political developments since the 1920s have altered their pasture rights, and headmen (*tselingata*), chief shepherds who ruled the families under them in autocratic fashion, have declined in power. Governmental policies have forced encampments to maintain closer ties with farming villages, thus giving them a more settled quality. Families find they need more cash than formerly, in part to pay grazing dues, but also to obtain goods which in agricultural villages they have found to be essential to family self-esteem (*philotimo*): items of manufactured clothing, factory-made tableware, and bread containing more wheat than maize (Campbell, 1964, 1–18; 1968, 145–146; Sanders, 1962, 109–112, 118–123).

Conservatism in the midst of a modernizing nation is bought at a price. Those who continue to keep sheep live fundamentally as they always have. But many have given up their flocks, for while they love independence with their flocks, they now prefer an occupation that will provide more cash and a modern style of life. In the face of these aspirations, and in the face of increasing difficulty in finding adequate pasture, the way of life of the Sarakatsani, as of other Balkan nomads, is in a state of decline (Campbell, 1963, 73–75; 1968, 145–146; Kavadias, 1965, passim; Sanders, 1962, 109–112, 118–123).

SEVEN

ATLANTIC COUNTRYMEN: PERSONALITY AND CHANGE

From Portugal to Norway, the great Atlantic Ocean laps against rocky, often precipitous shores, with only occasional stretches of sandy beach. In places some men fish, mostly from boats whose details of construction announce an ancient genealogy, whether it be the canvas-bottomed *curach* of Ireland or wooden-ribbed craft in Norway, Portugal, and elsewhere. In coastal villages and sheltered harbors, amidst nets and lines drying in the sun, weathered men in rubber boots look to the water, while inland, surrounded by green fields and forests, their neighbors and cousins scratch out a living on ancestral fields. In many places, the men who fish also farm, for the sea and the land can form two parts of a single existence as well as contrastive modes of life. But whether coastal or inland, the climate is the same, and must be reckoned with. Except for Portugal, cold stormy winters find only treacherous relief in short, wet, unpredictable summers which become wetter, though greener, the farther north one goes.

Along the western edge of Europe, ancient traits have survived in some places into the recent past and even into the present, a circumstance which led Swedish ethnologist Sigurd Erixon to designate the Atlantic fringe as a "relic area" (Erixon, 1938; Gailey, 1970). By that he meant that old customs have lasted there while they have become extinct in places more alive with change. In our time, it is this quality of backwardness, and the uniformities of mountain, sea, and climate, which most characterize the area, although the characterization does not apply equally in every part.

PORTUGAL

Recently in Portugal I examined with fascination a primitive kitchen in which cooking is done over an open hearth. The fireplace is reminiscent of prehistoric houses in which the smoke simply found its exit through crevices in the thatch or by way of a hole in the roof or upper wall. This fireplace is more developed, however, because a chimney is positioned high over the hearth, drawing off the free-flowing smoke through a rectangular, boxlike hood in which fish, meat, or sausages can be hung to cure. Looking at it gives one the sensation of having found the "missing link" between simple hearths and later fireplaces.

It is the late survival of culture traits such as the open hearth with chimney which led Erixon and others to speak of the Atlantic fringe as a relic area. As a matter of fact, within the last year or so I have also seen this kind of primitive hearth in other parts of the Atlantic area, namely in several peasant houses in the Netherlands as well as in one turf-roofed house from the Faroe Islands. It is significant, however, that while a number of traits survived until recent times, most now are no longer in use. The primitive kitchens I so recently examined all are located in museums. Even in remote, conservative areas, culture change takes place and always has.

As the British cultural geographer W. M. Williams points out, it is a mistake to think of rural societies as stable systems inherently or inevitably slow to change. When Williams undertook field work in a village in south-western England, a place located well within the Atlantic fringe, he found it was not the conservative, change-resistant community he had expected. Rather, he found it in a perpetual state of adjustment to "piecemeal" changes. And here he makes a point which others have made, including Stephen and Ethel Dunn in their work on the Great Russian peasant: It is necessary to distinguish two kinds of change; one is change within a social structure or cultural system which leaves the basic structure or system unchanged. Such change is relatively superficial. The other is more profound in its implications, for it involves change in the basic structure or system as such (Williams, 1963, xiv–xviii; see also Dunn and Dunn, 1963, 320; Firth, 1951, 84). Change of the first sort takes place in every culture all the time. Only the rate of change is variable. Change of the latter sort is less frequent, but is the quality of change involved in the process of modernization as we are examining it for Europe.

Hinterland communities in Portugal have not been changeless. High in the mountains of northern Portugal, human aeries built of stone identify settlements once connected with each other and the outer world by nothing better than footpaths which led travelers over terrain dominated by wolves, thieves, and steep drops. "The village was sequestered from the world by mountains and crags," recalls novelist Aquilino Ribeiro, and even now, where paved roads pass through, it remains backward in modern comparison (Ribeiro, 1964, 9–27). Electric lights and modern clothes have not much changed the outward appearance of these communities, in which women still throw used water off their porches, to the chagrin of unwary anthropologists in pathways below, and where adult men, in their best clothes, spend Sunday afternoons chatting in the shade of the church, just as their grandfathers did. Weekend dances at a farmhouse-tavern suggest an awareness of city life and its distractions, but the fact that farmers still thresh beans with flails indicates a primary allegiance to age-old customs (personal observations, 1969).

Yet structural alteration has occurred. Portuguese anthropologist Jorge Dias documented extensive change in the village of Rio de Onor in the mountains of the northern province of Tras-os-Montes (Dias, 1953; see also Dias,

1948; 1961, 69–89). There, where fields are cultivated for grain to make bread, grapes to make wine, and vegetables and fruits to round out the diet, there where the farmer also grazes goats and sheep on mountain pastures and where he harvests hay from natural meadows for his cattle, there much of the old way of life persisted to 1944, when Dias conducted his study, and to the present, so far as a more casual visitor can discern (Dias, 1953, 163–224). Yet even by the mid-forties, important changes had taken place, reflecting a first intrusion of modern values and new elements of social structure.

The fundamental social unit traditionally was a kind of joint-family household rather than the smaller domestic family limited to husband, wife, and children. Its integrity as a social unity depended upon keeping its land intact, along with associated rights in communally owned pasture, meadow, forest, and field. Much as in Ireland, in order to keep the land undivided as a single farm unit, but also to retain communal rights, only one son traditionally married, in Portugal usually the oldest, and that only when the father felt old enough to retire. Younger brothers, and those sisters not fortunate enough to marry, often remained to work and live, but not to raise families of their own. The typical family thus was three-generational, but in that special form of joint family known as a stem family, because only one son married and continued to live with his parents, even after children were born. The family included celibate adults (Dias, 1953, 134).

Change did not come to Rio de Onor through fundamental economic development in the mountains. Factories and industrial agriculture remain mere hopes for most of rural Portugal even today. Yet villagers have not been completely insulated from contact with modern Europe. For over half a century, paved roads led to urban centers. The government sent emissaries into the back country and took young men for military service in return. Discharged servicemen may reenter their home villages to take up life as it always was. But in the context of modern circumstances, they also may return with new ideas and a capacity to bring about some change. This occurred in Rio de Onor after 1914, when youths who served in World War I returned rebellious against marriage restrictions.

A number of returning servicemen at that time married earlier than was the custom. A few broke even more completely with the past, for they married when they should have stayed single. By the mid-1940s, 14 out of 43 families had been established by younger sons who lacked arable land. They survived by applying modern techniques, and especially new chemical fertilizers, to fields hacked out of the mountainside, formerly wild areas once shared by all as part of the village legacy. Though their lives remained insecure and precarious, with these fields they were able to support small families alongside the traditional stem families of their older brothers. But the creation of these small families undermined the delicate balance of communal integration. They led to further profound changes (Dias, 1953, 87, 135–136).

The family revolt challenged old customs of village organization. Each family possessed rights in communal land. These rights were supervised by the village council. The new families, though they gained some land, got no such rights in meadows, pastures, and other resources. They had no accepted place on the council and in village affairs. As their number grew, their presence increasingly undermined the authority of village government based on mutual interest in village-owned land. In 1944 Dias thought it likely Rio de Onor would go the way of a neighboring community where the traditional village structure had collapsed under comparable pressure (Dias, 1953, 136). Time was to prove Dias right, for in Rio de Onor, as throughout northern Portugal, communalism has disappeared (Jorge Dias, personal communication, 1969; see also Dias, 1953, 19).

It is well and good to analyze modernization in terms of cultural, social, and ecological variables. Ultimately, however, it is individuals who must make personal changes if a society is to develop. Every major theorist in the study of culture change recognizes this. "Gifted or unusual people . . . often play decisive roles in bringing about change," writes George M. Foster (1962, 112), and more broadly, Charles J. Erasmus sees some hope in the potentialities of "man's intelligence, . . . , and a self-interest. . . ." (Erasmus, 1961, 309; see Dunn, 1964, 397–398.)

The parish studied by Bernard J. Siegel in the Portuguese province of Estremadura provides a case in point. Located only 18 kilometers from Lisbon, it comprised communities further along the road of modernization than was Rio de Onor at about the same time. Following World War I, a small but growing number of individuals from the parish worked in Lisbon. By the mid-1950s, when Siegel did his work, about a third of the younger men commuted daily to the capital. In the reverse direction, city people also came to the parish, including teachers, policemen, public-health officials, and priests. Individuals who happen to move between town and country do not necessarily become the carriers of innovation, however. Only certain ones seem capable of that. "Awareness and knowledge of external values as well as attitudes toward them were basically communicated by a small group of influential men," Siegel observed. They were men who shared certain social characteristics (Siegel, 1961, 40).

Meeting frequently in the back room of a bar-restaurant owned by one of them, these were the official and unofficial village leaders. Their number included the president of the parish, but all had the power and prestige that comes with financial success and personal stature in a small community. One was a physician. One operated a medium-sized farm. The others were successful small businessmen. All were active adults between the ages of 30 and 45. All were educated at least through high school (Siegel, 1961, 40).

These men, then, had vigor, education, some leisure, economic well-being, and prestige. They also enjoyed the influence they had. For success as agents of modernization, however, they needed a further quality. In order to function as a bridge or hinge between urban and rural cultures, they had to participate to some extent in each, as Robert Redfield suggested some years ago (Redfield, 1956, 60–66).

Because they were either born in the parish or had lived there from childhood, they had the confidence of others in the community. At the same time, their education and business ties brought them into recurrent contact with the city, where they also met with people in an easy manner. Familiar with both subcultures, they functioned effectively in translating the one to the other. This facility extended even to language. They spoke both standard Portuguese and the parish dialect.

It was men of this type, it appears, who brought urban values to the community. We see success of this sort in the realm of medicine. A public-health doctor from outside offered free medical services. Thoroughly urban in his life style, he was frustrated in his efforts to reach sick people in the parish. The private physician had many patients. In addition, he frequently was asked for advice on nonmedical matters and had influence in local politics. He was able to function successfully as a hinge person because he was at home in both subcultures.

Again, in education, most teachers had an urban life style and were relatively ineffective as agents of modernization. The occasional teacher who had been brought up in the parish, however, had some success in leading pupils toward the goals of formal education (Siegel, 1961, 38–41).

IRELAND

Rectangular, thatch-roofed cottages built to house a family at one end and cattle at the other still are found in western Ireland. Men still are seen in the fields using shovels, sickles, and scythes. Many speak Irish Gaelic, and fairies are reputed to have their walkways and abodes in certain places. But people do not live with animals any longer. The longhouses that survive are partitioned, and former animal byres have been converted into bedrooms, storage areas, or dairies (Evans, 1957; Orme, 1970, 191–194). Children speak Irish Gaelic, but they are taught English as more useful in the outside world, and modernity has made belief in leprechauns and banshees unfashionable (Messenger, 1969, 97, 101, 129). In all, the past is much alive, yet much changed from what it was.

Many customs now dead or moribund still thrived in the early 1930s when Conrad Arensberg began his field work in County Clare, though even then change was apparent. He found still vivid a belief in fairies who peopled the countryside, for example. Not that people talked about fairies as something true and real. To do that was superstitious, as well they knew. Yet fairy paths traditionally were located on the west side of houses and, according to tradition, to block fairy paths was to court bad luck. Consistent with old tradition, not a single house in the county had a shed, building, or other house built at its western end. The belief was there, it just was not proper any longer to speak of it (Arensberg, 1968, 40).

The social structure of the parish was old-fashioned, too. People lived in terms of family ties and the intimacy of neighbors who had grown up together. Gatherings of adult farmers, a group formally recognized as the *cuaird*, were important in making decisions in the community. In some ways similar to the group of influential men who ran the village near Lisbon, the *cuaird* was made up of men who were vigorous, in control of local wealth and power, and endowed with prestige. They differed significantly, however, for they were not urban-wise.

The leadership asserted by the *cuaird* was adapted to traditional ends. "The topics brought up and debated upon are much the same from year to year and place to place," observed Arensberg (Arensberg, 1968, 129). Mostly they had to do with when to plow, sow, or harvest, with market prices for produce, and with other age-old topics. When they discussed innovations, they tended to favor the old, and when they dealt with the outside world, they tended to favor ways to preserve what was customary.

County Clare has changed in the nearly forty years since Conrad Arensberg and Solon Kimball carried out their study. In 1958, the government of Ireland began strenuous efforts to bring industry into the countryside, and by 1960 the program had enticed British, American, German, Dutch, and Japanese capital to finance 150 new factories. Twenty-three of these were established in County Clare, some centered around Shannon International Airport, but most dispersed throughout the countryside. As I write, Art Gallaher, Jr., is in the county to complete his study of these developments (personal communication; see Leyton, 1966, 1970). Until he has had the opportunity to assemble and analyze his data, Gallaher's conclusions can only be tentative. It appears, however, that changes in the role of hinge men have taken place.

Irish countrymen forty years ago relied mainly upon the local priest, doctor, and schoolmaster to intercede for them when they had to deal with townsmen. All three remain highly respected, but only the schoolmaster still is turned to in the old way as a hinge with outside authorities. New men serve this function more effectively now. The agricultural-extension agent and a local farmer active in the recently established national association of farmers appear to have become especially successful in this regard.

County Clare in the 1970s appears to be well along the road to modernity. Islands located only a few miles west remain more conservative. John C. Messenger finds on the one he studied that they still preserve customs made familiar in the work of Arensberg and Kimball, though some differ in detail. The *cuaird*, for example, never existed in that area (Messenger, 1969, 65, 73). In part, this conservatism results from ecological obstacles. Progress is limited by the small patches of man-made soil and fickle fishing grounds that are their heritage. It is unprofitable to mechanize, so they must continue to rely on digging sticks, spades, and scythes to cultivate crops and raise livestock as essentially subsistence operations. To foodstuffs raised for consumption they add small though significant amounts of cash earned from the sale of cattle and sheep, from seaweed collected along the beach, and from handcraft production, including knitted sweaters (Messenger, 1969, 2, 24–25).

The island is not unexposed to outside influence. Coast guard and lighthouse personnel are stationed there, and medical service is provided by a resident nurse as well as a doctor from a neighboring island. The community has long provided an elementary education for its children, following a curriculum set by national policy. From time to time outsiders come as tourists, as jobbers to buy livestock, as buyers and sellers on other business errands, and as emigrants returned for vacations. Almost every family has a radio, and since 1963 most watch television on a set located in the community "dance hall." An agricultural-extension agent resident on another of the islands visits the community from time to time to encourage the adoption of new farming techniques, particularly the proper use of fertilizers. In all, since the people regard themselves as "friendly, polite, and hospitable to outsiders," they seem to be greatly exposed to modern ideas (Messenger, 1969, 16–17, 54, 127).

Change of a superficial nature has taken place. Only three families were observed by Messenger still to eat from a shared dish atop the table, an avowedly "backward" custom. The homespun vests and trousers as well as the blue woolen shirts of the men, and the long red and blue woolen skirts as well as the shawls of the women are still in evidence, but gradually are being replaced by manufactured clothing. In all, although the standard of living is low, it has improved since the end of the last century (Messenger, 1969, 24, 42–43).

Basic change in the cultural system of the islands has not gotten very far, however. The social structure remains fundamentally what it was for ages, while values and norms have altered only in superficial ways. Ecological obstacles partially explain this conservatism, but in part individual factors must also be invoked.

The system of marriage and inheritance appears to lie at the heart of certain personality and role difficulties. A man cannot marry and take over management of a farm until his father is ready to retire. "Even at forty-five and fifty, if the old couple have not yet made over the farm, the countryman remains a 'boy' in respect to farm work and the rural vocabulary." (Arensberg and Kimball, 1968, 55.) In the Portuguese mountains, where we saw this syndrome, we saw young men break away after 1914. The syndrome also occurs in Norway, but there it is ameliorated by the custom of having lovers (Park, 1962; for more on Norwegian personality, see Hendin, 1964, 143–145). In Ireland, basic personality traits which include male inadequacy and a resistance to role appear to be the consequence (Opler, 1957, 5; Opler and Singer, 1956, 15–18). This type of personality lacks the kind of flexibility and aggressiveness individuals must have to adapt to new cultural demands (see Arensberg and Kimball, 1968, 112; Messenger, 1969, 59, 77, 107).

The failure to get direction and assistance from hinge people to the extent they need it constitutes still another obstacle. The priest, for example, is ideally placed to serve a bridge function. On the one hand, the priest has high prestige and power in the community. On the other hand, he is educated and knows the wider world of Ireland. Priests generally fail, however, for two reasons. First, those assigned to backward communities tend to be young men unhappy with their posts. They long to move on to more cosmopolitan places. Further, insofar as they attempt to shape people and their futures, they are committed to conservative orthodox goals. The average priest tends to concern himself far more with sexual morality than with modern adaptation (Messenger, 1969, 61–62).

In the 1960s, priests where Messenger worked seemed to be changing their attitude toward the island. From a concern which appeared mainly to focus upon enforcement of a puritanical code of conduct, they began to interest themselves in making the island a more exciting place to live. They have been successful in introducing some modern, if still modest, innovations. The islanders now are taught set-dancing and some music in the school. An annual inter-island competition in sports and dancing enlivens the year. Priests got a dance hall built where community functions can be held, and they saw to the establishment of a small lending library in the school (Messenger, 1969, 128). All of these changes, of course, are superficial. They suggest, however, the potentiality of a hinge role which otherwise has not functioned effectively to introduce modernity.

Sorbonne anthropologist Robert Cresswell provides an illustration of how farmers may vary in their response to modern circumstances. He documents this for the year 1956 in a parish that overlaps parts of counties Clare and Galway. In particular, he writes of a farmer named Finn who was traditional, though not backward, and of a farmer named Brian who was more open to change.

The smallness of Finn's farm placed severe strictures on his progress. All major changes took place within the limits of a traditional operation. In ten years he shifted from an emphasis upon animal husbandry to a primary investment in cereal and root crops, including more cash crops. But he still used a horse-drawn plow and other traditional tools and techniques, because his holding was too small to make mechanization feasible. He also continued to rely on the mutual aid of kinsmen and neighbors, unable to dispense with them or to participate in new forms of social organization. Finn seemed inevitably conservative under the circumstances. The finances of his farm did not permit him to modernize extensively. He seemed content that it be so (Cresswell, 1969, 284–294, 351–356).

The farm of Brian is bigger and more valuable than that of Finn. Brian owns all of the equipment a farmer needs, whereas Finn has only one horse when he should have two, and lacks other equipment as well. Further, Brian "is trying to modernize his holding as much as possible." (Cresswell, 1969, 356.) He has succeeded in adding modern equipment to his operation, including a Canadian harrow and a disc plow. The acquisition of new equipment appears to have undermined old social habits, moreover. He does not rely upon mutual aid as does Finn, so he is cut off from some of the intimacy of local life (Arensberg and Kimball, 1968, 68–69). This relative isolation is deepened by the lesser amount of time he has for leisure. Machinery in this case has not lightened his work, it has increased it, although production and wealth have increased even more. So Brian can enjoy more consumer goods than can Finn, but he works harder and has become something of a social isolate (Cresswell, 1969, 356–399).

Rural Ireland and rural Portugal seem alike in this. Among ordinary villagers, some individuals seem more open to change than others. In part, some have more opportunity. But personality factors also are important. From work done in the Netherlands we learn more about this.

THE NETHERLANDS

The best way to see the Netherlands is on bicycle in the summer. You may run into a head wind or a summer storm, but otherwise, the flat landscape and gentle sun make biking easy. Away from major highways, where it is quiet, you can see to the horizon in every direction, and the view is one of ripening fields, cool-flowing canals, and shady trees. It is also a view of magnificent old farm buildings, "Van Gogh" bridges, and ageless canal barges.

Yet, though the view remains decidedly rural in most places, it clearly is a view of a highly industrialized land. Small factories in the countryside reveal this, for not all industry is centralized in urban agglomerations. But the farms reveal this too. In the east, where John and Dorothy Keur studied a mixed-farming community in the early 1950s, one sees new buildings, scientific crop rotation, and farm machinery as well as abundant evidence of strong urban influence (Keur and Keur, 1955). In the west, where your bike takes you through the rainbow colors of vast fields of tulips, modernization is even more apparent. Flower-growing had been highly industrialized for over a century when, in the mid-1950s, rural sociologist I. Gadourek studied one of the bulb-growing communities located along the old highway that connects Leyden with Haarlem (Gadourek, 1956).

Some communities have been later to modernize than others, and one of the latest was Winterswijk near the German border, directly east of Arnhem. Until the turn of the century, Winterswijk was located in a region isolated by the nearly total absence of modern forms of transportation. Improved roads were built during the early decades of the twentieth century, but the IJssel River still kept the region partially isolated until just before World War II, since good bridges remained rare. Even as late as 1952, one main road was impassable at times during severe winters because the boatbridge that crossed it had to be removed while the ice was flowing (Benvenuti, 1961, 104). By the mid-1950s, however when Bernardo Benvenuti carried out a social survey, the region had become quite modern. Winterswijk is a service center for the surrounding countryside, and now has many of the characteristics of a modern town. We look, then, at farmers very much caught up in the modern world.

The Irish farmers Finn and Brian have their counterparts in Winterswijk. As a relatively unsuccessful farmer, there is the man we will call Mr. van Loon, age 36 years, the owner of a small farm with an old but well-maintained house. Dr. Benvenuti, an Italian scientist who speaks Dutch, found the van Loons "nice and helpful," but shy and ill-at-ease with strangers. He also found them very old-fashioned as individuals.

The old-fashioned orientation is visible in their home life. They still eat dinner from communal plates, and the only modern conveniences they enjoy are electric lights, running water, and an old radio. Tradition is visible in their dress, for they are never seen in anything other than heavy-duty work clothes devoid of frills or color. Tradition is visible in the things they live for: Farming for the van Loons is all they seem interested in. They do not take vacations and seldom leave the farm. Mr. van Loon owns a small motorbicycle which he uses occasionally to visit his married sister in a neighboring community or to go to town on an errand, but neither he nor his wife has ever been to Germany, which is located only two miles away.

The old-fashioned orientation is also visible in van Loon's farming habits. He has no silo and the few machines he owns consist of an old hayrake, an old hay snaffler, and an old mowing machine. Other machinery must be borrowed or rented. Mr. van Loon has no clear idea of what his income is, and no apparent idea of what his time is worth, for he does not keep books. In relations with outsiders, he seems unsure of himself: His wife and sister joke about his few efforts to travel, because he always worries so much about missing a train or bus that he fails to sleep at night (Benvenuti, 1961, 212–216).

The man we will call Mr. de Hoogh is very different. Thirty-two years old, his farm is even smaller than van Loon's, and his buildings are old and not too well kept. Yet, the interior of his home suggests a more acculturated individual. He has townlike furniture and uses electricity and piped water to provide his family with an electric iron, an electric washing machine, a shower, a flush toilet, and a kitchen sink. In the parlor, an old Dutch clock of carved wood, an oil painting, a carved-oak linen chest, and two polished hunting guns on the wall suggest middle-class tastes.

As individuals, the de Hooghs appear very modern and independent-minded. They conversed with Benvenuti without difficulty. At the time of the interview, Mrs. de Hoogh had just returned from a visit to town. She was dressed fashionably, with her hair set in the current vogue. Mr. de Hoogh was born on a farm, but is concerned about the outside world and keeps abreast of current events. Three years with the army in Indonesia gave him an interest in travel which he no longer indulges, since he cannot take time from his farm. He does, however, subscribe to a provincial newspaper in his effort to be part of the world beyond his farm.

The modern orientation of the de Hooghs is evident in farm management as well as in home life. Though rented, the farm is well equipped with silos and light farm machinery, so that only heavy equipment needs to be rented from the local cooperative. Mr. de Hoogh does not borrow from neighbors. His barn is fully modern, with separate mangers and automatic drinking troughs for the cattle. All equipment is in excellent repair, though the farm is somewhat unkempt, for, as de Hoogh put it, "A clean yard is nice, it is true; but I prefer spending my time in ploughing my soil deeper." Scientific management for de Hoogh includes careful bookkeeping and regular conferences with the local agricultural-extension agent (Benvenuti, 1961, 189–193).

The nature of leadership has changed in Winterswijk. In the late nineteenth and early twentieth centuries, two kinds of leaders were prominent. One consisted of bridge people: teachers, veterinarians, clergymen, and others who were nonfarmers but concerned themselves with farming problems. They were particularly influential in making the cooperative movement successful. The other consisted of leaders among the farmers themselves, and it is this type of leadership to which Benvenuti particularly gives his attention (Benvenuti, 1961, 134).

Formerly, leaders among the farmers came out of a local peasant aristocracy. The area for centuries had been occupied by the so-called Scholten farmers, families that enjoyed the prestige and power that comes from owning large farms and woods. Until 1941, when sharecropping was made illegal, they profited so much from tenants who farmed parts of their land that their own work involvement was largely managerial. In life style, they emulated the aristocracy, living in large homes, traveling, educating their children beyond the norm for farmers, hunting, riding, and in general assuming many of the attitudes of a landed gentry (Benvenuti, 1961, 115–120; see also Heeringa, 1934; Klokman, 1938).

Until recent decades, Scholten farmers dominated local affairs. They actively promoted the cooperative movement, individuals among them serving effectively on governing boards. Scholten farmers also served on school boards and in local church administration. Elections tended to favor them, so that aldermen were likely to be Scholten. In all, until World War II, local power rested in their hands, and no initiative could be taken without their support. In contributing leadership to the cooperative movement, they showed a capacity to give direction of a progressive nature, but they could as well have fostered conservative causes, since their influence was based upon hereditary prestige rather than personal qualities and the ideas they espoused (Benvenuti, 1961, 121).

So long as local life was regulated by traditional values and norms, the leading farmers remained Scholten. Now they are successful though not necessarily wealthy farmers like de Hoogh. Such men are looked to as models for change, they occupy formal leadership positions, and they tend to be the first adopters of innovation. These leaders, moreover, in some ways are alike as individuals.

The progressive farmer in Winterswijk is characterized by an orientation to the outside world, to contemporary middle-class standards. This orientation has a holistic quality in the sense that it involves the total personality, the individual's total view of the world. The leader tends to favor an urban adaptation in everything he does, in his whole life style, and not merely in farm management. Consistent with this, we find that de Hoogh and his family wear modern clothes, display modern tastes in household furnishings, and react as modern people in meeting strangers (Benvenuti, 1961, 383–384).

Not only is the personality orientation of the leader holistically modern, it is also characterized by what sociologist Daniel Lerner has termed "empathy," "an inner mechanism which enables newly mobile persons to operate efficiently in a changing world." (Lerner, 1958, 49–50.) A key feature of the person with empathy, as Lerner uses the term, is that he "is distinguished by a high capacity for identification with new aspects of his environment; he comes equipped with the mechanisms needed to incorporate new demands upon himself that arise outside of his habitual experience." (Lerner, 1958, 49.) Dr. Benvenuti found this capacity in men like de Hoogh, whose efficiency in culture change he attributes to "the degree of awareness of his personal position within the structure of which he is a part," and his "orientation towards the outside world." These elements, concludes Benvenuti, "are the result of the impact which modern western culture has had upon localist cultures in general." (Benvenuti, 1961, 383.)

NORWAY

With a couple of major exceptions, high mountains and dense forests confine tillable soil and human settlements mainly to narrow areas alongside the fjords that push deep into the peninsula and to the bottom lands and sloping sides of mountain valleys. In these scattered places, people earn their living primarily from agriculture and fishing. For centuries, until modern forms of transportation were perfected, most of rural Norway was isolated from urban centers. "To these communities, the city—with its swarming profusion of people and diversified activities, with its openness toward the world and its receptiveness to cultural impulses from the outside—was a distant and foreign world." (Munch, 1956, 32.)

The isolation of Norwegian peasant communities began to break down as early as the mid-1800s, however. Industrial needs for raw materials and a work force, as well as for a market for manufactured products, encouraged the construction of new lines of communication, including railways and steamships that brought urban centers and formerly remote peasant areas into an unprecedented confrontation. Urban-oriented individuals moved into nearly every rural community to work in country stores or small industrial workshops. Peasant emigrants found employment in industrial centers, giving countrymen close personal ties to individuals in towns and cities. The self-sufficiency of peasant production gave place to a growing commercial orientation. "And with all this came the whole complex of ideas and value attitudes," writes Peter A. Munch, "which in many points went directly against the value system of the old rural community." (Munch, 1956, 36; see also Munch, 1948, 76–111, 130–160; 1953.)

By the second half of the twentieth century, modernization has left the Norwegian countryman still different from his urban compatriots, but primarily as one must be different to live in a still rugged countryside and to be engaged in fishing and agriculture (Vorren, 1960; see also Brox, 1963, 26–29). Contemporary Norwegian countrymen are modern within these limits. They also have become thoroughly egalitarian. Great differences in wealth and status have not been part of Norwegian rural culture since the Norwegian Labor Party gained power in 1935 and the leveling of incomes and life chances got underway (Park and Soltow, 1961, 152–153; Barnes, 1954, 40). Within such communities, however, some individuals succeed better than others.

At the University of Bergen a few years ago, a group of anthropologists under the direction of Frederik Barth explored the role of the entrepreneur in social change in northern Norway. In this work, which draws upon the analysis of Cyril Belshaw of Canada, an entrepreneur is identified as "someone who takes the initiative in administering resources, and pursues an expansive economic policy." (Barth, 1963, 6; see Belshaw, 1955, 148.) Progressive countrymen, it appears, must orient themselves simultaneously to both traditional and modern cultures, or alternatively, to both the rural and the urban parts of a contemporary national culture. Their success, in short, requires empathy inward as well as outward.

Building upon concepts of game theory, but also upon some of Paul Bohannon's work in anthropological economics, Barth in part draws attention to the fact that different spheres of exchange may be identified in Norwegian society, just as they have been identified, say, in Africa (Bohannan, 1955). In primitive economic systems, the goods which may be exchanged often fall into two or more discrete spheres, each characterized by different ideas of what it is right and proper to exchange. For example, one may make gift exchanges of food for food, but it is not possible to barter food for the possession of a slave, since slaves are obtained only within their own separate sphere of exchange (Bohannan, 1965, 248–249).

Discrete spheres in Norway differentiate those goods exchanged in a money economy from noncommercial exchanges inherent in kin and neighbor interaction (Brox, 1963, 21–23). Above all, one must not commercialize the exchanges of intimates, nor rely solely on goodwill for success in commercial transactions. In the intimacy of a small, backwoods community, however, an entrepreneur may find it difficult to maintain the separation of these spheres. In one community, for example, Ottar Brox found that people were not loyal in bringing their trade to any one shopkeeper. Even a man's close relatives were not good customers. They apparently resented the commercial attitude of demanding set prices from all, regardless of friendship or kinship. "Neighbors give each other fish for the pot and help each other in pulling ashore boats," notes Brox, "but a shopman can hardly discriminate over the counter with respect to price or service." (Brox, 1963, 22.) The shopkeepers in that area were not very successful in meeting the demands of both commercial and traditional exchanges. (For the same problem in Melanesia, see Hogbin, 1958, 189–192.)

The case of Hans, who manages a local office of the post and steamship agency, is illustrative.

> Hans buys fish in the winter. But a lot of fishermen do not sell their fish to him, but to fish buyers in other fjords, even if this means an extra half an hour or more of time and fuel per day.
>
> Hans says that the Eastfjord people are so narrow-minded that they grudge a neighbour's earning a few kroner, and go far out of their way to avoid this. He is bitter, e.g., even an old friend with whom he once shared a motorboat, now sells his fish to a competitor. (Brox, 1963, 22–23.)

In a different community, an entrepreneur named Larsen has managed to maintain his clientele through a judicious balancing of the commercial ties of credit and neighborhood ties. To get families reestablished, at a time when they had to be relocated from an older settlement, he sold them fishing equipment which put them deeply in his debt. Because they owe so much, they feel obliged to sell him their catch. And because he sells everything they might buy, including electric appliances and other modern goods, they feel they cannot ask for large amounts of cash, but must apply their earnings to what they buy as well as to the debt. Under these circumstances, Larsen not only maintains his clientele, he is able to pay less for the fish he buys and charge more for the goods he sells. His customers are bound to him by the moral bonds of local obligation as well as the commercial bonds of business (Brox, 1963, 30–31).

Herring bosses, who must recruit crews to work their boats and nets, illustrate even more clearly the entrepreneur who succeeds in building upon both kinds of bonds. For the most part, the boss hires men and sells fish on a purely commercial basis. But occasionally he makes gifts of fish to families for their own consumption. Further, when the job does not require the employer to give orders, and the employee to obey, he interacts with his men as equals. "At cards, sharing a bottle or at a dancing party one will be the boss' equal, pal and neighbor." By making connections between spheres of exchange in this way, the herring boss assures himself crews and cooperation where money or personal bonds separately would fail or succeed less effectively (Brox, 1963, 25).

At present, we really cannot say more about how a person can display the sort of flexibility that allows him simultaneously to graft onto the outside world of commerce and the inside world of traditional obligations, to make connections, in the terms of Barth, between these two distinct spheres of exchange. It is clear, however, that empathy, a capacity to operate efficiently in a changing world, must include adjustments in both spheres if progressive men are to succeed in communities not yet fully industrialized or urbanized.

For the most part, lack of adequate published materials makes it impracticable to bring other parts of the Atlantic fringe into our discussion. This is true for Brittany (Marin, 1970), Normandy (Chaubet, 1921; Dalido, 1951), Scotland (Dorian, 1970; Evans and Gailey, 1961; Littlejohn, 1963), the Faroe Islands (Blehr, 1963; Rasmussen, 1950; Williamson, 1970), Iceland (Thompson, L., 1966; 1969, Chapter 9), Sweden (Blehr et al., 1968; Erixon, 1946; Hanssen, 1952; Izikowitz, Moberg, and Eskeröd, 1959; Lindstrom, 1951; Swedner, 1960; Yngvesson, 1970), and Finland (Doby, 1960; Haltsonen, 1960; Lander, 1970; Mead, W. R., 1953; Sweetser, 1964). Wales will be discussed in Chapter 10 as an ethnic enclave.

EIGHT

PLAIN COUNTRYMEN: POLITICS AND CHANGE

Moving through the plain of Europe, you do not get the sense of endless open space as in parts of the United States. Open areas exist, but for the most part the landscape is broken by gently rolling hills and forests. The color and shape of farm buildings, villages, and towns vary, too, as you move along, for each area bears the marks of its own folk heritage. Emerging from a forest, rounding a turn in the road, or coming over the top of a hill, you cannot see until you get there what the people will be like and the land that is theirs.

Farms and villages alternate with towns and factories. In many places, enormous cities spread asphalt and cement tentacles into the countryside for mile after mile, so that the line between town and country is blurred or obliterated. In other places, farmlands melt into forests and wilderness as though little had happened to multiply men and alienate them from the land. But for the most part, the plain has been the part of Europe, and of the world, that has been most changed by industrialization.

ENGLAND

George Kirkland, age 45, lived in a village in the south of England when he was interviewed in 1967. "I went from school to work as a shepherd boy on this farm," he mused, as he talked about changes affecting farm workers during the preceding few decades. "My father used to say that farm working was bad pay but a good life." (Blythe, 1969, 84, 85.) By that he apparently meant that field hands were no worse off economically than workmen in factories, and had some additional advantages from living in the country. As the years have passed, however, they have seen their wages fall behind. They also suffer the problem of the tied cottage: when a man leaves or loses his job at a particular farm, he loses his house as well.

Modernization in Europe must ultimately include the full participation of countrymen in modern political institutions, it may well be argued. Current change includes a growing opportunity for them to participate in politics.

Participation, however, tends to lag, especially among farm laborers,. It clearly lags in England, and in the village of Mr. Kirkland.

As secretary of the local union of farm laborers, Kirkland has been involved in attempts to get better union participation. He finds, however, that local men are not good about gathering to hear speakers brought in to discuss their problems or to advocate issues. "The trouble is that television and that sort of thing is keeping men away from the meetings," he says, and probably he is right (Blythe, 1969, 85). Even agitation for a 14-pound, 40-hour week, which should have been a popular issue, failed to raise enthusiasm (Blythe, 1969, 85–86).

The farm worker's lack of interest in politics is difficult to understand for older men who had to fight for their rights. A democratic form of government came to them from the outside. But the right to vote did not guarantee the right to a voice in government. Mr. Kirkland's father, who is still alive, recalls that most farm workers supported the Labour Party. Liberal leanings had to be kept secret in those days, however. "The farmers owned us then—or thought they did," recalls George Kirkland. "Father said there would be dreadful dos if the farmer found out that his men were going to a political meeting or a liberal talk." (Blythe, 1969, 86.) That was in the 1920s. In the 1960s men no longer were repressed so crudely. Yet they remained politically inactive.

The study of an agricultural community in southwest England (located in the Atlantic fringe, but British, and pertinent to this discussion) reveals much the same incompleteness of political participation. Rural sociologist E. W. Martin found that the traditional political structure survived until the end of World War I. By virtue of the land they owned, local squires controlled local government, including the leadership of borough, parish, village, school, and church. They found allies in the clergy, who often were the younger sons of squires, and nearly always shared their attitudes. This political structure left its mark on the life styles of both high and low (Martin, 1965, 8–9).

The personality of a squire tended to be similar for all in some ways. The children of the gentry were taught "the art, craft and language of local leadership and public display." (Martin, 1965, 9.) By the time he was an adult, a squire had learned to accept as his due the homage of countrymen. From his manor house, as far as he could see in every direction, he owned the land, the cottages, and in a sense, the people. Typically neither an enlightened patrician nor a domineering boor, he "knew himself to be a minor sovereign and behaved like one." (Martin, 1965, 29.) And he knew that it was part of his obligation to administer justice, to organize local defense forces in time of war, to undertake public projects, and to dispense charity (Martin, 1965, 15–29).

The countryman, for his part, also developed a life style and personality consistent with the political system. It never occurred to poorer individuals that a "touching of the forelock" to social superiors was not part of the natural order. "When I was small the master would tell father if we didn't make our curtsey," recalls one old lady, who added that her father, for his part, wanted "to make sure us poor children were brought up to respect their betters." (Martin, 1965, 98, 136.)

The community got a democratic form of government in 1885. "Rural democracy acquired a structure readily enough because it was prepared by national agencies, but it had little spirit or drive." (Martin, 1965, 116.) The country gentry had no difficulty in maintaining indirect if not direct control until 1918. Then men returned from the war with new ideas. They protested low wages, tied cottages, and the lack of opportunity for their children. The gentry, for their part, ceased to be the main employers and chief controllers of wealth, for legislation was ending their privileges.

Now, over fifty years later, the trend has moved far, with the farming population more knowledgeable, particularly since television has reached them. Yet participation in the democratic process remains incomplete, just as it does in the community of George Kirkland (Martin, 1965, 19, 110, 153). Specifically, elected and appointed officials are no longer aristocrats or their representatives, as was true after the first local election in 1889. But they are not farm laborers either. Only three manual workers and no agricultural laborers were elected to the county council in the last election. The rest were landholding farmers, businessmen, technicians, and professional people; in short, a kind of educated middle class. "They may be remote from Whitehall but they know more of policies and plans than county councillors; and they also care what happens to their town or village." (Martin, 1965, 128.) Those who most need help, though, are those least engaged in the democratic process.

It is said now that rural workers earn a "living wage." For most, however, this wage does not cover necessities. This is because their basic felt needs are greater than they used to be. Workers no longer are willing to live in damp, overcrowded cottages. They feel they must have modern sewer disposal, electricity, and running water. They want washing machines, clothes dryers, electric irons, telephones, and refrigerators. Many leave the countryside to get these things in urban centers. Those who remain have not yet learned to attack their problems with political weapons (Martin, 1965, 116, 135).

Gosforth is a country parish in northwestern England (Williams, 1956; see also Frankenberg, 1966, 65–85). (It, too, is part of the Atlantic fringe, but is best discussed in connection with other English communities.) "Folks just isn't interested in politics," said one informant to W. M. Williams, who found political matters seldom came up in the conversations he had with people in the parish. When asked why they voted for conservative candidates, most answered because "we all do," or because "me father did." It apparently did not occur to the average person to give reasons in terms of political policy (Williams, 1956, 175). Here again, we find the modern intrusion of a democratic form of local government has failed to elicit thorough participation. In the study of Gosforth, however, we also learn of another modern institution introduced to rural life. With a population of well under 800 people, the community has 31 formal voluntary associations (Williams, 1956, 121, 175; see Anderson and Anderson, 1959).

Like the right to vote, the freedom to form voluntary associations provides a modern mechanism for social involvement. By grouping in terms of some common interest, whether to establish a wrestling academy, a reading-room committee, a beagles and fox-hunting society, or a school-outing committee, individuals in Gosforth can gain the strength of numbers in pursuing goals to which they attach importance. Most of the goals are not political in the sense of having to do with formal government as such. At least seven of these associations are concerned with sports, and the dramatic association seems as important to the community as the Conservative Club, which has political objectives. Yet, whatever their manifest or overt functions, these associations constitute latent, covert elements in the political process.

From the analysis of Williams, it appears that local voluntary associations reinforce the hegemony of a local elite. The membership of an association may come from any stratum in the community, although lower-class individuals rarely join. But the leadership is always given to individuals of high status. With one exception, the president of every association in the parish is "upper-upper class" in status. Further, different associations tend to have the same individuals as officers. The result is that this modern, urban-derived institution, the voluntary association, reaffirms and reinforces the local power of a minority who already control power. It gives them additional organizational support and heightens their visibility. Thus associations fail in this instance to diffuse political involvement as theoretically they might (Williams, 1956, 121–139; see also Anderson and Anderson, 1962a).

The election of members of the upper stratum to leading offices in associations need not inevitably support them as power-wielders in the community. In another Atlantic fringe but British community, a Welsh settlement with a strong egalitarian ethic, Ronald Frankenberg found that ordinary people who made up the bulk of the population were split into factions, so that any issue was capable of bringing conflict in its train. It was not a problem of the haves versus the have-nots, but of Church people (Church of England in Wales) and Chapel people (mainly Baptists)—that is, those with an English cultural orientation and those loyally Welsh in culture.

Since disagreement within an association would easily split people along these factional lines, it helped maintain the peace to elect outsiders—that is, business and professional people not regarded as truly part of the community. With strangers in office, the blame for any disagreement could be placed upon them as scapegoats. In this way, the community obtained some of the advantages of associational organization, yet was saved from conflicts they might engender (Frankenberg, 1957, 18, 41, 65–66; see also Paine, 1963, 52).

Associations can also function to enhance rather than dampen local factionalism. Political or class divisions can gain organizational strength when each faction establishes its own separate associations, maintaining rival music societies or card-playing clubs, for example, or, alternatively, recruiting primarily from one element in the population, leaving others without an association for that purpose. Either way, cleavages within the community are enhanced rather than diminished as a latent function of voluntary associations (Anderson and Anderson, 1962a; Boissevain, 1969a, 88–89).

FRANCE

The community of Wissous, 16 kilometers south of Paris, proved well suited for a study of changing social structure. Today it is a suburb of Paris, having incorporated its surviving farming population into a thoroughly modern environment. But for long it remained a village surrounded by fields, significantly isolated from Paris by a lack of easy transportation. Suburbanization could not begin until the 1930s, when daily bus service allowed inhabitants to take employment in Paris and Parisians to live in Wissous as commuters (Anderson and Anderson, 1965).

When Wissous was a village, formal voluntary associations functioned much as in Gosforth. Manifestly they were nonpolitical, with goals in music and sports, for example. In the small, intimate community of that time, people were intolerant of those who deviated from accepted political views, and no one felt the need to have a local chapter of the political party the village supported. Latently, however, associations functioned to reinforce political control of the village by a traditional local elite (Anderson and Anderson, 1965, 197–204, 259–260).

Rapidly in the 1930s, politics in the village changed. Domination by a small number of farmers and their allies came swiftly to an end. With an influx of resident commuters and a new involvement of villagers in city life, old loyalties gave way to the competing demands of a larger, more heterogeneous population. Elections were contested by different local slates, each representing a different national political party, and new leaders emerged, often representing alliances of various special-interest groups. With these changes, the role of voluntary associations changed as well (Anderson and Anderson, 1965, 145–149, 242–243).

Many associations now overtly serve political functions. Only rarely, however, do they do so as the local branches of political parties. Rather, they mediate between local, often traditional, social groupings and individuals on the one hand, and agencies of the state on the other, helping individuals effectively to bring local concerns to national attention.

A governmental agency responsible for a canton, a department, or the nation as a whole cannot consider individually the wants of each family, each local church, or each village council. When people from such small groups express wishes or complain of needs, their voices are backed only by moral suasion. Faced by a myriad of such individual, often conflicting demands, government functionaries normally take no action. Elected officials find it equally impossible to respond to every individual in a constituency. Only by uniting into large groups with recognized spokesmen can individuals make themselves heard.

Such groups take shape as formal voluntary associations. In France, most associations are not purely local developments, but get established as national institutions with tables of organization that include national, regional, and local branches. Set up in this way, associations provide a structural correlate to state organization, which also has national, regional, and local branches. Such associations allow maximum effectiveness in representing the needs of villagers at all levels.

Higher branches of the government can be approached by the representatives of higher levels of a nationally organized association, whether it is a society for family betterment, Catholic Action, or the agricultural syndicate. The national headquarters of an association may function as a vociferous and well-financed pressure group. On the local level, an association can bring in legal representation and association experts with a backlog of experience and prepared arguments to help impress the wishes of the association on members of a communal council. Such advantages are not available to a purely local group.

This meshing of associational and political organization has allowed many traditional social groups to survive under modern circumstances. Local institutions—community, church, family, and business groupings—utilize associations or even become associations (develop a replicate social structure), as the most effective means of organizing social activity under modern circumstances (Anderson and Anderson, 1962b; 1965, 227–230; see also Stacey, 1960).

For the inhabitants of a small community to participate effectively in a modern nation, the social structure must incorporate relatively new institutions as facilitating mechanisms. Among plain countrymen, one such institution is some form of local democratic government and another is that of formal voluntary associations. A third, however, is equally important, for it concerns education.

The village school is not necessarily a wholly modern phenomenon. On the whole, peasants used to be illiterate, but in some parts of Europe, schooling is old and literacy has long been common. With the modern state, however, every nation in western Europe has set up a modern school system. Further, it is the intention of modern schools to bring to the community values, ideals, and knowledge which educational planners have concluded best will support effective government. French social scientists Lucien Bernot and René Blancard, in their study of a community in the north of France, cogently point out that "For nine years, from ages five to fourteen, boys and girls spend their time in two environments: in the home with their mother, father, brothers and sisters, and at school with their teachers and school mates." (Bernot and Blancard, 1953, 155.) The state supports, in other words, an institution capable of competing with that primordial institution of indoctrination, the family.

The family, of course, is a highly successful institution for indoctrination (Anderson, B. G., 1968; Métraux and Mead, 1954; see also Gorer, 1955, 1965; Gorer and Rickman, 1949). The church can also be highly influential, and it may contribute to a unique regional or national uniformity of character. As Jesse R. Pitts has pointed out, though many in Europe belong to the Roman Catholic church, "One may speak of a French Catholicism as against a Spanish or an Italian or an Irish Catholicism." (Pitts, 1963, 237.) Further, public schools are not without competition. Private schools provide alternatives, and not the least in France. Laurence Wylie studied a village in the west of France, for example, in which all but a few attended Catholic schools (Wylie, 1966, 288–300). On the whole, however, it is governmentally supervised public schools which shape education in ways purposefully contrived to inculcate agreed-upon skills, knowledge, and values.

Public schools in France aim to prepare children in various ways for success as adults (Wylie, 1964, 76). It is the school, above all, which teaches the facts of formal government. It is the school, too, which indoctrinates the beliefs, values, and attitudes that lie behind political behavior and give them force. Some anthropologists working on elementary education in Germany have particularly given attention to these aspects of the educational process.

In a hilly section of southwestern Germany, the community of Rebhausen long remained conservative by German standards. Agriculture, with a heavy emphasis on wine production, had only partly modernized. A cooperative to process and sell local wine was not established until 1934, and a substantial membership was not recruited until after the war, for many farmers were reluctant to give up the old custom of pressing their own grapes and fermenting the juice in their own casks. In the 1960s Rebhausen landowners still had not consolidated their scattered plots, although farmers in a neighboring village had.

In recent years local cultivators have gotten more fully caught up in the wider world of Germany. They face increasing competition from the wines of other member nations as the Common Market leads to the removal of tariffs. To cope with this threat they are updating farming procedures. In 1958 a chemical plant was built in the village, attracting the families of factory and office workers and resulting in a housing development (Warren, 1967, 3–24).

The school in Rebhausen got a new building in 1965. The teachers are state employees, bound by the constitution to teach children to be moral and charitable, to revere God, and to love country and home. In addition, they are obliged to teach political responsibility and commitment to a democratic form of government. Having undertaken an ethnography of the school, Richard L. Warren concludes that in part these political goals are achieved. When they leave school, children are able meaningfully to describe what a democratic system is and how it works. But in part, Warren feels the goals may remain unattained, for he does not feel confident of "their future ability to handle the functional, interpersonal relationships required to maintain the vitality of democratic government." (Warren, 1967, 46, 82.)

What concerns Warren is the evidence he found for indoctrination in the relationships of an authoritarian system. The prevailing classroom atmosphere places teachers in the authoritative role of directing, correcting, and judging pupils from whom obedience is expected. The traditional characterization of the German teacher as "king in the classroom" survives undiluted (Warren, 1967, 28, 70).

Each new teacher must serve three years of probation under the eyes of a county superintendent who makes classroom visits and administers the final teacher's examination. In this county, the superintendent is a man close to retirement age who retains attitudes from his own youth in the Nazi period. He embodies old notions about the prestige and authority of a bureaucrat, displaying an "almost merciless use of power." "The thrust of the power is never really blunted; it flows through the educational system and comes to rest in the classroom, where the student stands vulnerable, obligated to adjust to it, faced with no alternative." (Warren, 1967, 99.)

Another factor, not unrelated, also inhibits indoctrination to democratic values. Teachers feel that children are too young, inexperienced, and intellectually immature to practice democracy in the classroom. This point of view, however, is under attack. During the late sixties, national educational reform was in the wind throughout West Germany. By 1970 all state schools were to have an additional ninth year which would include emphasis on civic-political education. Since the county also soon will have a new superintendent, the Rebhausen school seems on the brink of change (Warren, 1967, 82, 104–110).

For twelve years, from 1959 to 1971, the Spindlers have carried out observations in a number of rural villages not far from the city of Stuttgart, in the same part of Germany as Rebhausen. Over the years, they have watched these communities urbanize in a dramatic way (Spindler, 1972b). Recently, they completed an ethnography of the school in Schönhausen, documenting adaptive efforts to prepare pupils for success in the modern world (Spindler, 1972a).

The prevailing atmosphere of the Schönhausen school is one of individual freedom. Younger, less experienced teachers sometimes demand strict order in their classes, insisting upon quiet because they demand it, and not because it seems necessary for the task at hand. Many teachers, however, and particularly those who are older and more experienced, allow self-direction, so much so that rooms sometimes are in near bedlam, though never out of control. Pupils still are punished for disobedience. A slap on the ear is not ususual, for freedom is balanced by constraint. But the emphasis is on freedom, and on the whole, it appears that teachers in Schönhausen are in revolt against the "deadly obedience and spirit" of the schools they went to as children, led by a principal whose philosophy is that to learn well, children must feel free. The authoritarian ethic has been replaced by one more congenial to a modern democracy (Spindler, 1972a; compare Lowie, 1954, 328–352; Spencer, 1965, 178–182; Wurzbacher, 1961).

On the European plain, as well as in other parts of Europe where the modernization of rural areas is well along, the quality of village life is greatly altered by grafting on new political institutions, including democratic forms of government, voluntary associations, and modern schools. These changes take place, however, as part of the larger process of urbanization, and that process, in the end, can lead to the final demise of differences between rural and urban settlements. In the valley where Schönhausen is located, it is expected that in time, the more than twenty villages and small towns now visible will become a single urban conglomeration. This, too, is part of what it may mean to live in a contemporary German community. Comparable change has already taken place in Denmark.

DENMARK

If you drive through Denmark today, you will find it still a land of gently rolling fields broken by an occasional lake, wood, or homestead. Industry is growing, but because it is an industry of small enterprises, it blends into the landscape. Farming is highly mechanized, but the fields are still visible. Villages have more houses than before, and around urban centers some communities clearly have become suburbs while others are wholly new, built up largely with apartment buildings. And with that, one does begin to recognize an urban revolution (Anderson and Anderson, 1964). The really impressive visual evidence, however, is different from what is found in places where heavy industry is present, as in the German Ruhr. It is not the massive urban-industrial concentration, but modern means of transportation which stand witness to what has happened.

Electric trains and busses radiate into the countryside from towns and cities. Special paths ease traffic for bicycles, including those with small motors. Motorcycles and motorscooters claim the edge lanes of paved highways. By such means, Danes have become remarkably mobile. Beginning in the late sixties, however, a wholly new dimension was added. Denmark entered the automobile age. For the first time, ordinary people, including those of the working class, could afford small automobiles.

Dispersed industry and effective means of transportation make it possible for workers, businessmen, and others to live in the countryside. The industrialization of the family farm releases members of farm families, sometimes the farmer himself, to find work in business and industry, often in towns, without leaving their farm homes, since they too are mobile. Urban and rural populations as a result are greatly interspersed now in nearly every corner of the nation. Farmers and former urbanites live side by side as neighbors. Under these circumstances, farmers acculturate readily. This is all the more so since they also are exposed to modern mass media, of which television is particularly influential, and are loyal to an egalitarian ethic, as American anthropologist Judith F. Hansen has pointed out (Hansen, 1970, 77–93; see also Anderson, R. T., 1972a, Chapter 14; Bidstrup and Kaufmann, 1963).

The modern farmer may like his work very much, but he now wants and gets the same things as other Danes. He and his family want to be near other people, shops, mechanics, central schools, communal offices, libraries, movie houses, sports arenas, beaches, restaurants, and cafés. Farming has become an occupation like any other. It has its advantages, which are appreciated. But its disadvantages—isolation, hard work, long hours, low pay, drudgery, and monotony—are unacceptable. Away from work, there remains little apparent difference between the modern farmer and his neighbor in the village who may be an office worker or a truck driver. Both are modern. They still face problems as they continue to adapt to changing circumstances. But they no longer face problems of culture change differently as rural and urban folk.

In other parts of Europe, particularly in the northwest, a comparable end to urban-rural differences either has been accomplished or now is taking place (e.g., Turney-High, 1953). It represents the ultimate product of a process of acculturation that has been underway for a century and more.

NINE

COMMUNIST
COUNTRYMEN:
IDEOLOGY AND
CHANGE

Eastern Europe comprises many peoples and terrains in addition to Russia, that mammoth among nations. It includes urbane Hungarians in Budapest, well-educated sophisticates in Czechoslovakia, mountain folk in parts of the Ukraine, and villagers in Rumania. Varieties of cultural background exist in profusion. Throughout, however, one senses common factors, whether one enters by train into East Berlin, by car into Yugoslavia, or by plane into Moscow. The common factors are not the climate, a shared history, or a single folk tradition, but socialist institutions and qualities they impart to human life.

Marxist ideology says little of totalitarian government with its system of secret police. Yet, when you enter an east European nation, the first and deepest impression you may expect is of the power and omnipresence of the police. You see them first in uniform as you pass through customs. You sense them later as plain-clothesmen and informers, as hotel clerks who keep watch on your movements, and as tourist guides who supervise your activities. You feel your lack of freedom and the invasion of your privacy as on one occasion after another you fill out forms and as time after time you take out identity papers on demand. This quality of restricted freedom and denied privacy is one commonality of eastern Europe in our time.

Another commonality is the drabness of life. Aside from extravagant monuments to socialist heroes and events, plainness of surroundings pervades these nations. Brightly colored lights, cheerful promenades, and villas or apartment houses that look like fun to live in do not exist, with but few exceptions. The dress of pedestrians tends to be dowdy and purely utilitarian, though some efforts to break away now are seen. Even in demeanor, people seem subdued in comparison with those in many parts of western Europe.

But if eastern Europe has drab, subdued qualities, it also is pervaded with self-confidence. Whether content with the government or not, and many clearly are content, the peoples of eastern Europe seem aware of enormous progress in raising living standards, of achievements in industry and advancements in agriculture and science which seem all the greater to older adults, because they remember the backwardness of presocialist times. Further, the man in the street tends to feel these achievements are his rather than those of a distant elite, for it is a quality of socialist culture that it belongs to all equally, at least in principle. So the appearance of eastern Europe can be misleading. If it is not a glad place, it is not sad either, and its people display a developed sense of self-esteem.

SOVIET UNION

Fifty-thousand villages cover the Soviet Union, yet we know little about them (Dunn, 1969; Simirenko, 1966). Ethnographers working out of the Miklukho-Maklai Institute of Ethnography carried out a study of Viriatino in central Russia, now known as the Lenin's Way Kolkhoz (Benet, 1970). But the results of this study are less than completely satisfactory. For one thing, the findings already are somewhat stale, since the field work was done around 1957. Again, the community is not representative of most kolkhozes, since it has enjoyed unusually good success in collectivizing. Finally, P. I. Kushner and his colleagues did their work as an official undertaking, and their published findings are more oriented to justifying governmental policies than to elucidating processes of culture change as such. The resultant view of Viriatino, then, is somewhat idealized, and even the interpretive powers of Stephen and Ethel Dunn cannot free it completely of this distortion (Dunn and Dunn, 1967).

Observations in the USSR by non-Soviet diplomats and journalists provide useful additional documentation (Maynard, 1962; Miller, 1961), as do the findings of anthropologists who have carried out what Margaret Mead has called the study of culture at a distance, using as data films, literary pieces, newspaper materials, and interviews with emigrants (Mead, M., 1966b; see also Gorer and Rickman, 1949). For the most part, however, these publications are now old, and in any case they lack the immediacy and depth of community studies or other direct findings. In the search, then, for information to balance that we have for Viriatino, I shall use that provided by a Soviet playwright.

Andrei Amalrik is one of what seems to be a growing number of intellectuals in the USSR today who, at great personal cost, criticize governmental acts they consider immoral, and insist they must have freedom in scholarly and artistic pursuits. They pay dearly for protests which in most of the West would seem moderate and reasonable. Some have been imprisoned. Others have been confined to insane asylums, perhaps on the assumption that only madmen defy the goliath of governmental fiat. Amalrik was made to work on a kolkhoz in Siberia. In an autobiographical account of his odyssey, he describes the Kalinin Kolkhoz in the years 1965 and 1966 (Amalrik, 1970).

What we know of Kalinin is in its own way as distortive as what we know of Viriatino. Located in Siberia, it represents a frontier environment where Soviet life is bound to be relatively rugged and primitive. Many of its people, like Amalrik, are there only because the police have expelled them from more desirable locations. Morality and motivation suffer. Kalinin, then, represents the least successful of kolkhozes. In addition, it is described for us by a critic of the regime.

The 32 families of Kaninin live in old cottages whitewashed on the inside and covered with straw roofs. Only a few have slate roofs and painted floors. Small windows which cannot be opened, even in the dusty heat of summer, allow a dim light to illuminate the interior, where iron bedsteads are found in a few as symbols of growing prosperity. Houses in general are furnished with a few mass-produced wooden items: a table, some chairs, a dresser, a bed. One house has a leather sofa, carefully protected with a dust cover and not intended for use except on special occasions.

The typical dwelling is divided into two rooms. The bedroom, not much used in the daytime, displays bedding and pillows piled high in testimony of well-being, an old peasant custom. Most display some inexpensive print on the wall, typically one depicting a white castle or a lady waving adieu to her knight. Icons also hang in nearly every house, although people seem totally indifferent to religion. "Who can tell if God exists or not?" the old men ask, and only one customarily goes to church in the town of Tomsk once a year to pray.

Every kitchen/living room has a large masonry oven lit occasionally when bread is baked. Small iron stoves otherwise serve for cooking and warmth. In summer, when the heat is oppressive, the stove is taken into the yard. Many have radios, but electricity to power them is usually supplied only at milking times: morning, noon, and night. Milking is done in separate outbuildings; pigs and new-born calves are kept in the houses with their owners, for they are products of the private enterprise that is allowed (Amalrik, 1970, 148–149).

The village offers very little for distraction. Apparently the most entertaining activity for adults is to visit the general store, where the eye can rove shelves of preserved foods and bottled goods, a small selection of clothing, household utensils, some items of furniture, and other goods displayed for sale. There, too, individuals gossip about the latest drunken fight or family quarrel (Amalrik, 1970, 174–177). In all, however, "the peasants' life was remarkably dull; all their free time was spent working on their private plots." Indeed, recalls Amalrik, "Their main distraction was drink, especially in winter, when they drank nearly every day." (Amalrik, 1970, 174–175.)

Young people frequent the largely unsupervised and unequipped village recreation room. In the summer, dances are held nearly every evening after work, particularly when students are in the village to help with the harvest. But the room lacks a record player, and the village accordion player knows only three pieces, so all dancing is done to the tune of a waltz, a Charleston, and a folk dance accompanied by hand-clapping and heel-stomping. A movie followed by a dance is programmed once a week, and becomes the only organized recreation in the winter. In spring and fall there is nothing, because film and equipment must be brought in by a motorcycle which cannot negotiate roads that become quagmires in the rain (Amalrik, 1970, 175, 176).

Viriatino seems only somewhat better than Kalinin in many ways. Families normally have only a two-room cottage much as in Kalinin, and many houses are occupied by two or three families, so that some have only a single room per family. Collective plans include four-room houses, each with a kitchen, dining room, living room, and bedroom, but so far, very few have been constructed.

In Viriatino, farmers do enjoy amenities not available in most places. In 1965, only 4 percent of all electricity consumed in the USSR went to rural users, according to the Dunns (Dunn and Dunn, 1967, 70). Yet electricity has been available in Viriatino since 1947. Some kolkhozniks own wardrobes, cupboards, dressers, sofas, book stands, and metal beds. Many, however, have no better furniture than do farmers in Siberia, and continue to store goods in trunks positioned along the walls or to hang clothing on walls with cloth coverings for protection.

Soviet investigators assert that gradually the culture and everyday life habits of villagers are becoming more like those of the city. They report that "the previously existing sharp division between village and city housing is being erased and new transitional forms are being established." (Benet, 1970, 229.) Apparently, however, this is a promise rather than a fact for most families (Benet, 1970, 223–229).

The communal facilities of Viriatino seem greatly superior to those of Kalinin. In 1957, a two-story brick building was built to serve in part as a village clubhouse. It includes an auditorium seating 300, a library, a reading room, a day nursery, and a game room. At the time of study, the second story was not yet finished, but plans included a sitting room, a classroom, a radio relay center, and a film booth.

Young people made the clubhouse and the square in front of it their favorite gathering place. Some participated in amateur theatricals and club meetings. In recent years young people have begun to learn ballroom dancing, chess, and sports such as skiing, volleyball, soccer, and track, though they lack equipment for these activities. At times they attend lectures on educational topics, including the evils of religion, or they sing in the choral group. Perhaps the most popular entertainment, however, remains movies, which have become a normal feature of rural life (Benet, 1970, 217, 295–300). These activities represent urban customs penetrating the countryside. "However, the gap is still considerable," as the investigators themselves conclude (Benet, 1970, 300).

In principle, a Russian community is governed as a free collective enterprise. Of Viriatino, it is said that the village soviet is elected following open procedures of nominating candidates, hearing them discuss their programs, and then casting secret ballots on election day. Within the soviet, committees take responsibility for special problems, such as political education or questions of hygiene, somewhat as committees or voluntary associations might do in the West (Benet, 1970, 280–282).

According to its charter, the collective farm, as distinct from the village as such, is a voluntary union of individuals who together own the means of production and who organize their labor on a joint basis in order to increase their productivity and create a better life for all. Policy decisions are decided in general meetings, while day-to-day affairs come under the management of an elected board of directors (Benet, 1970, 194, 200).

Although democratic in principle, village and kolkhoz affairs appear in practice to be run in a thoroughly authoritarian fashion. "The present kolkhoz system is based, in effect, on forced labor," argues Amalrik, "and the peasants are totally without rights." (Amalrik, 1970, 169).

To those who believe men have not been bound to the land since the Middle Ages, it comes as a surprise to learn that the custom exists in the USSR. To travel, a collective farmer must carry identity papers which are kept under lock in the kolkhoz office and can be gotten only with special permission. If he attempts to enter a city by stealth, he finds authorities have the power to arrest, jail, and deport those who lack residence permits (Amalrik, 1970, xi, 169, passim; George Y. Shkurkin, personal communication).

Workers on a farm, according to Amalrik, "have no say whatever in the so-called 'election' of the chairman . . . , the fixing of their rates of pay, or anything whatever." Further, kolkhozniks "are subject to a system of prohibitions and monetary fines, and they cannot sue the farm in case of a dispute." (Amalrik, 1970, 170.) Earnings have been going up, and collectives are shifting from a share system, in which settlements in money and kind are made only once a year, to a system of regular wage payments. Yet, kolkhozniks still cannot live on what they earn from the collective, and are forced to rely heavily on their private plots (Amalrik, 1970, 145, 156–160, 167, 248–251; see also Benet, 1970, 192).

Production under such circumstances suffers, in spite of the advantages one expects from larger, more industrialized undertakings. At least in the Kalinin kolkhoz, work often was carelessly done. Poles were raised for electric lines, for example, but nobody bothered to treat them to prevent rotting. In a few years they will fall. In a nearby kolkhoz, a tractor garage was begun but never finished, and gradually the timber was pilfered for firewood. "I imagine these things happen mainly because labor is paid so little that nobody thinks it worth economizing," Amalrik speculates (Amalrik, 1970, 163). For he found that men and women spent two or three weeks doing by hand what a tractor could have done in a day. If the collective owned a small mechanical mower for haying, the work of the villagers would be greatly eased in the harvest season. "Yet the kolkhozniks, or rather the kolkhoz authorities, appear unwilling to simplify their work even by such small mechanical gadgets as could be made in the kolkhoz repair shop." (Amalrik, 1970, 164, 157–165.)

It appears, in sum, that by western standards Soviet villages have not moved far in raising standards of living. As the Dunns point out, the "cultural screen" that separated peasants from urbanites used to be so dense that urban travelers in the countryside often felt they were in a different world. That screen still exists (Dunn and Dunn, 1967, 130; see also Amalrik, 1970, x–xi; Benet, 1970, 295–300).

HUNGARY

The high quality of ethnographic research in Hungary, and a recent willingness to allow foreign anthropologists to work there, allow us to know something of changes taking place in that nation (Bökönyi et al., 1970; Hofer, 1970; Maday, 1968, 1970). Above all, we have the case study of Atány carried out by Edit Fél and Tamás Hofer (Fél and Hofer, 1969).

The village of Atány, though large with its population of around 3,000, is fundamentally a Hungarian representative of the former open-field communities that existed throughout the great plain of Europe. In that, it also resembles the Russian village of Viriatino. It was late to be collectivized, however, and when Fél and Hofer began field work there in 1951, the community still preserved much that was traditional.

As late as that year, adobe, thatch-roofed houses of three or four rooms still preserved peasant customs in household use. People continued to wear clothes which distinguished them as villagers; only young women in prosperous families imitated urban fashions. On Sunday, the Protestant church remained filled as of old, with worshipers seated by tradition according to age, sex, marital status, and rank in the village hierarchy. In free hours, women and girls still did spinning and weaving while men gathered in the stables to chat. Most of the populace was not yet directly affected by the socialist revolution, though a few of the largest landowners and the church had been expropriated, and both school and village administration had been changed (Fél and Hofer, 1969, 70–74, 79, 277, 300, 381).

During the 1950s, the pace of change picked up. State-required deliveries of produce grew larger each year. The supervision of agricultural activities became increasingly strict. Rich farmers had their houses confiscated, and a few were put in prison. Cooperative groups were formed. The big change came, however, in 1959, when the village was reorganized into two collective farms and a state farm. With that, agriculturalists gave up private ownership of their land and shifted to working for labor credits, much as in the USSR. The revolution arrived (Fél and Hofer, 1969, 382).

In Atány today, a form of mixed farming similar to that practiced in the pre-communist period still employs men in the fields, though the workload is lightened by the economies of industrialized techniques. Tractor-drawn plows and combines accomplish efficiently what men with horses once did. Burdens lightened in one way are made heavier in others, however. Nearly half the income of farmers now is gotten from the intensive cultivation of private plots and privately raised livestock.

Old institutions have changed with these developments. The customary organization of labor by families is replaced by organization into brigades, and the joint family is under attack as taxation and agricultural delivery quotas make it advantageous for people to register as smaller domestic units. In a few cases, this is associated with the actual as well as legal dissolution of the joint family. The wider ties of kinship, godparenthood, and age group, formerly important, now have fallen into disuse. People are too busy to keep them up, and no longer feel the same need to do so.

The church, too, has lost its place in village life. Scarcely anyone attends Sunday services anymore, though most turn out for special holiday meetings. In choosing a husband or wife it no longer is felt necessary to find a fellow Calvinist from a farming family of comparable status, and new brides escape doing an apprenticeship under the watchful eye of a mother-in-law. Young people have become very independent of old family rules (Fél and Hofer, 1969, 383–384).

A massive and sudden urbanization of the community has taken place.

The local value system, with its emphasis on traditional, land-oriented activities, has been nearly obliterated by a new, urban focus. The old goal was to acquire land, obtain good stock, and secure buildings to provide the ingredients of a self-sufficient farm. Now, older people accumulate work credits on an industrialized farm, while younger people work in factories, move to town, or study to become craftsmen, skilled industrial workers, or salary-earning white-collar workers.

The strength of these new values is indicated by the things people work for. The new houses that are built are constructed according to urban models. Often they replace traditional structures which still are perfectly habitable, but no longer satisfy. And people furnish their houses with mass-produced products that appeal to urban tastes, including factory-made furniture, kitchen utensils, radios, and television sets (Fél and Hofer, 1969, 383).

It is difficult to estimate the personal costs of these changes. In part, they took place smoothly because they were long expected. By 1951, Atány already had become an anachronism insofar as many old-fashioned customs and attitudes were preserved long after they had disappeared in neighboring communities. Young people appear to have no regrets as they seek a new identity in the modern world. It is different for those who are older. The average age of those who belonged to the collective in 1964 was 57 years, and they acted rather discontented and uprooted. This comes out in their feelings of alienation from the bread they eat. Farmers' wives still bake at home, but the wheat they use comes from the collective now, and it is not the same. "We don't know when it was sown, or the time when it was reaped; the wheat is just brought." As one man put it, "One feels there is no summer anymore. It seems as if we [are] not in the same world where we used to live." (Fél and Hofer, 1969, 383–384; see also Enyedi, 1965; Erdei, 1970; Sárfalvi, 1965; Varga, 1970; Weinstock, 1964.)

POLAND

In most of eastern Europe, modernization has come to rural areas in the form of forced collectivization (Bohociu, 1966; Dunn, 1966a; Kayser, 1962; Sanders, 1949). Only in Poland and Yugoslavia has the family farm remained dominant.

Great differences in wealth no longer distinguish one countryman from another in Poland. As the agricultural economist Anna Szemberg has pointed out, most farmers work holdings of limited size, leasing or purchasing land from the state in order to bring their acreage up to standards (Szemberg, 1963, 10). Full-time farmers generally get about half of their output from cereal crops, potatoes, and sugar beets, and the other half from livestock and poultry. Equipment remains primitive by Western standards. In places, one still finds farmers harvesting with scythes, though many now own mowing machines. Tractors are uncommon, as are combines and other large pieces of equipment. The typical farm possesses only a plow, a harrow, a four-wheeled cart, and a horse for power (Barnett, 1958, 240–241; Franklin, 1969, 205).

Many farmers still inhabit small, old cottages in which the main room may contain a cast-iron stove for cooking and heating, a table and chairs for taking meals, and a bed along the wall for one or two of the children. A small bedroom to the side, with just enough room for two beds, may constitute the remaining part of the house, and the most prominent decoration may consist of colored curtains over the window. Clothing generally is rugged. Meals are substantial, but plain (Benet, 1951; Kuhn and Kuhn, 1958; Thomas and Znaniecki, 1927).

In recent years, living standards have improved. Although most farm income is needed to pay for food, clothing, and household needs, some surplus has become available. Much of this is invested in housing and farm buildings rather than in improving productive facilities as such. Homes are not so likely to be expropriated. New cottages, especially, have given the countryside a more prosperous look in recent years (Franklin, 1969, 205–216).

This pattern of investment may be changing. According to official surveys, the amount of surplus put into machinery and improvement of the land has tended to increase, reflecting, perhaps, a growing confidence in the future of the family farm. One finds no tendency, however, for successful farmers to increase their holdings beyond about six hectares. And on the whole, those doing well apply their surplus to the raising of living standards: eating better food, wearing better clothing, and purchasing more consumer durables. In this, they display urban tastes (Franklin, 1969, 206).

Several developments have encouraged this urbanization of values in the countryside. The growing, if still limited, financial capacity clearly is significant. Equally important, however, is an increasing familiarity of countrymen with city ways. This seems a product in part of the growth of industry in the countryside.

Many countrymen have found industrial employment within commuting distance of their farms as worker-peasants. In many families, one adult, often the head, works in construction, transportation, manufacturing, or artisanry. Although worker-peasants produce one-fifth less income on their farms, they live relatively well, since wage income is added to farming profits. Cultural geographer S. H. Franklin concludes that for these individuals and their neighbors, industry "widens the view and alters the mode of life, assisting in the establishment of the urban way of life as the model generally aspired to in the village." (Franklin, 1969, 212.)

The Polish peasant has come a long way from the harsh conditions described by sociologists William I. Thomas and Florian Znaniecki in the 1920s. Village life is being transformed, even though it has not been collectivized. Young people and adult males are leaving farming for industrial work, resulting in a growing feminization of the agricultural work force, much as one finds in many places in the West. The old classes have disappeared as land holdings have been equalized. Standards of consumption have risen. Urban ways are being adopted. Polish farmers remain poor if comparisons are made to English, German, or Danish farmers, but they have moved far from the primitivity many still alive remember from their childhood (Franklin, 1969, 205; Galeski, 1964a, b).

YUGOSLAVIA

The village of Orašak lies tucked in among the meadows, fields, and orchards of Serbia, one of the major ethnic regions of Yugoslavia. When Joel and Barbara Halpern first did field work in the village in 1955, they made their entrance by ox cart over the dirt road that led from the town of Arandjelovac four miles distant. Small factories had already set the town on its way toward urban-industrial modernization, but in Orašak, the Halperns were struck more with the villagelike quality of the area than with the fact that they had come to live in a contemporary socialist community.

At that time, they encountered an atmosphere of simple farming activities. Men worked their fields with little time for relaxation. When some errand brought one into the village center from his fields and farmstead, he stopped on the road or over a glass of plum brandy at the tavern (*kafana*) to chat with a fellow villager, took care of his business, and returned to his farm again. On Sundays, only a few went to church even though the priest was known to all, but some of the older men relaxed in the sun and gossiped in front of the tavern, folk dancers did their turns in the afternoon to the accompaniment of accordion and flute music, and boys played soccer by the church. In the fall, several wedding parties shattered the quiet each Sunday with their happy shouting and horseplay. On the whole, it was a bucolic existence, a way of life oriented to fields and families (Halpern, 1967, xix, 1, 37–40).

When they returned twelve years later, the Halperns found Orašak had not yet become a suburb of the nearby town. Perhaps it never will. Yet life in the community had undergone a fundamental sort of change as the effects of urban influence were thoroughly felt (Halpern, 1967, 301).

Superficially, the community looks much as it did before. Folk dancing still takes place on Sundays, men still chat over plum brandy at the kafana, and fall remains the season for weddings. Small cottages with red tile roofs dot the gentle slopes of the countryside as before, and one even encounters women and girls spinning wool as they keep watch over their sheep. But whereas culture change formerly tended to leave the village different from the city as an enclave of farming culture, now it brings the village closer to life styles of the city, obliterating the contrasts of urban and rural (Halpern, 1967, 302–303).

The residents of Orašak have new aspirations and habits. Some have television sets and motorcycles. Many possess flashlights, and most have become so accustomed to electricity that they no longer keep kerosene lamps handy for power failures. Activities are planned only after getting the weather forecast on the radio, and meals may include dehydrated chicken soup and other new foods. Even funerals display new features in an old context. When a young worker was killed in an accident in 1966, a motor-truck served as his hearse, and his fellow workers carried red-star-decorated plastic wreaths to his grave. At the cemetery, a young man spoke reverently of the qualities of the deceased as a worker and a communist, and only then did the mourners turn to a traditional memorial feast of roast, bread, and brandy served by the grave site (Halpern, 1967, 225–231, 304–305).

Still early in the process of modernization, the people of Orašak find their hopes are not always realized as easily as first expected. Electricity often fails, because the lines are not yet up to standard. New plumbing does not work properly. Farm machinery breaks down, and inexperience results in accidents.

The paved road to Arandjelovac began to buckle not long after it was constructed, enamel ware utensils chip easily, glass cracks, spray guns fail to work, and plastic bags of sugar split, pouring their contents on the ground. Villagers get angry and discouraged over inefficiencies and failures, and comment bitterly upon them. Yet, on the whole, they seem to regard these as problems associated with growth and modernization. They see them as difficulties in development, not as the eternal drawbacks of a failing system (Halpern, 1967, 306–307).

With the proximity of industry, worker-peasants have become more numerous. In a village survey, Halpern found that children, with the approval of their parents, show "a keenly felt desire to escape from peasant agriculture as an occupation and a way of life, and to a lesser extent to get out of the village mud. . . ." (Halpern, 1967, 315.) They look down on farming as hard and unremunerative. As a result, young people are leaving the village, and many who might have become full-time farmers are becoming worker-peasants instead (Halpern, 1967, 305–316, 320).

In progressive communities such as Orašak, Yugoslav countrymen appear to have moved significantly from pre-communist norms and habits without yet having become fully modern. In backward, mountainous areas, poverty remains widespread and modernization has not yet gotten under way (Blanc, 1967, 198–218). This persistence of the old is apparent when one examines changes in social structure. Kinship practices, for example, are changing. Yet the wider ties of kinship, real and fictive, continue to be important.

From a field survey in various parts of the nation, Eugene Hammel concludes that contemporary Yugoslav countrymen turn to one or the other of three kinds of traditional relationship. Mutual rights and obligations may be established or carried out in terms of the ties of male descent (agnatic relationships), in terms of connections through marriage (affinal relationships), or in terms of godparenthood (*kumstvo*) ties (ritual relationships). (Hammel, 1968, 91.)

Agnatic ties, the ties of a man through his father, are much stronger and more important than those in the uterine line. This especially is apparent in the establishment of a larger household group, the *zadruga*. The family that owns and works a large farm may grow beyond the domestic family to include the wives and children of a man's son or sons. When a joint family of this sort lasts for a couple of generations, instead of splitting up when it gets large as often is the case, the adult men who form its nucleus are related as patrilateral cousins. Such families can be quite large. Although the smallest may comprise only an old couple with one or more of their married sons, or two brothers with their wives, a large zadruga may have as many as 80 members, all working their jointly owned property under the leadership of a family head, and all contributing to and drawing from a common budget (Hammel, 1968, 13–14; see also Hammel, 1969a, 82).

Beyond domestic and patrilateral joint families, Yugoslavs maintain cohesion in a larger agnatic group or lineage known as the *bratstvo* (from *brat*, brother). Individuals united in a lineage share the lineage name and a patron saint (*slava*), whose feast day they celebrate. Lineages are grouped into *plemena* or clans on the basis of presumed or actual descent from a founding ancestor.

Clans used to have recognized leaders as well as courts in which members could be tried according to clan mores. Occasionally they united in feuding with other clans. But lineages and clans seem little more than names now, and even the joint family is in decline. In the 1970s, fewer farms are managed on the zadruga principle, and those that survive are smaller. The family remains very important, but increasingly it is the stem family and the nuclear family which function as the fundamental unit (Erlich, 1966; Halpern and Anderson, 1970, 97; Hammel, 1968, 14, 23).

Ties of marriage are also important. Formerly, affinal ties were so strong that when breached by premature death, the levirate or sororate was practiced. If a man died, his widow married one of his brothers (levirate). An older woman might be inherited in this way within a zadruga, a younger man marrying the widow of his father's brother. Through levirate marriage, the original bride price did not have to be redeemed when a woman lost her husband.

If a woman died, the converse of the rule applied (sororate). The deceased wife's sister became the new wife of the widower. In some cases, perhaps in anticipation of a potential levirate succession, men had sexual realtions with their brothers' wives. "Together we eat, together we rut," one man is reported to have said (Hammel, 1968, 33). But the sexual sharing of an anticipatory levirate probably never was widespread, and the levirate itself, along with the sororate and bride price, is not practiced in modern parts of Yugoslavia (Hammel, 1968, 32; see also Coon, 1950; Durham, 1910).

Ties of godparenthood may be established when individuals become sponsors at a baptism, marriage, or, less commonly, the ritual first haircutting of a child. Unlike other parts of Europe, however, the ties of godparenthood tend to be inherited from one generation to the next and to unite one zadruga with another as the donor and the recipient of sponsors, respectively. That is, in its simplest form, the members of one zadruga always supply sponsors to members of another. The latter, for their part, supply sponsors to a third, and so on. Further, since any member of the zadruga which supplies godparents may function as sponsor on any particular occasion, though usually it is an adult, the relationship has a collective quality. Members of the donor group are related to members of the recipient group collectively as sponsors and sponsored (Hammel, 1968, 8, 45).

Godparenthood affects the way individuals interact with one another. Deference is due to the sponsor himself, and to any member of his family. As a Macedonian proverb puts it, "When the godparent (kum) comes into the house, even the ground under the threshold trembles." (Hammel, 1968, 79.) In underdeveloped areas of Yugoslavia, where the expression of deference is strongest, the whole family kneels bareheaded in front of the house to greet the godparent when he comes. They may even spread linen on the ground for him to walk on. One of the women may wash his feet, all will kiss his hand, "and grizzled heroes of the Turkish wars kiss the hand even of a small boy sent to officiate at a baptism," according to Hammel (1968, 80).

Avoidance behavior is invoked to perpetuate such deference. It is felt desirable that the sponsor live in a different village, since daily contacts can lead to quarreling. One should never have business dealings with a godparent, and it would be considered incestuous for a marriage to take place with a baptismal godparent, or even with anyone closely related to the godparent. In western Yugoslavia, relationships are more casual, and the godparent is regarded more as a friend or benefactor. Yet there, too, godparenthood provides guidelines to acceptable behavior (Hammel, 1968, 81, 85).

In contrast to village practices, godparenthood in Yugoslav towns and cities functions as it does throughout the Mediterranean area. It is used to establish individual ties, generally with one's social equals, the important relationship being that of godfather and father rather than godfather and child. Groups are not involved, and a man may seek godparents for his children from as many families as possible in order to build up a wide network, since the tie often is exploited for patronage. Town practices have apparently long been different from those of the countryside (Hammel, 1968, 70).

Godparenthood practices are proving persistent in the countryside. Extreme forms of deference have long been absent from most of the nation, but recent decades have not brought any marked further weakening of the institution. Countrymen continue to establish ties in traditional ways and to respect their obligations. Even when a farmer migrates from one rural area to another, efforts usually are made to keep up the old relationship. Sometimes a godparent will travel halfway across the nation to attend the wedding of a migrant. Only when he moves to the city does he abandon old ideas (Hammel, 1968, 70).

In all, Yugoslavia today is modernizing rapidly in some areas, even though differences between urban and rural ways of life continue to be prominent (see Halpern, 1965; Lockwood, 1965, 1970). It surely makes a difference that modernization is taking place within the framework of a communist ideology. Yet it is difficult to see clearly what the difference is. Since most farms are not collectivized, the most striking contrast between communist and non-communist systems is removed. The encouragement of cooperative efforts seems basically similar to strong efforts made to make the cooperative movement work in the West, so the difference does not lie there. A tendency for joint families to decline in size or to disband, and a broader tendency for kinship ties to weaken, seem directly to reflect urban-industrial influences rather than an especially communist program (Halpern, 1967, 301). More and more countrymen are becoming worker-peasants, but worker-peasants are also becoming more numerous in parts of the West. Underdeveloped regions and unemployment occur throughout the Mediterranean. In all, culture change in Yugoslavia does not seem greatly different from change in the West, except for the rhetoric.

TEN

MINORITY ENCLAVES:
ETHNICITY AND CHANGE

Some nations in Europe were founded as political unions of ethnically diverse peoples. Czechoslovakia, for example, unites Czechs and Slovaks, but also includes Germans, Magyars (Hungarians), Ukrainians, Jews, Poles, and others. Yugoslavia brings together Serbs, Croats, and Slovenes, and adds Germans, Magyars, Albanians, Rumanians, Italians, Bosnians, and Montenegrans, the latter two minorities within the Serbian-speaking population.

Other nations seem ethnically less diverse, yet they too incorporate minorities. Refer to a Scotsman, Welshman, or Irishmen as English rather than British, and you will learn in no uncertain terms that ethnic diversity is an important part of the contemporary British scene. Even in a country as homogeneous as Denmark, minorities are found. As Danish anthropologist George Nellemann points out, the average citizen is likely to wonder, "Do we have minorities in Denmark?" (Nellemann, 1970b, 289.) Yet, a recent issue of an ethnographic journal devoted to the subject carried articles on Greenland Eskimos, Faroe Islanders, Germans, Jews, Poles, Gypsies, and two newer kinds of minority, resident foreign workers, including Germans, Englishmen, Turks, and Yugoslavs, and settled political refugees, including East Germans, Hungarians, and Chinese (*Jordens Folk*, 6(3), 1970; see also Rose, 1969).

The distinctiveness of ethnic enclaves ranges from scarcely different at all from the majority population to very thoroughly different. Most ethnic groups, however, occupy a middle position. Like their neighbors of the majority population, they usually are countrymen who till the soil, herd cattle or sheep, fish, or work the forest. Though different from fellow citizens, the differences are no greater than those that distinguish the countrymen of one nation from those of the nation next door.

BASQUES

Basques, located on both the Spanish and French sides of the western Pyrenees, are familiar as an often-mentioned ethnic enclave. Except for being better known to the general public, however, their distinctiveness is no greater than that of many minorities in Europe. For the most part, they resemble neighboring Spanish and French farmers and fishermen.

If you visit the modern seaside resort towns of Biarritz in France or San Sebastian in Spain, you may not even be aware that you are in Basque territory. Perhaps you will come to realize it if you attend a bull fight and witness members of the Basque fishermen's guild parade into the arena in red shirts and berets, carrying oars and a massive wooden chest on their shoulders, on top of which a young man in black frock coat and white trousers balances with a top hat in one hand and a red flag in the other. You may realize it if you see an exhibition of touristic folk dancing, with music provided by a man playing a flute with one hand and a drum with the other. Anyone will tell you it is Basque dancers who do a dramatic leaping dance on the edge of a filled wine goblet (but note Gallop, 1970, 65). Otherwise, as you walk along the street or by the beach, probably nothing will strike you as particularly strange to the French or Spanish scene (note Greenwood, 1972).

Except for when they put on folkloristic displays, men, women, and children dress in modern clothing. The beret originally marked men as Basques, but for years it has been widely popular throughout Spain and France.

Housing may be distinctive. In towns, a few old three- and four-story houses with wrought-iron balconies or ox blood red shutters survive as testimonials to traditional Basque varieties of architecture. In the countryside, some gabled farmhouses with the dwelling located over a ground-floor stall also survive as part of the old Basque tradition, though in gross form they are Iberian or south European in type. Most Basques, however, inhabit buildings indistinguishable from those of non-Basques (Gallop, 1970, 203–214.)

The extent of Basqueness in material culture is illustrated in the ox-drawn cart with its two wheels of solid wood. It is so clearly an antique, even where it still is in daily use, that it seems to represent a distinctive tradition. Yet basically it is the same old two-wheeled cart one finds throughout the Iberian peninsula and beyond. Only the sheepskin hats the oxen are fitted with are unusual.

From the work of William Douglass, we learn that in social structure, too, Basques are much like their neighbors (Douglass, 1969). The small family is basic as in all of Spain, with social obligations a matter of family rather than individual responsibility. The most distinctive trait is that individuals belong to kindreds which impose special rights and obligations on relatives on both sides of the family as far as second cousins. These ties have no obvious functions in daily life, which explains, perhaps, why they only recently were described. But Douglass found they are activated for rites of passage and when a hamlet celebrates its saint's day. In particular, members of the lineage are invited to a banquet for a child's first communion or a wedding. Urban members visit their country cousins on weekends or holidays, and in return, countrymen visiting the city get food, shelter, and advice when they need it (Douglass, 1969, 166–189). Basques also have a "closest neighbor" relationship not found in Spanish and French communities (Freeman, 1970, 1112–1113).

Above all, Basques differ from other Europeans in their language, which has no proven relatives, and in special qualities of personality and temperament, as seen in part in art and literature. Folklorist Rodney Gallop speaks of their "independence and reserve." Very few, he concludes, "see through this dour mask to the light-heartedness and sly, whimsical humour which lie beneath." (Gallop, 1970, 63.)

The total inventory of distinctively Basque traits is not great. Yet the differences that exist are very significant, because they function as symbols of ethnic identity. Having failed to carve out a nation of their own, Basques resist complete absorption into the societies that surround them by clinging to what remains of a distinctive heritage. This effort to perpetuate a separate identity has grown stronger since 1968, for it is reinforced now by active revolt.

WELSHMEN

The Welsh also failed to establish an independent nation, and they too perpetuate a separate identity as an ethnic enclave. When Alwyn D. Rees described the results of his community study in Wales, he gave prominence to those characteristics that distinguish rural Welsh culture from the rural culture of England. "The contrast with the village traditions of the greater part of England," he concluded, "is striking." (Rees, 1961, 162.) A trait-by-trait comparison of rural English and Welsh culture would suggest that Rees exaggerated, however. The differences are on the order of those that distinguish Basques from Frenchmen or Spaniards, and they are not great as such. Yet the statement is accurate in this sense: the contrast is striking insofar as distinctive Welsh traditions have important symbolic functions.

From her study of Llan, a community in north Wales where cultural conservatism is most persistent, Isabel Emmett concludes that the key to understanding the Welsh is to realize that they are motivated by a strong anti-English feeling, a deep resentment of that foreign society which sends its agents to govern them. This feeling makes partisans of the northern Welsh. They are fighters for their ethnic identity, and without compromise. "You are either Welsh and in that case you fight," observes Emmett, "or you are trying to be English, in which case you are on the other side." (Emmett, 1964, 22.) The very definition of Welsh culture under these conditions requires the ability to conjure up a contrasting definition of English culture (Emmett, 1964, 43).

If a man elects to remain Welsh, he will probably become a laborer or farmer, for manual work brings prestige in the Welsh value system, though not in that of the English. A man can take pride in being strong and in working with his hands. It links him with the ruggedness of an old way of life. Working with his hands, he will wear working clothes rather than the suits and ties of Englishmen. As late as 1962, Emmett found young workers still dressed as their fathers had dressed a half century earlier in nondescript assortments of patched trousers, sometimes wearing two pairs at once, one over the other, the costume pieced out with odds and ends of army dress. And, as Ronald Frankenberg and others also have observed, he will remain in the country. Townsmen are English in culture (Emmett, 1964, 32–33; Frankenberg, 1957, 24).

The man who elects to remain Welsh will also speak his native tongue.

Nearly all Welshmen now are bilingual. But for the most part they feel uncomfortable with English, which remains for them a foreign language. Many have a limited vocabulary. They do not understand less common words, official terms, slang, and nuances. Often they have great difficulty with regional accents or dialects. A Welshman consulting his doctor may find he cannot state exactly his complaint, and if he phones a hospital to inquire of a sick relative, he may find he cannot clearly understand the nurse. To avoid such embarrassment, many avoid English-speaking situations. Some neglect to see a doctor, or simply avoid official meetings. In some cases, Welshmen have not claimed benefits due them, because they cannot bear the humiliation which language difficulties can cause. Good English ranks high on the English scale of values. Only Welsh matters on the Welsh scale (Emmett, 1964, 33–35).

The man who elects to be Welsh often is deeply religious. Further, he will belong to one or another of the independent Protestant chapels rather than to the official Church of England in Wales, which is the center for Englishmen and anglicized Welshmen. The chapel, whether Baptist, Methodist, or other, is the rallying point for Welsh-speaking workers and farmers, or at least has been in the past. Puritanism, a love of Welsh hymns, and support of Sunday school, may be part of being Welsh and not English (Emmett, 1964, 76, 96–100).

The nonconformist chapel was never the sole public arena for Welsh culture, however. If the Welsh love of music found expression in chapel hymns, it also was revealed in folk songs, and in singing in public houses and competitions (*Eisteddfodau*). If being puritanical was Welsh, so too was a lighthearted tolerance of sex permissiveness before marriage and the tradition of night-courting. "The Welsh people used to court in bed: sometimes with a bolster interposed and sometimes with nothing but faith between the courting couple." (Emmett, 1964, 106.) Always, as David Jenkins points out, the life style of "religious people" has coexisted with that of "tavern people," those who drink, relax on Sundays, ride motorcycles, and loiter on street corners (Emmett, 1964, 11, 97; Jenkins, 1960, 12–23).

But the two life styles are not as different as at first they appear. Many a religious man will take a drink from time to time, and the chapel will not be harsh with an unwed mother and her illegitimate child. Religious and tavern people mix socially in the community. Their children often intermarry. In short, some go regularly to chapel and some do not, but all tell the same stories, admire the same Welsh heroes, and "do not feel part of the 'respectable' or 'disreputable' groups so much as they feel part of the Welsh-speaking community of North Wales." (Emmett, 1964, 12.)

To be Welsh, then, is to be a partisan in bloodless warfare. The weapons of defense are culture traits taken to symbolize social allegiance. And though the battle is bloodless, it is not passive. Individuals must actively decide which society they will belong to. Getting a higher education, moving to the city, taking factory employment, or joining the Church of England are steps one takes to acculturate, to anglicize. Becoming a farmer or laborer, staying in the countryside, neglecting to improve one's command of English, and remaining loyal to the chapel are steps one takes to remain Welsh.

In some ways, Welsh partisans use guerrilla tactics in the war of symbols.

Every Welshman poaches, for example. This is curious, because fishing does not attract that many enthusiasts where it is permitted. It probably is not done just to have fish. The first few salmon provide welcome relief from a daily fare of boiled potatoes, fried eggs, bread, and butter. But a salmon diet itself grows monotonous and continued poaching appears to function, at least in part, as a way in which the Welsh confront the English.

In the intimacy of a thinly populated countryside, people know their neighbors' activities and the movements of police. This information flows rapidly through links of women shopping in the village store, men passing on the road, or boys cutting across a field. The whereabouts of poachers is common knowledge, and they are alerted when danger threatens, so they almost never get caught. Hindering the police serves manifestly to make poaching possible. It functions latently, however, to unite Welshmen in a conspiracy against their enemy, symbolizing their separateness and unity (Emmett, 1964, 69–73).

The Welsh win skirmishes of this sort, but they seem to be losing the war. So long as they remained attached to the land, whether in agriculture or in mining, they lived side by side with the English and yet remained Welsh in culture. The land, however, supports them poorly. Many mines have proved unprofitable in modern times, and have closed. Since World War II, England has come closer to the Welsh homeland with faster transportation and television sets—but above all, with jobs. When young people find work in modern industry, they enter the world of the English, where pressures to adopt English values are overwhelming. Many parts of Wales already have thoroughly acculturated. It seems but a matter of time before the rest will as well (Emmett, 1964, 139–141; Frankenberg, 1957, 24; Rees, 1961, 168).

LAPPS

If it is winter when you step down from the train in Kiruna, Sweden, the town which boasts the northernmost streetcar line in the world, then you surely will feel yourself totally removed from the Europe of Mediterranean islands, German vineyards, and English downs. You are north of the arctic circle, and when you leave the mining and marketing center that is Kiruna, you enter forests and tundra that make up the heart of Lapp territory. Your sense of being out of Europe will grow all the stronger if you strike out on skis, away from Swedish farming settlements, to search out a Lapp village.

Twenty years ago, you still might encounter an encampment of tipi-shaped tents at the edge of the forest. I remember one that George Nellemann and I visited in 1950. It looked almost exactly as it would have a hundred years earlier, and people lived in it in much the same way. The floor was covered with twigs for comfort and insulation. In the center burned a fire over which thin slices of frozen reindeer meat were boiled to produce a somewhat flat-tasting but warming and filling meal. Above all, the coffee pot simmered there, to give cheer and comfort in the cold, its flavor strongly affected by powdered reindeer chese blended in.

People in the several tents wore contemporary work-a-day versions of Lapp costume, largely distinctive from Swedish dress. For the men this included visored caps with large red pompons, blue or green jackets embellished with red and yellow bands of ribbon, and reindeer hide shoes with curving pointed toes and native hay in place of socks. The women were equally non-Swedish in their dress.

Reindeer nearby testified to their occupation as herders, and boatlike sledges standing on end to keep from being buried in the snow revealed the continuing reliance of these people on draft-reindeer. Inside a tent, at the edges, small wooden chests of traditional sort were in use for storage, and even the large gold watch and a rifle with cartridges that hung from nails on the tent poles could have dated from a century before, though they were much newer than that. The only really discordant element was one you could not long ignore. To the left on entering the tent, where you would fail to notice it until you had sat down for a while, a bright red portable radio was installed.

Twenty years ago, tent camps in the snow already were uncommon. Most reindeer Lapps settled each winter in small hamlets. In places, tipi-shaped wooden huts of distinctive Lapp design served this purpose, but where we were, wooden cabins and farmhouses of Swedish design were in use. Inside the house of a family we stayed with, heat was provided by an old-fashioned corner fireplace of a type once common among Swedish peasants. The furniture, too, was Swedish, though mattresses were stuffed with reindeer hair. The life style, however, was thoroughly Lappish. Reindeer herders in their winter camp were neighbors to Swedish and Finnish farmers, yet in daily life as well as on holidays they spoke Lappish, dressed Lappish, acted Lappish, and were concerned with Lappish things. Above all, they were concerned with their herds of reindeer.

The living habits of reindeer Lapps have changed greatly during the last century. Particularly is this so in the last few decades. As Lapp anthropologist Israel Ruong has pointed out, with modern transportation, subsistence herding has given place to a cash economy, and while reindeer still are slaughtered for food, much now is bought which formerly was manufactured of reindeer and forest products. Herding techniques have changed, too, helped in part by radios, automobiles, trucks, and trains. This in turn makes it possible for families to maintain fixed homes, although the men still must spend long periods in the fields keeping guard over their herds. In the old days, whole families migrated as true nomads (Ruong, 1960, 27–28; see also Ruong, 1967, 1969).

From the community he studied, Swedish anthropologist Adolf Steen reports that in the early 1960s some individuals still wove their own cloth and made winter clothing of reindeer skins, but most bought cloth and made their own Lapp-style tunics, trousers, and caps on sewing machines. Only underwear was bought ready-made. Traditional wooden household objects, woven belts, footwear, hunting knives, and other objects were still made during quiet hours in the camp or village, but mostly for sale to tourists (Steen, 1963, 116–117).

It is important to realize that Lapp culture has changed, but it is equally important to realize that it has remained distinctively Lapp. Clothing may be made now of factory-woven goods, but it remains unmistakably Lapp in design. Trucks, snowmobiles, flashlights, Coleman lanterns, steel blades, modern medicines, two-way radios, and many other products of contemporary industry are integrated elements of Lapp culture, still focused upon the movements of herds and the challenges of a rugged outdoors. The Lapps have been Christians for centuries, yet their view of the world, their values, and in many ways their beliefs are peculiar to them (Gjessing, 1954, 62).

No doubt, the persistence of a distinctively Lapp culture is due importantly to ecological factors. Living as reindeer herders, people cannot fail to be very different from settled farmers, coastal fishermen, mine workers, and others. Yet, symbolic functions also play a role. Reindeer Lapps clearly feel the need to remain culturally different beyond what is required by their occupation. They take obvious delight in tramping into coastal settlements in their colorful costumes, proud leaders of their herds, pleased to be seen as the bearers of traditions which often are old, but which always are those that mark them as aristocrats of the wilderness, the masters of a harsh environment.

Many Lapps are settled now as fishermen and farmers. They live side by side with Norwegians in coastal communities in the north. In some villages they are a minority, but in many they comprise most of the population. Norwegian anthropologist Harald Eidheim worked in one village in which all but six of the approximately 150 people were Lapps. Yet, when he first entered the community, not only did he not find the bright colors of Lapp costume, he found people so apparently Norwegian in culture that a major clue to their Lapp identity was that they acted more Norwegian than the Norwegians. That subtlety, along with traces of a Lapp accent in the speech of many and features of body and face which, though caucasaoid, appear more among Lapps than Norwegians, provided the only clues that the population was Lapp rather than Norwegian (Eidheim, 1969, 41–43).

Gradually, residents began to realize that Eidheim spoke Lappish and did not look down on Lapp ways, as so often is the case in Scandinavia. Hesitantly at first, they opened up to him, until finally he saw revealed a version of Lapp culture still very much alive behind the Norwegian culture he originally had been shown. Yet, Norwegian culture is not merely a façade. These people have developed a life style which incorporates elements of both cultures. To that extent it is an acculturated hybrid. But insofar as behavior symbolizes allegiance to one society or the other, they move adroitly from behavior which completely emphasizes their Norwegian adherence to behavior still importantly Lapp in quality.

When the coastal steamer comes into harbor or when strangers otherwise are present, local individuals take care to give no indication they are anything other than completely Norwegian. In chatting with fellow Lapps aboard the steamer or in other places where they might be overheard, they speak Norwegian. It seems clear they want to hide their Lapp identity, and they succeed. According to Eidheim, "an outsider, paying a casual and short visit in the area, will most likely notice no signs of ethnic diversity. . . ." (Eidheim, 1969, 41.)

The same behavior is characteristic, however, when any of the six local

Norwegians are around. Under such circumstances there can be no question of hiding true ethnic identity. The community is too small for that. Even so, Lapps chatting together will shift instantly from Lappish and Lapp topics of conversation to Norwegian language and themes whenever a Norwegian comes within earshot. They try, though not entirely with success, to keep secret from resident Norwegians that they wear Lapp moccasins in their homes, are fond of certain Lapp foods, place amulets or coins in the foundations of new houses, and pronounce spells when an animal is slaughtered or the first time a net is set each year. They avoid being seen with reindeer Lapps when they can, and have grown increasingly resentful of those who arrive each spring with their herds on the way to summer pastures on nearby islands (Eidheim, 1966; 1969, 56).

The symbolism of Lapp custom under these circumstances is very different from that of reindeer Lapps, to whom they have close historical ties. Both groups live among peoples who regard them as low-bred or uncivilized. Reindeer Lapps meet this challenge head-on by denying the allegation, in effect, and by insisting upon their dignity as a people. An aggressive display of Lappishness provides symbolic reinforcement (Pelto, 1962, 175–176; Whitaker, 1955, 92–96).

Coastal Lapps, however, seem unable to cope with discrimination in this way. Perhaps they compromised themselves too much when they abandoned a traditional Lapp technology to settle down as farmers. That alone cannot be causal, of course, for in that event, Basques, Welshmen, and many others who retain their ethnic identity would long since have disappeared as distinctive enclaves, since economically they also do not differ in any pronounced way from the majority population. But coastal Lapps did more than adopt Norwegian technology. Apparently they also accepted the common Norwegian deprecation of Lapp culture. To some extent, no doubt with ambivalence, their image of themselves is negative. They seem to feel keenly embarrassed to be recognized as Lapps by strangers, and to behave as Lapps in the presence of resident Norwegians, because, at least subconsciously and to some extent, they agree with the majority that Lapps and Lapp ways are inferior (Eidheim, 1969, 44).

Such an attitude is not conducive to cultural survival. In the long run, if they continue as they are, they will undoubtedly become completely Norwegian. As late as the 1930s their parents and grandparents lived in Lapp-style huts and wore Lapp clothes. By the 1940s these habits had died out, except for Lapp footwear. By the 1950s language remained the only major surviving trait. At that time, 40 out of the approximately 50 households still spoke Lappish as a domestic language, while in the other ten, at least one person in each spoke it in other social contexts. But at that time, many families had decided that their children would be better off if they did not learn the language, so they taught them only Norwegian. It seems only a matter of time before this trend will have run its full course (Eidheim, 1969, 44, 55).

Lapp culture symbolizes a disparaged status that coastal Lapps prefer to avoid when in the company of Norwegians. When by themselves, however, the symbolic message of Lapp culture changes. Negative connotations become irrelevant for the most part, and Lapp ways become symbolic of in-group solidarity. Without question, members of the community feel at their ease when speaking Lappish, wearing moccasins, and for a few, when eating with their fingers in the old manner. To be more at one's ease is reason in itself for shifting from Norwegian to Lapp custom when alone. But beyond that, the shift to Lapp custom seems to be attractive because it symbolizes the integrity of their society. Insofar as they share in-group secrets, insofar as they speak Lappish and act like Lapps, they symbolize for themselves the solidarity of Lapps vis-à-vis the dominant society. So for the time being, at least, the Lapps use two symbolic codes, one in the public sphere which is purely Norwegian, and another in the private sphere which is still importantly Lappish (Eidheim, 1969, 49–53).

The contrast between coastal and reindeer Lapps in their allegiance to Lapp culture has implications for politics. Since around 1950, two factions have emerged to compete for leadership and influence in northern Finnoscandia. One has established Lapp voluntary associations in Sweden, Norway, and Finland as well as an inter-Scandinavian association, *Nordisk Sameråd*. Led by a small elite of Lapps and a larger body of non-Lapps, mostly intellectuals, this faction supports a program that aims to maximize the integrity of Lapp society as a viable ethnic enclave. The other faction is committed to solving Lapp social problems through rapid and complete assimilation, and thus to end an ancient ethnic identity (Eidheim, 1963, 70–71).

As Lapp culture change has taken on political dimensions, the survival or disappearance of Lapp culture traits has become, in part, a political issue. Above all, educational questions are involved, since the two factions are opposed over whether or not Lappish should be taught in the elementary schools of Lapp districts (Eidheim, 1963, 71).

Politicians on the local level play on cultural issues in their efforts to get power and keep it. In the coastal areas where Eidheim worked, for example, two opposing politicians did this. Although most settled Lapps do not display Lappishness in the public sphere, many, for a variety of reasons, favored the candidate who supported Lapp values. His opponent countered by opposing Lappish language instruction in the schools, which he claimed would make it increasingly difficult for children to learn Norwegian properly and to assimilate. He claimed it is romanticism to try to keep Lapps isolated and, as he put it, to "preserve them as a minority for eternity." (Eidheim, 1963, 76.)

The challenger got some support. The winner, however, proved more adroit in manipulating issues and controlling newspapers. He further assured his success by getting support from about one-fifth of the electorate who are reindeer herders and do not normally exercise their rights of suffrage. They turned out to vote in this election, many hiring taxis to cover the 180 miles from their autumn pastures, because they felt it was important to support a political program favoring Lapp cultural integrity (Eidheim, 1963, 72–79).

GYPSIES

Cultural traits that function as ethnic symbols may carry one meaning for the minority and a very different one for the majority. Often, to each it is the other that is seen as inferior. Basques, Welshmen, and reindeer Lapps look down on their neighbors, to some degree at least, but their neighbors also look down on them. Part of the success of communication by means of the symbolic codes of ethnic confrontation may depend on this built-in ambiguity of meaning, a fact that seems particularly true regarding Gypsies.

Gypsies resemble reindeer Lapps more than Basques or Welshmen insofar as their life style differs thoroughly from that of other Europeans and is based on underlying differences in economy. Some are settled, and in parts of southern Europe whole neighborhoods of Gypsies can be found in the poor parts of towns and cities or even in large villages. Often the people of such neighborhoods are not true Gypsies at all, but merely pimps, prostitutes, entertainers, and others attempting to capitalize on romantic, exotic beliefs. Many who are indeed Gypsies prefer to disguise their identity much as coastal Lapps do, and for the same reason. They are looked down on as dirty and uncivilized. Under these conditions urban-settled Gypsies tend to intermarry with non-Gypsies of low status, and eventually to assimilate to the lowest level of urban society, the *Lumpenproletariat* (Bloch, 1953, 48–52; Fél and Hofer, 1969, 247; Halpern, 1967, 288; Starkie, 1961). The Gypsies we are interested in, however, are the many who remain nomads.

Speaking their own language—one or another dialect of Romany, an Indo-European tongue—they wander almost at random, buffeted about by hostile authorities and unfriendly citizens. They may practice what writer Jan Yoors has characterized as subsistence thieving, meeting their basic daily needs by pilfering from a non-Gypsy world which they regard as entirely in the public domain. But they also follow traditional trades. In the south and east where industrialism is still underdeveloped, they function as horse traders, peddlers, tinsmiths, beggars, musicians, dancers, carnival workers, and fortune tellers. In other areas, some have taken on new occupations as auto mechanics, body-and-fender men, and used-car salesmen—logical extensions of tinkering and horse trading. They no longer line the highway with their horse-drawn caravans, a familiar sight in the past, but still move from place to place in vans and housetrailers, able to cover more ground faster than before (Clébert, 1967, 129–158; Marrimer, 1966; Yoors, 1967, 7).

For the most part, local populations appear to have no difficulty in recognizing Gypsies when they arrive. Even when they come into a large, urban setting where strangers are common, and even if they are not overheard speaking Romany, they are easy to recognize because they assume cultural poses which non-Gypsies consider dirty, immoral, unnatural, criminal, and primitive.

They are considered to be liars and thieves, and often they are. Many storekeepers will not let Gypsies into their shops because they are notorious shoplifters. Farmers know them as chicken thieves who will cheat them all they can, pasturing their horses surreptitiously at night to get free feed. Carnival-goers encounter them as swindlers, selling shoddy merchandise or tricking them out of their money. When we speak of a "gyp," we are reflecting an old view of the Gypsies (Lepowsky, 1971, 6–17; see also Halpern, 1967, 289; Reeve, 1958).

They are well-known beggars, pestering passers-by or visitors to their camps with skirt-tugging and arm-pulling in a way that shows an apparent total lack of pride. Though often suspected of possessing great secret wealth, they give the appearance of being impoverished, living in shabby vans or road-worn trailers, their camps slovenly and filthy (Dodds, 1966; Halpern, 1967, 289; Pitt-Rivers, 1954, 60–61; Reeve, 1958).

In the past, Gypsies often were identifiable by their clothing. As travelers, they might wear items of apparel from distant places which had a garish look. Mostly, they wore older, more ragged clothing than that common to those among whom they traveled, or they wore clothes long out of style. In many cases, they favored more vivid colors and richer ornamentation, including jewelry. In our time, distinctive dress is less common. Men not only look like others in the area, but may appear quite elegant. In the south and east, their wives and daughters often still clothe themselves in a distinctively Gypsy manner, affecting long skirts, handsome aprons, heavy jewelry, or bright blouses different from what others wear. But if dress is less distinctive now, it still in places keeps up an old tradition of being shabby or bizarre (Clébert, 1967, 219–222).

Gypsies are dirty-looking and smell bad. Many do not wash, and the heavy scent of body odor gives an unmistakable clue to their presence. They may have oily skins, and women have been known to slick back their hair with hands greasy from food as a way to achieve a well-oiled sheen (Yoors, 1967, 30).

Perhaps most disgusting of all in the eyes of non-Gypsies, women give the appearance of being lewd and immoral. Gypsy women, and particularly professional dancers, seem not to mind that the low neckline of their blouses reveals a cleavage in shameless display. They seem indifferent to what men see of their bodies. Sexual looseness is also inferred from the brazen way they accost men, just as prostitutes do, when they beg, sell, or solicit for fortune telling. As professional entertainers, by that fact alone they are assumed to be immoral in many areas (Pitt-Rivers, 1954, 174, 198; Starkie, 1961).

Gypsies have maintained their ethnic discreteness for hundreds of years. Yet many of the symbols of their discreteness are symbols as well of inferior social status. How then do they manage to maintain the sense of self-respect which probably is essential if people are to resist acculturation and assimilation? How do they avoid the fate of the coastal Lapps who appear to have adopted a negative image of themselves, and consistent with that, to have moved in the direction of ethnic extinction? The answer, perhaps, is that Gypsies have not lost their sense of dignity; they have not internalized a negative self-image because they do not share the outsiders' low evaluation of the things they do.

Behavior regarded as degraded by others is seen as perfectly acceptable in the eyes of Gypsies. Success in lying and stealing, for example, provides evidence of cleverness, and just retribution against a hostile and often vicious population. It also reflects a very different sense of property values. In Gypsy belief, it is not right that a person should be denied the necessities of life, so stealing or cheating to get what one needs is acceptable. Begging provides an alternative way of bilking strangers, and thus also demonstrates superiority (Yoors, 1967, 34).

Gypsies in their own view are not dirty, except rarely when their defense against hostility is to inspire fear by looking purposely disheveled and witchlike. In fact, their vans and trailers usually are reported to be very clean by contemporary standards. It is true that many do not wash. But often they have good reason, since travelers on the road do not have easy access to toilet facilities. Successful traveling requires an ability to get along this way, and certain beliefs support the habit. It is felt that unwashed or greasy skin is healthy or takes care of itself. And for Gypsies, far more important than regular showers are the ideas they have about ritual cleanliness.

It is believed that a woman is unclean from the waist down. Her lower body and her clothing defile men, kitchen utensils, and food. Women take care, therefore, to remain ritually clean, to respect taboos that prevent the touching of a woman's skirts, for example. But while they are careful about ritual cleanliness, they find disgusting such non-Gypsy practices as the common one of washing women's clothes with those of men, and even with tablecloths that come into contact with food. Even taking a bath is indecent, since it has a person wash his face and upper body with water defiled by the lower body (Clébert, 1967, 229–230; Yoors, 1967).

Finally, the fact that non-Gypsies regard their women as immoral is merely one more proof for them that "peasants" (*Gaje*) are gullible and simple-minded. In fact, Gypsy women are subject to very strict sexual taboos. Girls marry young, and are subject to categorical injunctions against sexual looseness. "Gypsy" prostitutes in towns are usually highly acculturated, settled Gypsies, outcasts, or simply not Gypsies at all (Bloch, 1953, 106; Clébert, 1967, 208–209; Yoors, 1967).

In sum, traits which non-Gypsies regard as degraded carry no such connotation among the Gypsies themselves. On the contrary, such traits may connote superiority of intellect and initiative and they always indicate how ignorant and insensitive non-Gypsies can be. Far from constituting challenges to ethnic pride, they provide strong support for it.

The Gypsy way of life probably will endure for some time to come. Yet it is not without threat. Under the Nazis some 400,000 Gypsies were exterminated in the same program that destroyed Jewish communities in much of Europe. In Germany and the east they have never fully recovered from that loss. In eastern Europe since the war, communist policy has favored isolating them as families and forcing them to settle. They may find it impossible to resist.

When Europe was largely agrarian in economy, horse traders, tinkers, and itinerant peddlers played a needed role. Even traveling entertainers provided welcome diversion in the centuries before moving pictures and television. A modern society has no need for such services. Further, legislation in many countries makes it difficult if not impossible for Gypsy nomads to survive. Camping sites are closed to them, or only short stays are permitted. They encounter difficulties in crossing national frontiers. In the end, external forces in both east and west may overwhelm them. But to date, they survive remarkably intact (Clébert, 1967, 248–256; see also Kenny, 1971).

JEWS

No country in Europe today lacks ethnic enclaves. Some resemble the Basques and the Welsh in that they differ from the majority population in language and other traits of great symbolic importance, yet economically and technologically are similar to their neighbors. Bretons in France, Scotsmen in Great Britain, Faroe Islanders in Denmark, Corsicans in France, and Sardinians in Italy are some of the better-known of this general sort (e.g., Musco, 1969). They exist in communist Europe, too, as Ukrainians, Mordvins, Letts, Lithuanians, and others (Benoist-Méchin, 1941; Dunn, 1966a, b).

Many who once were ethnically distinctive have lost nearly all that was unique. George Nellemann's study of settled Polish field hands in Denmark reveals a population nearly completely absorbed now into Danish culture (Nellemann, 1967, 91–94; 1970a). The study by A. L. Maraspini of Greek-speaking villages in southern Italy shows communities so similar in culture to Italian-speaking ones that the ability to speak a Greek dialect on the part of older people seems merely to give the population an antiquarian interest. In no other way do they constitute a distinctive enclave anymore (Maraspini, 1968).

At the opposite extreme, some ethnic groups differ greatly in basic ecological adaptation, and with that maintain a culture greatly different from that of the larger population that surrounds them. Lapps and Gypsies illustrate this condition, as also do the Sarakatsani, Koutsovlachs, and Karagouni of Greece. Ethnic enclaves in Europe, in all, can be placed along a continuum of distinctiveness which ranges from nearly totally assimilated to the majority culture, through those who are different in many ways, to societies nearly totally different. And this brings us to European Jews. Their style of life has included the whole range of possible adaptations.

Before World War II and the Nazi program of genocide, the Jews of eastern and central Europe lived in ghettos where they maintained a culture that was highly distinctive. From the work of anthropologists Mark Zborowski and Elizabeth Herzog, we learn that they spoke their own Germanic language, Yiddish, wore clothes and groomed their hair in a Jewish manner, and shared a value system and view of the world completely suffused with the tenets of their own religion. Both on the surface, where culture acts as a symbol of social integrity, and beneath the surface, in the way people think and the things they believe, Jews of the ghetto were as different from neighboring Poles, Russians, Germans, and others as Lapps and Gypsies are different from their neighbors (Zborowski and Herzog, 1962).

Their whole way of life, in effect, symbolized their discreteness from other Europeans. As Stanley A. Freed has pointed out, moreover, the social structure of the Jewish ghetto enhanced their capacity to adapt to changing times and to participate in the modern business world without sacrificing differentness. This took shape as a system of social stratification (Freed, 1957).

Men of learning, the *sheyneh yidn* (literally, "beautiful Jews"), had the highest prestige and formed the highest stratum. As scholars, they were dedicated to preserving the Jewish heritage and keeping it potent in Jewish life. Living as scholars, their activities and interests centered on the synagogue and the school. They had so little to do with people beyond the ghetto that in some cases they very poorly spoke the language of the country in which they lived. Insofar as community leaders were *sheyneh yidn*, they were insulated from acculturative influences.

The highest stratum also included men of wealth, who had succeeded in a world of business that brought them into contact with the outside world. These men might have become agents of acculturation—that is, hinges—since they were familiar with non-Jewish ways and successful to some extent in coping with them. To attain prestige in the ghetto, however, they had to transform their wealth into prestige that derived from religion and religious learning. They were morally compelled to share with the poor. In addition, they gained status by becoming the patrons of scholarship, supporting students by giving them meals in their homes, for example. Ideally, a rich man married his daughter to a promising intellectual, whose continuing studies he supported either by the gift of a large dowry or by an agreement to subsidize the couple for some years. One way or the other, however, rich men found they had to support traditional values if they were to gain respect and status. Not to use money in these conventional ways was to be thought low-bred by others in the community, a strong sanction in a closed society.

People of high status either lived in isolation from the outside world (the beautiful Jews) or were under pressure to commit themselves to traditional values in order to be granted prestige and status (rich men). Most Jews were people of lower status, and those most tempted to abandon Jewish for Gentile habits tended to be poor Jews (*prosteh*) (Freed, 1957, 57–58). In part, then, because those most likely to attempt to introduce Gentile traits were low-status individuals, but in part also, as I interpret the evidence, because by the very act of emulating the outside world they lost prestige in the ghetto, the carriers of change would easily be ignored. "If a person from the lower class did something that was contrary to the ways of [the town of] Stozcek, people would say, 'What can you expect from a plain person?'" (Rosenthal, 1954, 181.) Over the centuries, many new traits did become part of Jewish culture (Caster, 1955), but the community maintained a kind of unconscious veto power over such innovations insofar as, within the community, the supporters of tradition enjoyed high prestige and those who supported change had none.

The ghetto solution to maintaining an ethnic identity no longer exists in Europe. Almost everywhere, Jews are city people, for they rarely became farmers; but the tendency to form closed neighborhoods is countered by the practice of establishing homes where they can find suitable apartments or houses, whoever their neighbors may be. The synagogue remains central to their sense of being different, and they remain distinctive in those values and norms central to religious belief, particularly in concepts of private and family morality. But many now speak only the language of the country in which they are citizens, or speak Yiddish (less commonly Sephardic Spanish) mainly as a domestic language, dress as do others, and engage in occupations that are not ethnically distinctive. They remain apart as Jews, but no longer so completely. And many have abandoned their Jewish heritage entirely (e.g., in Denmark, Blum, 1970; in Sweden, Ek, 1971).

We are speaking here of people whose customs distribute them along a continuum. While some remain nearly as different as the inhabitants of prewar ghettos, and while many constitute an ethnic enclave with differences on the order of those that distinguish Basques and Welshmen, many are greatly acculturated, differing only slightly or not at all from the national majority among whom they live. Jewish ethnicity in the twentieth century has covered the range from one extreme of the continuum to the other.

ELEVEN

MODERN EUROPE

The central feature of an anthropological perspective is that we make comparisons, a sound if not entirely original method. Poet Mark Van Doren describes it as the universal technique for gaining wisdom: "There are two statements about human beings that are true: that all human beings are alike, and that all are different. On those two facts all human wisdom is founded."

In the effort to gain a perspective on Modern Europe, we have systematically compared the present with the past. Taking the eighteenth century as a baseline, we have documented both likenesses (continuity) and differences. (change). Insofar as these are likenesses and differences in human behavior as such, they are difficult to evaluate. That is, individual culture traits throughout history have always had a tendency to change, so alterations or replacements cannot be taken as diagnostic in themselves of the appearance of a new kind of civilization.

Modern Europe, however, differs qualitatively from Traditional Europe. It is that different because Europe has changed as a cultural system. Major continuities in custom and belief should not obscure the magnitude of this systemic change. The cultural parts that make up the civilizational whole relate differently to one another now.

Traditional Europe as a system comprised three major class cultures: aristocratic, burgher, and peasant. Cultural differentiation kept them distinct. Acculturation tended to take place within classes and to keep them uniform. By the eighteenth century, these relationships had endured for hundreds of years. The system was quite stable.

Modern Europe as a system is dominated by a single culture. Because it is so widely shared, it has often been termed "mass culture." In historical perspective, however, it is not found to have emerged somehow out of amorphous European folk origins. Rather, it appears as the old culture of the aristocracy in modern form, and is not different because its content has changed. Content has always been subject to change, particularly in aristocratic culture. It is different because its relationship to other cultures has changed. In the interaction of class cultures, the process of cultural differentiation has been replaced by that of acculturation.

We see the effects of systemic adjustment in aristocratic culture as such. It is structurally different now in three significant ways. For one, it has come to include a large middle-class component characterized by standards which emphasize those patterns of behavior that do not require large amounts of wealth, power, and leisure to fulfill. Again, the social structure of cultural creativity is different. Innovation and diffusion take place now through commercial, governmental, and other channels rather than largely within the structure of upper-class society as such. Finally, the emergent form of upper-class culture initiated acculturation by the lower classes when dominant members of society set out to help raise standards of living among the poor. Now, the lower classes freely emulate the upper.

With the growth of industrialization, burgher culture virtually disappeared as such, its place taken by a proletarian way of life. Exploitation under early capitalism reduced the growing working class to great depths of poverty. Working-class culture in its early years was impoverished as a way of life. Improvement was slow to come, and did not greatly quicken in pace until the 1950s.

When economic development finally reached the working class, their culture began to change rapidly. So recent is this that the process is still underway. Workers are adopting the middle-class version of upper-class culture. Acculturation of this nature is only partially visible in old proletarian neighborhoods. It is much more apparent in new housing developments. There, in some cases, it has left workers indistinguishable from members of the middle class. This, at least, is the preliminary conclusion one can draw from the limited amount of research carried out so far.

Peasant culture, like burgher culture, has disappeared. At about the time that burgher culture was superseded by that of the working class, peasant culture was displaced by that of farmers—for just as factories led to great changes in the life style of townsmen, factory products led to great changes in the life style of countrymen. The similarity does not stop there. Farmers now also display a tendency to acculturate to the middle class. They vary greatly in the extent to which the process is complete.

Four major kinds of farm culture can be identified in western Europe. First, in highly urbanized regions such as Denmark and the Netherlands, one finds farmers with substantial holdings who belong essentially to the middle class. Second, perhaps in most places, family farms perpetuate a distinctive subculture. Third, where countrymen find employment as workers in industry yet maintain small holdings as a subsidiary occupation, one finds a way of life we have identified as that of the worker-peasant. Finally, in underdeveloped areas, substandard farming and an impoverished way of life persist whether it is that of smallholders, of women, children, and old people managing family holdings while adult males work in factories elsewhere, or of old farmers without successors. In many such places, rural development eventually will allow these people to become worker-peasants, successful family farmers, or middle-class farmers. Not all will succeed in those directions, however, and those who remain may end up with a fifth and final kind of farm culture, that of park-keepers (Franklin, 1969, 220, 221). Park-keepers run inefficient operations but are supported by government subsidy or with income from the tourist trade because their farms constitute a resort area where urbanites can spend vacations in rustic surroundings. Park-keepers may live as well as successful family farmers.

Communist Europe does not differ as much as one might suppose in the direction culture change is taking. In spite of an ideological insistence upon the virtues of a proletarian style of life, members of the so-called new class—those with relative wealth, leisure, and power—have shown themselves susceptible to a middle-class version of aristocratic ideas about the good life. Workers and countrymen, for their part, seem inclined to emulate the new class of managers and bureaucrats, although they are still far from "middle class" in life style.

Two of the types of farm culture characteristic of western Europe can be identified in Poland and Yugoslavia: family farmers and worker-peasants. But for the most part, eastern Europe is dominated by two styles of life virtually unknown on the other side of the Iron Curtain: collective farmers and workers or managers of state industrial farms. The general tendency of acculturation may be the same in both east and west, but the expression of it now, and in the foreseeable future, is quite different.

It does not appear that the growing dominance of bourgeois culture will result in complete homogeneity, for cultural differentiation is still a process to be reckoned with. We still find cultural differentiation at work in ethnic enclaves. But it is equally effective within the new mass culture as such. It lies behind the different life styles of men and women. It works powerfully to create quite different age cultures, through which each person may pass as a part of his own life cycle. And just as importantly, it is inherent in the efforts of individuals to break away from mass conformity, and to attract others to join them. Bohemians in the twenties and hippies in the sixties were not merely age groups, they were also self-generated deviant societies.

Modern Europe as a system contrastive to that of traditional Europe is not fully developed. The acculturation of workers and farmers is not yet complete, and may never be. The process is well underway, however, and if present trends continue, the system should one day have the following dimensions. Europe will probably comprise various cultures or part-cultures defined in terms of the criteria of age, sex, occupation, ethnicity, region, nationality, or personal inclination. Some life styles may become as different from mass culture as the three cultures of Traditional Europe were different from each other. Through the process of cultural differentiation, each will create and maintain its distinctiveness. Through the process of acculturation, each will ensure homogeneity among its bearers. And just as individuals underwent secondary enculturation as they moved from one culture to another in Old Europe, secondary enculturation will take place as individuals move in and out of contemporary and future cultures. Even now, the relationship of the parts is very different from what it was, but the forces that keep the parts in their places—cultural processes—appear to remain immutable.

134

APPENDIX

BIBLIOGRAPHY

Aceves, Joseph
  1971   Social change in a Spanish village. Cambridge, Mass.: Schenkman.

Amalrik, Andrei
  1970   Involuntary journey to Siberia. New York: Harcourt, Brace, Jovanovich.

Anderson, Barbara Gallatin
  1956   A survey of Italian godparenthood. Kroeber Anthropological Society Papers, 15.
  1957   Il comparaggio: the Italian godparenthood complex. Southwestern Journal of Anthropology, 13.
  1968   How French children learn to drink. Trans-action, June.

Anderson, Robert T.
  1965   From Mafia to Cosa Nostra. American Journal of Sociology, 71.
  1971   Traditional Europe: a study in anthropology and history. Belmont, Calif.: Wadsworth.
  1972a Denmark: the success of a developing nation. Cambridge, Mass.: Schenkman, to appear.
  1972b Europe, introduction. Encyclopedia Americana, to appear.
  1972c Europe: folk culture of the European plain. Encyclopaedia Britannica, to appear.

Anderson, Robert T., and Barbara Gallatin Anderson
  1959   Voluntary associations and urbanization: a diachronic analysis. American Journal of Sociology, 65.
  1962a The indirect social structure of European village communities. American Anthropologist, 64.
  1962b The replicate social structure. Southwestern Journal of Anthropology, 18.
  1962c Voluntary associations among Ukrainians in France. Anthropological Quarterly, 35.

1964   The vanishing village: a Danish maritime community. Seattle: University of Washington Press.

1965   Bus stop for Paris: the transformation of a French village. Garden City, N. Y.: Doubleday.

Anfossi, Anna, Magda Talamo, and Francesco Indovina
1959   Ragusa: comunita in transizione. Torino: Taylor.

Arensberg, Conrad M.
1963   The old world peoples: the place of European cultures in world ethnography. Anthropological Quarterly, 36.
1968   The Irish countryman. (First published, 1937.) Garden City, N. Y.: Natural History Press.

Arensberg, Conrad M., and Solon T. Kimball
1968   Family and community in Ireland, rev. ed. (First published, 1940.) Cambridge, Mass.: Harvard University Press.

Banfield, Edward C.
1958   The moral basis of a backward society. New York: Free Press.

Barnes, John A.
1954   Class and committees in a Norwegian island parish. Human Relations, 7.

Barnett, Clifford R.
1958   Poland, its people, its society, its culture. New York: Grove.

Baroja, Caro Julio
1946   Los pueblos de España: ensayo de ethnologia. Barcelona: Editorial Barna.
1966   Honour and shame: a historical account of several conflicts. J. G. Peristiany, ed., Honour and shame: the values of Mediterranean society. Chicago: University of Chicago Press.

Barth, Frederik, ed.
1963   The role of the entrepreneur in social change in northern Norway. (Årbok for Universitetet i Bergen, Humanistisk Serie, 3.) Bergen and Oslo: Norwegian Universities Press.

Barzini, Luigi
1964   The Italians. New York: Bantam.

Belshaw, Cyrus
1955   The cultural milieu of the entrepreneur: a critical essay. Explorations in Entrepreneurial History, 7.

Bendix, Reinhard
1969   Nation-building and citizenship. Garden City, N. Y.: Doubleday.

Benedict, Ruth
1946   Rumanian culture and behavior. New York: Institute for Intercultural Studies (mimeo.).

Benet, Sula
1951   Song, dance and customs of peasant Poland. London: Dobson.

Benet, Sula, tr. and ed.
1970   The village of Viriatino: an ethnographic study of a Russian village from before the revolution to the present. Garden City, N. Y.: Doubleday.

Benoist-Méchin
1941   L'Ukraine: des origines à Staline. Paris: Albin Michel.

Benvenuti, B.
1961   Farming in cultural change. New York: Humanities Press.

Bernard, H. Russell
1968   Kalymnos: economic and cultural change on a Greek sponge fishing island. Ph.D. dissertation, University of Illinois.
1970   Paratsoukli: institutionalized nicknaming in rural Greece. Ethnologia Europaea, 2–3.

Bernatzik, Hugo A.
1954   Die neue grosse völkerkunde, vol. 1. Frankfurt/Main: Herkul G.M.B.H.

Bernot, Lucien, and René Blancard
1953   Nouville, un village français. Travaux et Memoires de L'Institut d'Ethnologie, 57.

Berthoud, Gérald
1967   Changements économiques et sociaux de la montagne. Bern: Francke Verlag.

Bidstrup, Knud, and Erik Kaufmann
1963   Denmark under forvandling. (Denmarks radios grundbøger.) Copenhagen: Fremad.

Black, Cyril E.
1960   The transformation of Russian society: aspects of change since 1861. Cambridge, Mass.: Harvard University Press.

Blanc, André
1967   La Yougoslavie. Paris: Armand Colin.

Blehr, Otto
1963   Action groups in a society with bilateral kinship: a case study from the Faroe Islands. Ethnology, 2.

Blehr, Otto, et al.
1968   Vad Sker i Glesbygden? (Nordisk Etnologisk-Folkloristisk Arbejdsgruppes Skriftserie (NEFA) nr. 2.) Luleå, Sweden: Norrbottens Museum.

Bloch, Jules
1953   Les Tsiganes. Paris: Presses Universitaires de France.

Blom, Jan-Petter   **137**
  1969   Ethnic and cultural differentation. Frederik Barth, ed., Ethnic groups
         and boundaries: the social organization of culture difference. Boston:
         Little, Brown.

Bloomfield, Paul
  1955   Uncommon people: a study of England's elite. London: Hamish Ha-
         milton.

Blum, Jaques
  1970   Jøderne. Jordens Folk, 6.

Blythe, Ronald
  1969   Akenfield: portrait of an English village. New York: Random House.

Bohannan, Paul
  1955   Some principles of exchange and investment among the Tiv. Ameri-
         can Anthropologist, 57.
  1965   Social anthropology. New York: Holt, Rinehart and Winston.

Bohociu, Octavian
  1966   Folklore and ethnography in Rumania. Current Anthropology, 7.

Boissevain, Jeremy F.
  1962   Maltese village politics and their relation to national politics. Journal
         of Commonwealth Political Studies, 1.
  1965   Saints and fireworks: religion and politics in rural Malta. London
         School of Economics, Monographs on Social Anthropology, 30.
  1966a Patronage in Sicily. Man, 1.
  1966b Poverty and politics in a Sicilian agro-town. International Archives
         of Ethnography, 1.
  1969a Hal-Farrug: a village in Malta. New York: Holt, Rinehart and Winston.
  1969b Some aspects of two total networks. Paper read at the seminar on
         network approaches. Leiden.

Bökönyi, Sándor, et al.
  1970   On Hungarian anthropology. Current Anthropology, 11.

Booth, Charles
  1882   Life and labour of the people in London, 2nd. ed., 9 vols. London:
  to 1897 Macmillan.

Bott, Elizabeth
  1957   Family and social network. London: Tavistock.
  1971   Urban families: conjugal roles and social networks. (Reprinted from
         Human Relations, 8, 1955.) Yehudi A. Cohen, ed., Man in adaptation:
         the institutional framework. Chicago: Aldine.

Briggs, Asa
  1963   Victorian people. (First published, 1955.) New York: Harper & Row.

Brogan, D. W.
  1963   The French nation from Napoleon to Petain, 1814–1940. (First pub-
         lished, 1957.) New York: Harper & Row.

138   Brox, Ottar
         1963   Three types of north Norwegian entrepreneurship. Frederik Barth,
                ed., The role of the entrepreneur in social change in northern Nor-
                way. (Årbok for Universitetet i Bergen, Humanistisk Serie, 3.) Bergen
                and Oslo: Norwegian Universities Press.

         Brøgger, Jan
         1971   Montevarese: a study of peasant society and culture in southern Italy.
                Oslo: Universitetsforlaget.

         Brudner, Lilyan A.
         1972   The maintenance of bilingualism in southern Austria. Ethnology, 11.

         Brügge, Peter
         1966   Die reichen in Deutschland. Der Spiegel, 20 (37, 38, 39).

         Brunhes-Delamarre, Mariel Jean
         1970   Le berger dans la France des villages: bergers communs à Saint Véran
                en Queyras et à Normée en Champagne. Paris: Editions du Centre
                National de la Recherche Scientifique.

         Buchanan, R. H.
         1961   Folklife in the highlands. Ulster Folklife, 7.

         Bull, Edvard
         1929   Sammenlignende studier over bondesamfundets kulturforhold, et ar-
                beidsprogram. Instituttet for Sammenlignende Kulturforskning, serie
                C, 2.

         Burns, Robert K., Jr.
         1959   Saint Vérain, France's highest village. National Geographic, 115.
         1961   The ecological basis of French alpine peasant communities in the
                Dauphine. Anthropological Quarterly, 34.
         1963   The circum-alpine culture area: a preliminary view. Anthropological
                Quarterly, 36.

         Campbell, J. K.
         1963   The kindred in a Greek mountain community. Julian Pitt-Rivers, ed.,
                Mediterranean countrymen. The Hague: Mouton.
         1964   Honour, family and patronage: a study of institutions and moral
                values in a Greek mountain community. Oxford: Clarendon.
         1968   Two case studies of marketing and patronage in Greece. J. G. Peris-
                tiany, ed., contributions to Mediterranean sociology. The Hague:
                Mouton.

         Cancian, Frank
         1961   The south Italian peasant: world view and political behavior. Anthro-
                pological Quarterly, 34.

         Cantor, N. F., and M. S. Werthman, eds.
         1968   The history of popular culture since 1815. New York: Macmillan.

         Carrier, E. H.
         1932   Water and grass. London: Christophers.

Caster, Theodor H.
1955 Customs and folkways of Jewish life. New York: William Sloane.

Chapman, Charlotte Gower
1971 Milocca: a Sicilian village. Cambridge, Mass.: Schenkman.

Chaubet, Stéphen
1921 La Normandie ancestrale—ethnologie, vie, coutumes, meubles, utensiles, costumes, patois. Paris: Boivin.

Chombart de Lauwe, Paul
1956 La vie quotidienne des familles ouvrières. Paris: Centre National de la Recherche Scientifique.
1959 Famille et habitation, vol. 1. Paris: Centre National de la Recherche Scientifique.
1960 Famille et habitation, vol. 2. Paris: Centre National de la Recherche Scientifique.

Chombart de Lauwe, Paul, et al.
1952 Paris et l'agglomeration parisienne, vol. 1. Paris: Presses Universitaires de France.

Clébert, Jean-Paul
1967 The Gypsies. (First published in French, 1961.) Baltimore, Md.: Penguin.

Cobban, Alfred
1965 The social interpretation of the French revolution. Cambridge: University Press.

Coing, Henri
1966 Rénovation urbaine et changement social: l'ilot no. 4 (Paris 13e). Paris: Éditions Ouvrières.

Cole, John W.
1969 Economic alternatives in the upper Nonsberg. Anthropological Quarterly, 42.
1970 Inheritance processes and their social consequences: a case study from northern Italy. Sociologia, Rivista di Studi Sociali, n.s., 4.

Coon, Carleton S.
1950 The mountains of giants. Peabody Museum of American Archeology and Ethnology, Papers, 23.

Coppock, John O.
1963 North Atlantic policy: the agricultural gap. New York: Twentieth Century Fund.

Cornelisen, Ann
1969 Torregreca: life, death, miracles. Boston: Little, Brown.

Cresswell, Robert
1969 Une communauté rurale de l'Irelande. (Travaux et Mémoires de l'Institute d'Ethnologie, 74.) Paris: Institut d'Ethnologie.

Cronin, Constance
   1970   The sting of change: Sicilians in Sicily and Australia. Chicago: University of Chicago Press.

Cvijic, Jovan
   1918   La péninsule balkanique, géographie humaine. Paris: Payot.

Dalido, Pierre
   1951   Jersey, île agricole Anglo-Normande, étude de sociographie. Arradon: chez l'auteur.

Denitch, Bette S.
   1969   Social mobility and industrialization in a Yugoslav town. Ph.D. dissertation, University of California, Berkeley.

Derruau, Max
   1958   L'Europe. Paris: Hachette.

Dias, Jorge
   1948   Vilarinho da Furna: una aldeia comunitaria. Instituto de Alta Cultura, Centro de Estudos de Etnologia Peninsular.
   1953   Rio de Onor: comunitarismo agro-pastoril. Instituto de Alta Cultura, Centro de Estudos de Etnologia Peninsular.
   1961   Portuguese contributions to cultural anthropology. Johannesburg: Witwatersrand University Press.

Djilas, Milovan
   1957   The new class: an analysis of the communist system. New York: Praeger.

Doby, Harry R.
   1960   A study of social change and social disorganization in a Finnish rural community. Ph.D. dissertation, University of California, Berkeley.

Dodds, N.
   1966   Gypsies, Didikois and other travellers. London: Johnson.

Dorian, Nancy C.
   1970   A substitute name system in the Scottish highlands. American Anthropologist, 72.

Douglass, William A.
   1969   Death in Murelaga: funerary ritual in a Spanish Basque village. Seattle: University of Washington Press.

Dunn, Stephen P.
   1964   Logical deduction, unconscious inference, and cultural change: a caveat. American Anthropologist, 66.
   1966a Cultural process in the Baltic area under Soviet rule. Research Series, 11. Institute of International Studies. University of California, Berkeley.
   1966b Review of Issledovaniia po material'noi kul'ture mordovskogo naroda

by V. N. Belitser and K. A. Kotkov, eds. American Anthropologist, 68.

Dunn, Stephen P., ed.
1969   Sociology in the USSR: a collection of readings from Soviet sources. White Plains, N.Y.: International Arts and Sciences Press.

Dunn, Stephen P., and Ethel Dunn
1963   The Great Russian peasant: culture change or cultural development? Ethnology, 2.
1967   The peasants of central Russia. New York: Holt, Rinehart and Winston.

Durham, M. E.
1910   High Albania and its customs in 1908. Journal of the Royal Anthropological Institute, 40.

Eckersley, C. E., and L. C. B. Seaman
1949   Pattern of England, book 2. London: Longmans, Green.

Eidheim, Harald
1963   Entrepreneurship in politics. Frederik Barth, ed. The role of the entrepreneur in social change in northern Norway. (Årbok for Universitetet i Bergen, Humanistisk Serie, 3.) Bergen and Oslo: Norwegian Universities Press.
1966   Lappish guest relationships under conditions of cultural change. American Anthropologist, 68.
1969   When ethnic identity is a social stigma. Frederik Barth, ed., Ethnic groups and boundaries: the social organization of culture difference. Boston: Little, Brown.

Ek, Sven B.
1971   Nöden i Lund: en etnologisk stadsstudie. Lund, Sweden: C. W. K. Gleerup.

Emmett, Isabel
1964   A north Wales village: a social anthropological study. London: Routledge and Kegan Paul.

Enyedi, Irene
1965   The "Kossuth" collective farm of Bekescasaba in the southern part of the great Hungarian plain. Geographia Polonica, 5.

Erasmus, Charles J.
1961   Man takes control: cultural development and American aid. Indianapolis: Bobbs-Merrill.

Erdei, Ferenc
1970   The changing Hungarian village. New Hungarian Quarterly, 38.

Erixon, Sigurd
1938   West European connections and culture relations. Folk Liv, 2.

    1946   Kila. En Östgötsk skogsby. En byundersökning 1912–1913. (Instituttet for Folklivsforskning, Etnologiska Källskrifter.) Stockholm: Hakan Ohlssons Boktryckeri.

Erlich, Vera Stein
    1966   Family in transition: a study of 300 Yugoslav villages. Princeton, N.J.: Princeton University Press.

Evans, Estyn E.
    1957   Irish folk ways. London: Routledge and Kegan Paul.
    1968   Europe. Encyclopaedia Britannica, 8.

Evans, Estyn E., and A. Gailey.
    1961   The evolution of rural settlement in Scotland and beyond. Ulster Folklife, 7.

Fél, Edit, and Tamás Hofer
    1969   Proper peasants: traditional life in a Hungarian village. Chicago: Aldine.

Firth, Raymond
    1951   Elements of social organization. London: Watts.

Firth, Raymond, ed.
    1956   Two studies of kinship in London. London School of Economics, Monographs on Social Anthropology, 15.

Firth, Raymond, and J. Djamour
    1956   Kinship in South Borough. Raymond Firth, ed., Two studies of kinship in London. London School of Economics, Monographs on Social Anthropology, 15.

Foster, George M.
    1951   Report on an ethnological reconnaissance of Spain. American Anthropologist, 53.
    1953   What is folk culture? American Anthropologist, 55.
    1962   Traditional cultures and the impact of technological change. New York: Harper.
    1965   Peasant society and the image of limited good. American Anthropologist, 67.

Frankenberg, Ronald
    1957   Village on the border: a social study of religion, politics and football in a north Wales community. London: Cohen & West.
    1966   Communities in Britain: social life in town and country. Baltimore, Md.: Penguin.

Franklin, S. H.
    1969   The European peasantry: the final phase. London: Methuen.

Freed, Stanley A.
    1957   Suggested type societies in acculturation studies. American Anthropologist, 59.

Freeman, Susan Tax
1968 Religious aspects of the social organization of a Castilian village. American Anthropologist, 70.
1970 Review of Death in Murelaga by William A. Douglass. American Anthropologist, 72.

Friedl, Ernestine
1959 The role of kinship in the transmission of national culture to a rural village in mainland Greece. American Anthropologist, 61.
1962 Vasilika: a village in modern Greece. New York: Holt, Rinehart and Winston.
1963 Some aspects of dowry and inheritance in Boeotia. Julian Pitt-Rivers, ed., Mediterranean countrymen: essays in the social anthropology of the Mediterranean. The Hague: Mouton.
1968 Lagging emulation in post-peasant society: a Greek case. J. G. Peristiany, ed., Contributions to Mediterranean sociology: Mediterranean rural communities and social change. The Hague: Mouton.

Friedl, John
1971 Economic and social change in a Swiss alpine village. Ph.D. dissertation, University of California, Berkeley.

Friedmann, Fredrick G.
1960 The hoe and book: an Italian experiment in community development. Ithaca, N.Y.: Cornell University Press.

Frödin, John
1940 Zentraleuropas alpwirtschaft. Instituttet for Sammenlignende Kulturforskning, serie B, 38.

Fustel de Coulanges, Numa
1956 The ancient city. (First published, 1864.) Garden City, N.Y.: Doubleday.

Gadourek, I.
1956 A Dutch community: social and cultural structure and process in a bulb-growing region in the Netherlands. Leiden: H. E. Stenfert Kroese N. V.

Gailey, Alan
1970 Cultural connections in north-west Britain and Ireland. Ethnologia Europaea, 2–3.

Galeski, B.
1964a From peasant to farmer. Polish Sociological Bulletin, 2.
1964b Sociology of the village. Polish Perspectives, 7.

Gallop, Rodney
1970 A book of the Basques. (First published, 1930.) Reno: University of Nevada Press.

Geyl, P.
1949 Napoleon: for and against. New Haven: Yale University Press.

Gjessing, Gutorm
    1954   Changing Lapps: a study in culture relations in northernmost Norway. London School of Economics and Political Science, Monographs on Social Anthropology, 13.

Goffman, Erving
    1959   The presentation of self in everyday life. Garden City, N.Y.: Doubleday.

Gorer, Geoffrey
    1955   Exploring English character. London: Cresset.
    1965   Death, grief and mourning in contemporary Britain. London: Cresset.

Gorer, Geoffrey, and John Rickman
    1949   The people of Great Russia, a psychological study. London: Cresset.

Granick, David
    1961   The Red executive: a study of the organization man in Russian industry. Garden City, N.Y.: Doubleday.

Graves, Robert, and Alan Hodge
    1963   The long week-end: a social history of Great Britain 1918–1939. New York: Norton.

Greenwood, Davydd J.
    1972   Tourism as an agent of change: a Spanish Basque case. Ethnology, 11.

Guérard, Albert
    1965   France in the classical age: the life and death of an ideal. (First published, 1928.) New York: Harper & Row.

Halpern, Joel M.
    1965   Peasant culture and urbanization in Yugoslavia. Human Organization, 24.
    1967   A Serbian village: social and cultural change in a Yugoslav community, rev. ed. New York: Harper & Row.

Halpern, Joel M., and David Anderson
    1970   The zadruga, a century of change. Anthropologica, 12.

Haltsonen, Sulo.
    1960   Some interests and tasks of Finnish ethnography. Ethnografia Polska, 3.

Hammel, Eugene A.
    1968   Alternative social structures and ritual relations in the Balkans. Englewood Cliffs, N.J.: Prentice-Hall.
    1969a The Balkan peasant: a view from Serbia. Philip K. Bock, ed., Peasants in the modern world. Albuquerque, N.M.: University of New Mexico Press.
    1969b The pink yo-yo: occupational mobility in Belgrade, ca. 1915–1965. University of California, Berkeley, Institute of International Studies.

Hammond, J. L., and Barbara Hammond
1920 The town laborer, 1765–1832. London: Longmans, Green.

Hansen, Judith Friedman
1970 Danish social interaction: cultural assumptions and patterns of behavior. Ph.D. dissertation, University of California, Berkeley.

Hanssen, Börje
1952 Österlen. Stockholm: L. T.'s Forlag.
1953 Fields of social activity and their dynamics. Transactions of the Westermarck Society, 2.

Havighurst, Alfred F.
1962 Twentieth century Britain. New York: Row, Peterson.

Heeringa, Tetje
1934 De Graafschap, een bijdrage tot de kennis van het cultuur-landschap en van het Scholten-probleem. Dissertation, University of Utrecht.

Hendin, Herbert
1964 Suicide and Scandinavia. Garden City, N.Y.: Doubleday.

Hervo, Monique, and Marie-Ange Charras
1971 Bidonvilles, l'enlisement. Paris: Maspero.

Hill, Rowland G. P., ed.
1960 The Lapps to-day in Finland, Norway and Sweden. École Pratique des Hautes Études, Sorbonne, Sixième Section: Sciencés Economiques et Sociales, Bibliotheque Arctique et Antarctique, 1.

Hobsbawn, E. J.
1968 Industry and empire. New York: Random House.

Hofer, Tamás
1970 Anthropologists and native ethnographers at work in Central European villages. Anthropologica, 12.

Hoffman, Susanna Martina
1971 A cultural grammar of a peasant society. Ph.D. dissertation, University of California, Berkeley.

Hogbin, H. Ian
1958 Social change. London: Watts.

Honigmann, John J.
1963a Bauer and arbeiter in a rural Austrian community. Southwestern Journal of Anthropology, 19.
1963b Dynamics of drinking in an Austrian village. Ethnology, 2.
1964 Survival of a cultural focus. Ward H. Goodenough, ed., Explorations in cultural anthropology. New York: McGraw-Hill.
1970 Rationality and fantasy in Styrian villagers. Anthropologica, 12.

Izikowitz, K. G., Carl-Axel Moberg, and Albert Eskeröd
1959 Anthropology in Sweden. American Anthropologist, 61.

Jenkins, David
  1960 Aber-Porth: a study of a coastal village in south Cardiganshire. David
      Jenkins, Emrys Jones, T. Jones Hughes, Trefor M. Owen, eds., Welsh
      rural communities. Cardiff: University of Wales Press.

Kavadias, Georges B.
  1965 Pasteurs-nomades Méditerranéens: les Saraçatsans de Grèce. Paris:
      Gauthier-Villars.

Kayser, B.
  1962 Les problemes de l'agriculture Bulgare. Études Rurales, 4.

Kearney, Michael
  1969 An exception to the "image of limited good." American Anthro-
      pologist, 71.

Kenny, Michael
  1960 Pattern of patronage in Spain. Anthropological Quarterly, 33.
  1966 A Spanish tapestry: town and country in Castile. (First published,
      1961.) New York: Harper & Row.
  1968a Parallel power structures in Castile: the patron-client balance. J. G.
      Peristiany, ed., Contributions to Mediterranean sociology. The Hague:
      Mouton.
  1968b Review of Belmonte de los Caballeros. American Anthropologist, 70.
  1971 Gypsy. Encyclopaedia Britannica.

Keur, John Y., and Dorothy L. Keur
  1955 The deeply rooted: a study of a Drents community in the Nether-
      lands. Monographs of the American Ethnological Society, 25.

Klein, Julius
  1920 The mesta: a study in Spanish economic history, 1273–1836. Cam-
      bridge, Mass.: Harvard University Press.

Klokman, G. J.
  1938 De Achterhoekers. P. J. Meertens and A. de Vries, eds., De Neder-
      landsche volkskarakters. Kampen: n.p.

Krader, L.
  1960 The transition from serf to peasant in Eastern Europe. Anthro-
      pological Quarterly, 33.

Kuhn, Ferdinand, and Delia Kuhn
  1958 Poland opens her doors. National Geographic, 114.

Lander, Patricia Slade
  1970 Cleavages and convergences in a Finnish parish. Paper read at the
      annual meeting of the American Anthropological Association, San
      Diego, November.

Landes, David
  1965 The place of businessmen in the nineteenth century French class

structure. Bernard Barber and Elinor G. Barber, eds., European social
class: stability and change. New York: Macmillan.

Lee, Dorothy Demetracopoulou
1955   Greece. Margaret Mead, ed., Cultural patterns and technical change.
       New York: New American Library.

Lefebvre, Henri
n.d.   Untitled comments. Georges Friedmann, ed. Villes et campagnes: civi-
       lisation urbaine et civilisation rurale en France. Paris: Armand Colin.

Lepowsky, Maria
1971   Attitudes of nomadic Gypsies and sedentary peoples of Europe toward
       each other. Senior honors thesis, Department of Anthropology, Uni-
       versity of California, Berkeley.

Lerner, Daniel
1958   The passing of traditional society: modernizing the Middle East. New
       York: Free Press.

Levander, Lars
1944   Vaamhusfjärdingen. Folklivsskildringar, Kungl. G. Adolfs Ak.

Levi, Carlo
1947   Christ stopped at Eboli. New York: Farrar Straus.

Lewis, Oscar
1968   La vida: a Puerto Rican family in the culture of poverty—San Juan
       and New York. New York: Random House.

Lewis, Roy, and Angus Maude
1950   The English middle classes. New York: Knopf.

Leyton, Elliot H.
1966   Conscious models and dispute regulation in an Ulster village. Man,
       n.s., 1.
1970   Spheres of inheritance in Aughnaboy. American Anthropologist, 72.

Lindstrom, David E.
1951   The changing rural community in Sweden. Rural Sociology, 16.

Lison-Tolosana, Carmelo
1966   Belmonte de los Caballeros: a sociological study of a Spanish town.
       Oxford: Clarendon.
1968   Social factors in economic development Spain. J. G. Persistiany, ed.,
       Contributions to Mediterranean sociology. The Hague: Mouton.

Littlejohn, James
1963   Westrigg: the sociology of a Cheviot parish. New York: Humanities
       Press.

Lockwood, William G.
1965   The market place as a social mechanism in peasant society. Kroeber
       Anthropological Society, Papers, 32.

1970   *Selo* and *carsija*: the peasant market place as a mechanism of social integration in western Bosnia. Ph.D. dissertation, University of California, Berkeley.

Lopreato, Joseph
1965   How would you like to be a peasant? Human Organization, 24.
1967   Peasants no more: social class and social change in an underdeveloped society. San Francisco: Chandler.

Lowie, Robert H.
1954   Toward understanding Germany. Chicago: University of Chicago Press.

McConochie, Roger
1971   Household resources in a diversifying high alpine economy. Paper read at the annual meeting of the American Anthropological Association, New York, November.

McVean, D. N., and J. D. Lockie
1969   Ecology and land use in upland Scotland. Chicago: Aldine.

Maday, Bela C.
1968   Hungarian anthropology: the problem of communication. Current Anthropology, 9.
1970   Hungarian peasant studies. Research Reports, 6. Department of Anthropology, University of Massachusetts, Amherst.

Maraspini, A. L.
1968   The study of an Italian village. Paris: Mouton.

Marrimer, D.
1966   Searching for Gypsies in the Tyrol. Journal of the Gypsy Lore Society, 45 (3, 4).

Marsh, David C.
1958   The changing social structure of England and Wales, 1871–1951. London: Routledge and Kegan Paul.

Martin, E. W.
1965   The shearers and the shorn: a study of life in a Devon community. London: Routledge and Kegan Paul.

Maynard, John
1962   The Russian peasant and other studies. (First published, 1942). New York: Collier.

Mazour, Anatole G.
1962   Russia: tsarist and communist. New York: Van Nostrand.

Mead, Margaret
1966a New lives for old: cultural transformation—Manus, 1928-1953. (First published, 1956.) New York: Dell.
1966b Soviet attitudes toward authority: an interdisciplinary approach to

problems of Soviet character. (First published, 1951.) New York: Schocken.

Mead, Margaret, and Rhoda Métraux
1953   The study of culture at a distance. Chicago: University of Chicago Press.

Mead, W. R.
1953   Farming in Finland. London: University of London, Athlone Press.

Messenger, John C.
1969   Inis Beag: isle of Ireland. New York: Holt, Rinehart and Winston.

Métraux, Rhoda, and Margaret Mead
1954   Themes in French culture. Hoover Institute Studies, series D.

Miller, Wright
1961   Russians as people. New York: Dutton.

Mira, J. F.
1971   Mariage et familie dans une communauté rurale du Pays de Valence (Espagne). Études Rurales, 42.

Moore, Barrington, Jr.
1966   Social origins of dictatorship and democracy: lord and peasant in the making of the modern world. Boston: Beacon.

Morin, Edgar
1970   The red and the white: report from a French village. New York: Pantheon.

Moss, Leonard W., and Stephen C. Cappannari
1960   Patterns of kinship, comparaggio and community in a South Italian village. Anthropological Quarterly, 33.
1962   Estate and class in a South Italian hill village. American Anthropologist, 64.

Moss, Leonard, and Walter H. Thompson
1959   The South Italian family: literature and observations. Human Organization, 18.

Mowat, Charles Loch
1955   Britain between the wars—1918–1940. Chicago: University of Chicago Press.

Mumford, Lewis
1961   The city in history. New York: Harcourt, Brace & World.

Munch, Peter A.
1948   Landhandelen i Norge. Oslo: Halvorsen & Larsen.
1953   The peasant movement in Norway, a study of class and culture. British Journal of Sociology, 4.
1956   A study of cultural change: rural-urban conflicts in Norway. Studia Norvegica, 9.

Musio, Gavino
    1969   La cultura solitaria: tradizione e acculturazione nella Sardegna ar-
           caica. Bologna: Il Mulino.

Naroll, Raoul, and Frada Naroll
    1962   Social development in a Tyrolean village. Anthropological Quarterly,
           35.

Nef, John U.
    1963   Western civilization since the Renaissance. New York: Harper & Row.

Nellemann, George
    1967   Den Polske indvandring til Lolland-Falster. Copenhagen: Nationalmu-
           seet.
    1970a The introduction of the sugar beet as a cash crop in Denmark and
           the immigration of Polish rural workers. Anthropologica, 12.
    1970b Minoriteter i Danmark. Jordens Folk, 6.

Netting, Robert
    1971   Of men and meadows: constraints and options in alpine land use.
           Paper read at the annual meeting of the American Anthropological
           Association, New York, November.

Novak, Joseph
    1964   The future is ours, comrade. New York: Dutton.

Opler, Marvin K.
    1957   Schizophrenia and culture. Scientific American, August.

Opler, Marvin K., and J. L. Singer
    1956   Ethnic differences in behavior and psychopathology: Italian and Irish.
           International Journal of Social Psychiatry, 2.

Organization for European Economic Cooperation.
    n.d.   Land consolidation: cheaper and more simplified methods. European
           Productivity Agency. Paris: OEEC
    1959   The small family farm: a European problem. Methods for creating
           economically viable units. Project No. 199/2, European Productivity
           Agency. Paris: OEEC

Orme, A. R.
    1970   Ireland. Chicago: Aldine.

Paine, Robert
    1963   Entrepreneurial activity without its profits. Frederik Barth, ed., The
           role of the entrepreneur in social change in northern Norway. (Årbok
           for Universitetet i Bergen, Humanistisk Serie.) Bergen and Oslo: Nor-
           wegian Universities Press.

Park, George K.
    1962   Sons and lovers: characterological requisites of the roles in a peasant
           society. Ethnology, 1.

Park, George K., and Lee Soltow
1961   Politics and social structure in a Norwegian village. American Journal of Sociology, 67.

Pelto, Pertti J.
1962   Individualism in Skolt Lapp society. Kansatieteellinen Arkisto, 16.

Pérez Díaz, Victor
1966   Estructura social del campo y éxodo rural, estudio de un pueblo de Castilla. Madrid: Editorial Tecnos.

Peristiany, J. G.
1966   Introduction. J. G. Peristiany, ed., Honour and shame: the values of Mediterranean society. Chicago: University of Chicago Press.

Pfautz, Harold W.
1967   Charles Booth on the city. Chicago: University of Chicago Press.

Pitt-Rivers, Julian A.
1954   The people of the Sierra. New York: Criterion.
1966   Honour and social status. J. G. Peristiany, ed., Honour and shame: the values of Mediterranean society. Chicago: University of Chicago Press.

Pitts, Jesse R.
1963   Continuity and change in bourgeois France. Stanley Hoffmann et al., eds., In search of France. New York: Harper & Row.

Pomponi, Janine
1962   La vie rurale de deux communes corses: Serra di Scopamene et Sotta. Faculté des Lettres, Aix-en-Provence, série Travaux et Mémoires, 26.

Portal, Roger
1969   The Slavs: a cultural and historical survey of the Slavonic peoples. New York: Harper & Row.

Rasmussen, Holger
1950   Faêröske kulturbilleder omkring aarhundred-skiftet. Copenhagen: H. P. Hansens Bogtrykkeri.
1963   Landsbyliv. Copenhagen: Gyldendal.

Raup, Philip M.
1969   Constraints and potentials in agriculture. Robert H. Beck et al., eds., The changing structure of Europe: economic, social, and political trends. Minneapolis: University of Minnesota Press.

Reader, W. J.
1964   Life in Victorian England. London: Batsford.

Redfield, Robert
1956   Peasant society and culture: an anthropological approach to civilization. Chicago: University of Chicago Press.

Rees, Alwyn D.
      1961   Life in a Welsh countryside: a social study of Llanfihangel yng Ng-
             wynfa. (First published, 1950.) Cardiff: University of Wales Press.

Reeve, D.
      1958   Smoke in the lanes. London: Constable.

Reinton, Lars
      1955   Saêterbruket i Norge, I., saêtertypar og driftsformer. Instituttet for
             Sammenlignende Kulturforskning, serie B, 48.

Ribeiro, Aquilino
      1964   Aldeia: terra, gente e bichos. Lisbon: Livraria Bertrand.

Rickard, J. A.
      1951   An outline of the history of England. New York: Barnes & Noble.

Rodnick, David
      1948   Postwar Germans: an anthropologist's account. New Haven: Yale Uni-
             versity Press.

Rose, Arnold M.
      1959   Indagine sull'integrazione sociale in due quartieri de Roma. Universi-
             tà de Roma, Instituto di Statistica, studi e inchieste, nuova serie,
             sezione di sociologia, 1.
      1969   Migrants in Europe: problems of acceptance and adjustment. Min-
             neapolis: University of Minnesota Press.

Rosenthal, Celia S.
      1954   Deviation and social change in the Jewish community of a small
             Polish town. American Journal of Sociology, 59.

Roubin, Lucienne A.
      1970   Chambrettes des Provençaux: une maison des hommes en Méditer-
             ranée septentrionale. Paris: Plon.

Ruong, Israel
      1960   The relation between culture and means of livelihood in Lapland.
             Rowland G. P. Hill, ed., The Lapps to-day in Finland, Norway and
             Sweden. École Pratique des Hautes Études, Sorbonne, Sixième Section:
             Sciences Economiques et Sociales, Bibliotheque Arctique et Antarc-
             tique, 1.
      1967   The Lapps in Sweden. Stockholm: The Swedish Institute for Cultural
             Relations with Foreign Countries.
      1969   Samerna. Stockholm: Aldus/Bonniers.

Russell, Richard Joel, and Fred Bowerman Kniffen
      1951   Culture worlds. New York: Macmillan.

Sanders, Irwin T.
      1949   Balkan village. Lexington: University of Kentucky Press.
      1962   Rainbow in the rock: the people of rural Greece. Cambridge, Mass.:
             Harvard University Press.

Sárfalvi, Béla
1965   The village of Csepreg in western Hungary. Geographia Polonica, 5.

Sauvigny, G. de Bertier de
1955   La restauration. Paris: Flammarion.

Schein, Muriel
1971a Only on Sundays. Natural History, 80.
1971b Social stratification in a Greek village. Transactions of the New York
       Academy of Sciences.

Schnapper, Dominique
1971   L'Italie rouge et noire. Paris: Gallimard.

Siegel, Bernard J.
1961   Conflict, parochialism and social differentiation in Portuguese socie-
       ty. Journal of Conflict Resolution, 5.

Silverman, Sydel F.
1965   Patronage and community-nation relationships in central Italy. Eth-
       nology, 4.
1966   An ethnographic approach to social stratification: prestige in a cen-
       tral Italian community. American Anthropologist, 68.

Simić, Andrei
1970   Cultural factors in Yugoslav industrialization. Ph.D. dissertation, Uni-
       versity of California, Berkeley.

Simirenko, Alex, ed.
1966   Soviet sociology. Chicago: Quadrangle.

Solheim, Svale
1952   Norsk saetertradisjon. Instituttet for Sammenlignende Kulturforsk-
       ning, serie B, 47.

Spencer, Robert F.
1965   The German paradox (a problem in national character). Journal of
       the Minnesota Academy of Science, 32.

Spindler, George D.
1972a Schooling in Schönhausen: a study of cultural transmission and
       instrumental adaptation in an urbanizing German village. George D.
       Spindler, ed., Education and cultural process. New York: Holt, Rine-
       hart and Winston, to appear.
1972b Burgbach: an urbanizing German village (Working title). New York:
       Holt, Rinehart and Winston, to appear.

Stacey, Margaret
1960   Tradition and change: a study of Banbury. London: Oxford Universi-
       ty Press.

Stanislawski, Dan
1963   Portugal's other kingdom: the Algarve. Austin: University of Texas
       Press.

154   Starkie, Walter
      1961   Spanish raggle-taggle: adventures with a fiddle in north Spain. (First published, 1934.) Baltimore, Md.: Penguin.

Steen, Adolf
      1963   Masi, en Samebygd. Norsk Folkemuseum, Samiske Samlinger, 4.

Steensberg, Axel
      1945*a* Bondegaarden. M. P. Ejerslev, ed., Den Danske bonde: kulturbilleder. Copenhagen: Nordisk Specialforlag.
      1945*b* Bondens hverdag. M. P. Ejerslev, ed., Den Danske bonde: kulturbilleder. Copenhagen: Nordisk Specialforlag.

Sturmthal, Adolf
      1968   Labor movements and collective bargaining in Europe. International Encyclopedia of the Social Sciences, 8.

Swedner, Harald
      1960   Ecological differentiation of habits and attitudes. (Lund Studies in Sociology.) Lund: Gleerup.

Sweetser, Dorrian A.
      1964   Urbanization and the patrilinial transmission of farms in Finland. Institute of Sociology, University of Helsinki.

Szemberg, Anna
      1963   Changes in agrarian structure. Polish Perspectives, 6.

Tardieu, Suzanne
      1964   La vie domestique dans le Mâconnais rural pré-industriel. (Institut d'Ethnologie.) Paris: Musée de l'Homme.

Thomas, William I., and Florian Znaniecki
      1927   The Polish peasant in Europe and America, 2. New York: Knopf.

Thompson, J. M.
      1952   Napoleon Bonaparte: his rise and fall. Oxford: Blackwell.

Thompson, Laura
      1966   Core values and diplomacy: a case study of Iceland. Human Organization, 19.
      1969   The secret of culture: nine community studies. New York: Random House.

Turney-High, H. H.
      1953   Château-Gérard: the life and times of a Walloon village. Columbia: University of South Carolina Press.

Valkenburg, Samuel van, and Ellsworth Huntington
      1935   Europe. New York: Wiley.

Varga, Gyula
      1970   A cooperative village: Aparhant. New Hungarian Quarterly, 38.

Volin, Lazar   **155**
  1960 The Russian peasant: from emancipation to kolkhoz. Cyril E. Black,
        ed., The transformation of Russian society. Cambridge, Mass.: Har-
        vard University Press.
  1970 A century of Russian agriculture: from Alexander II to Khrushchev.
        Cambridge, Mass.: Harvard University Press.

Vorren, Ø., ed.
  1960 Norway north of 65. Tromsø Museums Skrifter, 8.

Wace, A. J. B., and M. S. Thompson
  1914 The nomads of the Balkans: an account of life and customs among
        the Vlachs of northern Pindus. London: Routledge.

Wagner, Richard V.
  1969 Social cohesion in a French alpine society. Ph.D. dissertation, Univer-
        sity of California, Berkeley.

Warren, Richard L.
  1967 Education in Rebhausen: a German village. New York: Holt, Rinehart
        and Winston.

Weinstock, S. A.
  1964 Motivation and social structure in the study of acculturation: a Hun-
        garian case. Human Organization, 23.

Weiss, Richard
  1946 Volkskunde der Schweiz. Erlenbach-Zürich: Eugene Rentsch Verlag.

Whitaker, Ian
  1955 Social relations in a nomadic Lappish community. Norsk Folkemu-
        seum, Samiske Samlinger, 2.

Wikman, K. Rob. V.
  1937 Die einleitung der ehe, eine vergleichend ethnosoziologische unter-
        suchung über die vorstufe der ehe in den sitten des schwedischen
        volkstums. Acta Academiae Aboensis, Humaniora, 11.

Williams, W. M.
  1956 Gosforth: the sociology of an English village. Glencoe, Ill.: Free Press.
  1963 A west country village, Ashworthy: family, kinship, and land. Lon-
        don: Routledge and Kegan Paul.

Williamson, Kenneth
  1970 The Atlantic islands, rev. ed. London: Routledge and Kegan Paul.

Wolf, Eric R.
  1962 Cultural dissonance in the Italian Alps. Comparative Studies in Socie-
        ty and History, 5.
  1966 Kinship, friendship, and patron-client relations in complex societies.
        M. P. Banton, ed., The social anthropology of complex societies. Lon-
        don: Tavistock.

1970   The inheritance of land among Bavarian and Tyrolese peasants. Anthropologica, 12.

Wright, Gordon
1960   France in modern times: 1760 to the present. Chicago: Rand McNally.

Wurzbacher, Gerhard
1961   Das dorf im spannungsfeld industrieller entwicklung. Stuttgart: Ferdinand Enke Verlag.

Wylie, Laurence
1964   Village in the Vaucluse: an account of life in a French village. New York: Harper & Row.
1966   Chanzeaux: a village in Anjou. Cambridge, Mass.: Harvard University Press.

Yngvesson, Barbara Belton
1970   Decision-making and dispute settlement in a Swedish fishing village: an ethnography of law. Ph.D. dissertation, University of California, Berkeley.

Yoors, Jan
1967   The Gypsies. New York: Simon and Schuster.

Young, Michael, and Peter Willmott
1957   Family and kinship in east London. Glencoe, Ill.: Free Press.

Zborowski, Mark, and Elizabeth Herzog
1962   Life is with people: the culture of the shtetl. (First published, 1952.) New York: Schocken.

INDEX